Palgrave's Critical Policing Studies

Series Editors
Elizabeth Aston
School of Applied Sciences
Edinburgh Napier University
Edinburgh, UK

Michael Rowe
Department of Social Sciences Newcastle City Campus
Northumbria University
Newcastle upon Tyne, UK

In a period where police and academics benefit from coproduction in research and education, the need for a critical perspective on key challenges is pressing. Palgrave's Critical Policing Studies is a series of high quality, research-based books which examine a range of cutting-edge challenges and developments to policing and their social and political contexts. They seek to provide evidence-based case studies and high quality research, combined with critique and theory, to address fundamental challenging questions about future directions in policing.

Through a range of formats including monographs, edited collections and short form Pivots, this series provides research at a variety of lengths to suit both academics and practitioners. The series brings together new topics at the forefront of policing scholarship but is also organised around who the contemporary police are, what they do, how they go about it, and the ever-changing external environments which bear upon their work.

The series will cover topics such as: the purpose of policing and public expectations, public health approaches to policing, policing of cybercrime, environmental policing, digital policing, social media, Artificial Intelligence and big data, accountability of complex networks of actors involved in policing, austerity, public scrutiny, technological and social changes, over-policing and marginalised groups, under-policing and corporate crime, institutional abuses, policing of climate change, ethics, workforce, education, evidence-based policing, and the pluralisation of policing.

More information about this series at
http://www.palgrave.com/gp/series/16586

Graham Smith

On the Wrong Side of The Law

Complaints Against Metropolitan
Police, 1829–1964

Graham Smith
Manchester, UK

ISSN 2730-535X   ISSN 2730-5368   (electronic)
Palgrave's Critical Policing Studies
ISBN 978-3-030-48221-3   ISBN 978-3-030-48222-0   (eBook)
https://doi.org/10.1007/978-3-030-48222-0

This Palgrave Macmillan imprint is published by the registered company Springer Nature Switzerland AG.
The registered company address is: Gewerbestrasse 11, 6330 Cham, Switzerland

Foreword

There is no conflict between effective investigation of allegations of misconduct by police officers and effective law enforcement and crime prevention. Indeed one is dependent on the other. The public will only comply with the law and cooperate with the police by providing information and assistance if they see the police as being legitimate and accountability is a key feature of that accountability. I would contend that the vast majority of the public do not see that accountability in terms of structures, targets or statistics but their own personal experience of police encounters and that of their friends and family and their view of high-profile cases that have generated public concern. Only repressive and para-military policing can guarantee compliance with the law if the public feel that police officers and indeed others in positions of power are above that law. Sir Robert Peel who founded the Metropolitan Police in 1829 fully appreciated this and indeed it is the underlying philosophy behind his Principle of Policing laid down on the formation of the 'new police'.

In my 34 years of policing the debate about the complaints system has been a running sore which has hindered efforts to improve both policing and public confidence in the police. At times, measures which would have aided the police to arrest and convict more criminals were opposed because of lack of confidence in the police to use those measures legitimately. On the other hand standing back I would have to say that every measure that increased independent oversight of the police and greater transparency and accountability improved policing and led to more effective law enforcement.

Unfortunately the various attempts to reform the complaints system since the Royal Commission on the Police in 1962, described by Graham Smith in the introduction to this book, have not in my view taken us in that direction. They have not created the desired confidence in the public that the police are accountable when things 'go wrong' or indeed the confidence among police officers that the system is thorough and fair. The various reforms have not led to police culture being more open and less defensive; in fact I would argue the opposite. Along the road the system has become more cumbersome, bureaucratic and lengthy and the best route for complainants in more serious cases remains to be through civil justice or the support of national media.

The whole complaints system including discipline hearings themselves has become more legalistic and less complainant focused and the investigation process inhibits the ability of policing to admit mistakes and to ensure that lessons are learnt in a timely fashion. The system struggles to distinguish between poor service, poor professional practice, organisational failings and wilful misconduct. In the words of Elton John (or in fact Bernie Taupin) often 'Sorry seems to be the hardest word'. In all this, it has to be said that race is an enduring theme including in respect of members of the police force who want to complain about colleagues or indeed the organisation itself.

I first met Graham Smith the author of this book when as Chief Constable of Greater Manchester Police I commissioned him to carry out research as to why ethnic minority officers featured disproportionately in complaints and discipline cases (a trend which sadly continues to this day). His research and his authorship of this work benefits from his background as a community activist and a victim of police misconduct as well as his willingness to speak truth to power. We have not always agreed on the conclusions of his research but I have always found him to be someone who appreciates the dilemmas and tensions in day-to-day operational policing and he has become a good friend if also a critical one.

In this first volume of his study Graham charts the development of the complaints system between the formation of the Metropolitan Police and the Royal Commission of 1962. It shows that as so often in UK policing, reform is the result of high-profile cases generating public and political concern or of developments that have happened haphazardly without any firm political direction and not seemingly cognisant of the longer-term impact. I found it fascinating to discover that the police role in the investigation of crime and creation of the CID happened in such a fashion, and that it was not part of the original design of Peel. It has always puzzled me why police ownership and direction of investigations has not been more questioned when in so many other jurisdictions investigations are directed by examining magistrates or state attorneys. This responsibility for investigations then developed into responsibility and ownership of the criminal prosecution process until the advent of the Crown Prosecution Service in 1986, which was so very late in the development of English public administration (the Procurator Fiscal was established in Scotland in 1867).

Graham also charts how democratic oversight of policing effectively went into reverse during the nineteenth and twentieth centuries moving away from some of the bedrocks established by Peel and again how the concept of operational independence arguably came about by happenstance and not a conscious political direction or adequate public consultation. It now seems remarkable that statistics on police complaints were not published for so many years before the 1962 Commission but the work outlines how the police were able to take more control of the whole complaints system during this period, This is not only a fascinating history of the police complaints system but a history of key elements of policing itself and to a degree a social history.

Whatever internal systems and processes an organisation establishes together with the systems of external oversight and direction, a crucial test of accountability to its customers, in this case to the public, is the effectiveness of procedures for dealing with situations where the power of the organisation or its members causes harm to individuals or fails to protect them. In my time as a police leader, I saw many many times the remarkable ability of policing to transform the lives of individuals and communities, to show incredible degrees of bravery and self-sacrifice and to show enormous compassion, patience and care. On the other hand, I have also seen in the UK and elsewhere the enormous damage to communities and individuals which the power of the state can do when transmitted through the power of the police and individual members of the police force and the impact of the failure of the police to protect the individual or control the activities of the criminally minded. This includes instances where the power of the organisation has been used against its own members, especially those who have tried to raise concerns about police practice or their colleagues or tried to challenge the prevailing culture. I have also experienced personally and seen in others the stress caused to officers under investigation when they do not have confidence in the fairness or professionalism of that investigation or where it is allowed to drag on for many months or needs. In my time I introduced an element of independent oversight into the complaints system by establishing an office of Independent Ombudsman for Complaints an initiative which ultimately failed as it did not fit into the nationally defined process. While Graham and others have long argued that the police are resistant to more independence in the police complaints system I would point out that the Police Federation have advocated a totally independent system of complaints investigation since the 1980s. Despite the various iterations and renaming of complaint oversight bodies it remains the case that the vast majority of complaints continue to be investigated by the police themselves.

This first volume teasingly finishes with the Royal Commission of 1962 and at the advent of a period of enormous social turmoil which saw the make-up of the population of the UK radically change and the end of the traditional deference to authority and the establishment which previously had characterised our society. Inner city riots, public protests, the impact of inequality and the impact of the loss of traditional industries and job prospects brought the police further into conflict with ordinary people affected by these changes and the lack of accountability in the complaints system heightened the levels of resentment and anger exacerbating that level of conflict. This first volume shows how the foundations laid down in previous decades, some planned and intentional, some reacting to personalities and events left the police poorly prepared to maintain public confidence and legitimacy in the face of this upheaval.

Manchester, UK   Sir Peter Fahy

Preface and Acknowledgements

This book, the first of a two-volume study of complaints against officers serving with the Metropolitan Police, is informed by nearly 40 years of experience in the field as complainant, civil rights activist, researcher and international consultant. Having served in recent years as an expert on international human rights law to the Council of Europe and advising on the prohibition of torture and ill-treatment, it is evident that the need to combat impunity for human rights abuse is not restricted to authoritarian regimes or transitional states. Stable democracies, notably the United States of America and United Kingdom in their treatment of terrorist suspects and policing ethnic minority communities, for example, are not beyond reproach when it comes to holding law enforcement and security personnel accountable for their conduct.

The jurisprudence of the European Court of Human Rights requires independent and effective investigation of allegations of serious human rights abuse, and citizen oversight of police has been promoted as a fundamental protection against impunity. Yet, despite the existence of a succession of independent police complaints bodies in England and Wales, Scotland and Northern Ireland for close to half-a-century, accusations continue that a culture of impunity protects UK police officers. In examining complaints against officers serving with the Metropolitan Police, between inception in 1829 and codification of complaints in 1964 in this first volume, and the period when independent oversight bodies have been in operation in the second, the overarching purpose of this study is to ground a study of police misconduct in the experiences of complainants.

Traumatised as the result of an encounter with officers serving with the Greater Manchester Police in 1983, I have since worked closely with complainants, civil society activists, lawyers, journalists, politicians, scholars, police officers and overseers. Their experiences, knowledge and commitment to calling out police misconduct have been invaluable to the complainant standpoint developed in this study. Pride of place goes to members of Hackney Community Defence Association (HCDA) who were victimised by police in the 1980s and 1990s. Too many to mention, my apologies to those that I fail to acknowledge, and particular mention is made of Annette Monerville who started the ball rolling in spearheading a campaign in support of her nephew Trevor after his detention in Stoke Newington police station; with a rich history of activism Martin Walker lent his experience to the fledgling Association; stalwart Rudolf Hawkins would go into police stations to enquire after the welfare of persons detained in custody and acted as McKenzie's Friend in the local magistrates' court; Maria Franklin shared with the group the knowledge she acquired on post-traumatic stress disorder following her encounter with a mounted police officer and his horse; Chas Loft tirelessly investigated cases and played a major role in obtaining evidence against a group of Stoke Newington officers eventually dismissed from the Met; and Russell Miller introduced innovative intelligence gathering and data storing ideas which improved capacity to monitor the police.

Other HCDA members, civil rights activists, politicians, professionals and scholars to whom I am in debt include Ralf Alleweldt; Vicky Anning; Rodney Austin; David Best; William Bevin-Nicholls; Tim Bianek; Anja Bienert; Dave Bombroffe; Hazel Bruno-Gilbert; Tom Bucke; Duncan Campbell; Tanzil Chowdhury; Louise Christian; Deborah Coles; Jeremy Corbyn MP; Isabelle Cox; Steve Cragg; Simon Creighton; Charles Crichlow; Jane Deighton; Unmesh Desai; Shamik Ditta; Bill Dixon; Geoff Eaton; Phil Edwards; Ben Emmerson; Clive Emsley; Chuck Epp; Liz Fekete; Ken Fero; Margarita Galstyan; Elaine Genders; Joanna Gilmore; Jean Gould; Courtenay Griffiths; Harry Hagger Johnson; Peter Hall; Tony Hall (deceased); Barnor Hesse; Audley Harrison; John

Harvey; Brian Heaphy; David Hoffman; Tamar Hopkins; Mark James; Kapil Juj; Rennie Kingsley; Julia Kozma; Mick Lavery, Nicholas Long; John McDonnell MP; Bozhena Malanchuk; Saffa Mir; John Monerville; James Morton; Tine Munk; Jim Murdoch; Fiona Murphy; Tony Murphy; Mahir Mushteidzada; Ida Oderinde; Nogah Ofer; Anne Owers; Pragna Patel; Gareth Peirce; Scott Poynting; Hugh Prince; Tony Pryce; Maurice Punch; Gwen Quigley; Robert Reiner; Pauline Roach; Imani Robinson; Jonathan Rogers; David Rose; Ian Russell; Steve Savage; Mark Scott; Stafford Scott; Phil Scraton; Toby Seddon; Brian Sedgemore MP (deceased); Helen Shaw; Tommy Sheppard; Joe Sim; Lauri Sivonen; Andrew Smith; Nick Stanage; Keir Starmer; John Stewart; Gary Stretch; Eric Svanidze; Leslie Thomas; Debbie Tripley; Shaun Waterman; Pete Weatherby; Frances Webber; Patrick Williams; Tom Williamson (deceased).

I am especially grateful to the close friends and family whose support and advice have been essential over the years. Longstanding friends Chris Roberts and Matt Hawkins were present before I embarked on what has proved to be my life work. Mark Metcalf, Celia Stubbs and Malcolm Kennedy (deceased) played a major part in HCDA and, then, the Colin Roach Centre, which was an independent community centre that survived on voluntary subscriptions for over six years. More recently I have learned much from close working relations with Andrew Sanders, Peter Fahy and Craig Futterman, two professors and a former chief constable who are committed to the pursuit of excellence and social justice. Most of all, I owe a great deal to a 30-year friendship with Raju Bhatt. We started our careers at the same time—him an activist turned civil rights lawyer and me a civil rights activist—and spent many hours together discussing cases and perfecting strategies for holding police to account.

Finally, this book is dedicated to my wife Bex and our two sons Joe and Sam. Without their love and support this book would not have been written.

Manchester, UK   Graham Smith

Contents

Contents

List of Tables

1

Standpoint

Launched on 8 January 2018 the Independent Office for Police Conduct (IOPC) is the fourth body established in England and Wales with a remit to oversee the police complaints system. Over the course of the last half-century or so police misconduct and the remedies available to victims have attracted public criticism and there has been major legislative reform on five occasions.

The police complaints system was first codified under the Police Act 1964. In the late 1950s there was an absence of transparency surrounding internal investigations of police misconduct, and the climate of secrecy contributed to widely held perceptions that police officers were not accountable for their conduct. Following a series of scandals around the United Kingdom, and eventually triggered by disquiet surrounding settlement by the Commissioner of the Metropolitan Police (commonly referred to as the Met) of a civil action against a constable which was not accompanied by disciplinary proceedings against the officer, the Royal Commission on the Police (1960–62 Commission 1962) was appointed. The primary purpose of the Commission was to consider arrangements for the governance of police, and much of the 1964 Act was devoted to implementing the recommendation of the Commission to establish a

© The Author(s) 2020
G. Smith, *On the Wrong Side of The Law*, Palgrave's Critical Policing Studies,
https://doi.org/10.1007/978-3-030-48222-0_1

tripartite arrangement between the chief officer of police (Chief Constable of a provincial force and the Commissioner in the case of the Metropolitan and City of London forces), local police authority and Home Secretary. Under their terms of reference the 1960–62 Commission were also asked to consider police public relations and procedures for handling public complaints against the police. Acknowledging the decline in deference to authority that together with an increasing awareness of civil rights had begun to define police public relations, the Commission recognised the need for legislative reform. On the recommendation of the majority of Commissioners a statutory internal police complaints system modelled on the Met system was created under Section 49 of the 1964 Act. The chief officer of police, who served as disciplinary authority for all officers below chief officer rank,[1] was given responsibility for the investigation of complaints. In addition, provision was made for the Director of Public Prosecutions (DPP) to determine whether, following investigation of a complaint, criminal proceedings should be brought against an officer. Under Section 48 of the Act a vicarious liability rule in the laws of tort was introduced which permitted victims to claim damages from the chief officer of police, and Section 50 required police authorities and inspectors of constabulary to keep themselves informed of the way in which complaints were handled.

Significance attaches to the Police Act 1964 for introducing a misconduct package under sections 48 to 50 which set out remedies in criminal, civil and administrative proceedings and provided for oversight. Since formation of the Met as the first modern police force under the Metropolitan Police Act 1829, the two legal remedies were available to victims of misconduct at common law, and police regulations provided for discipline and complaints procedures. In the mid-nineteenth century victims would bring criminal charges against constables by application to a police court magistrate for a summons or indictment; officers were occasionally to be found in the civil courts having to defend themselves against a claim for damages; and records show that constables were regularly punished for offences against discipline. In the absence of records, it is not known what the outcomes were of public complaints that were handled internally. By the mid-twentieth century criminal and civil remedies were largely inaccessible to victims and officers were rarely brought before the courts, quasi-judicial disciplinary proceedings with the right of appeal to the Home Secretary[2] were less frequent and there was no evidence to suggest the operation of an effective complaints system. Alongside the internal complaints system, inclusion in the 1964 misconduct package of statutory roles for the DPP in criminal proceedings and chief officers of police in civil proceedings were presented as means by which victims of serious misconduct could access legal remedies. Decisions on criminal proceedings would be made by the DPP independently of the police, and the chief officer would be liable in civil proceedings regardless of whether the claimant knew the identity of the constable responsible for the damage they had suffered.

Three members of the 1960–62 Commission were not persuaded that the public interest in tackling police misconduct could be sufficiently met by legislating for police investigations of complaints that were not independently monitored. Concerned that police would not be able to reassure the public that internal procedures were effective and fair to both complainants and officers, the minority recommended appointment of a Commissioner of Rights to oversee the complaints system (1960–62 Commission 1962). Rejected by government, the minority proposal represented an early contribution to what has developed into a highly contested international complaints discourse, in which the proposition that police cannot be trusted to impartially investigate police is countered by the assertion that only police can effectively investigate police (Prenzler and Ronken 2001).

In accordance with Section 50 of the 1964 Act, the Chief Inspector of Constabulary (1964) and Met Commissioner (1965) commenced regular publication of complaints statistics in their annual reports of 1963 and 1964, respectively. The figures confirmed the perception that complaints against officers were rarely substantiated and seldom resulted in criminal or disciplinary proceedings. Allegations of police racism, which had come to the fore in the late 1950s and were to escalate in the 1960s (Hunte 1966; Lambert 1970), were increasingly met by African Caribbean and Asian communities mobilising in support of their members (Humphry and John 1971; Sivanandan 1982; Trew 2015). The Home Office quickly revisited the operation of the complaints system and appointed a Police Advisory Board Working Party, which reported in

1970,[3] and the Select Committee on Race Relations (1972) urged the government to consider introduction of an independent element to the system. Created by the Police Act 1976 and launched on 1 July 1977, with limited powers to review completed reports of police investigations of complaints and direct a chief police officer to bring disciplinary charges against an officer, the Police Complaints Board (PCB) was to survive for eight years as the first independent oversight body.

The PCB was criticised for rarely resorting to their disciplinary powers (Hewitt 1982), and the clamour for complaints reform continued unabated. Black and ethnic minority communities were particularly vocal and campaigns were launched in response to a spate of controversial deaths during or following contact with the police (Benn and Warpole 1986; Scraton and Chadwick 1986), and in opposition to stop and search and 'Sus', the power of police to arrest and charge a suspected person under Section 4 of the Vagrancy Act 1824 (Demuth 1978). An inquiry by Lord Scarman (1981) into the Brixton and other inner city disturbances of 1981, a Working Party chaired by the Chairman of the PCB, Lord Plowden (1981) and an inquiry by the House of Commons Home Affairs Committee (HAC 1982) were each to conclude that greater independence in the police complaints system was required.

At the same time that momentum was gathering for further complaints reform, police powers and responsibilities to investigate crime and prepare criminal prosecutions were under scrutiny. Appointed to inquire into a 1972 investigation by Met officers into the death of Maxwell Confait and the prosecution of three young men, whose convictions were subsequently overturned by the Court of Appeal, Sir Henry Fisher (1977) found that the Met investigation and prosecution were seriously flawed. He proposed that a more general examination of the criminal justice process was required and the Royal Commission on Criminal Procedure (1981) was subsequently appointed to examine police criminal investigation responsibilities, safeguards for suspects and the conduct of prosecutions. On their recommendation police powers, which had previously been developed at common law, were codified by the Police and Criminal Evidence Act 1984.[4] In addition, Part IX of the Act provided for the PCB to be replaced by the Police Complaints Authority (PCA) with additional powers to supervise police investigations of complaints. Launched on 1

April 1985, and despite widespread public concern with PCA effectiveness at a time when the Court of Appeal was overturning a succession of convictions that relied on tainted police evidence (Walker and Starmer 1999), the much-criticised oversight body lasted for 19 years.

From a low baseline when publication of figures commenced in the mid-1960s, annual complaints and discipline statistics, which were collated and published by the Home Office between 1990 and 2003/04, revealed a declining substantiation rate across England and Wales reaching a low of 2% of the total number recorded in 1995/96 and the following four years (Povey and Cotton 2001). In contrast, with claimants relying on Section 48 of the Police Act 1964 civil actions emerged as a viable remedy for police misconduct. In the three years 1994/95 to 1996/97, 863 claims against the Met Commissioner (1997) were successfully concluded with more than £6 million paid out to claimants in settlements and court awards. In the same three years three Met officers were convicted of a criminal offence and disciplinary charges were proved against 50 officers arising from public complaints (excluding traffic offences). Furthermore, in 1997 decisions by DPP Dame Barbara Mills not to prosecute police officers after two people died following contact with Met officers and the 'plastic bagging' of a suspect by West Midlands officers were challenged in three joined judicial reviews (Smith 1997, 2001). The DPP agreed to review decisions in the two death in custody cases and was directed by the Divisional Court to review the plastic bagging decision (*R. v. DPP Ex parte Treadaway* [1997] EWHC Admin 741).[5] The HAC (1998) took notice of these developments and recommended urgent reform of police disciplinary procedures, and that the Home Office commission feasibility research on independent investigation of complaints (KPMG 2000).[6] These proposals were endorsed by the Council of Europe Committee for the Prevention of Torture (2000) following a 1997 visit to the United Kingdom and Lord Macpherson (1999) in his Stephen Lawrence Inquiry Report. As part of a wider reform programme that significantly reshaped the policing landscape (Savage 2007) Part II of the Police Reform Act 2002 provided for radical reform of the complaints process. For the first time in the history of the police of England and Wales investigative powers were available to a lay oversight body which was also to serve as an appellate authority.

The Independent Police Complaints Commission (IPCC) commenced operations on 1 April 2004. With the vast majority of complaints against officers still investigated by police, 31 independent investigations were opened and 8 completed in their first operational year; and out of a total of 1033 appeals against police decisions received from complainants, 768 were ruled valid (IPCC 2005). The total number of IPCC investigations only managed to increase to 100 opened and 82 completed investigations in 2007/08 (IPCC 2008) and, with 3592 out of 4171 appeals (86.12%) found to be valid, it was evident that the IPCC was having little impact on internal police complaints procedures. In 2008 the National Audit Office (NAO 2008) criticised the IPCC for giving insufficient consideration to the interests of complainants, and a couple of years later the HAC (2010) suggested further reform was required. Reiterating the concerns of the NAO, the HAC inquiry into the work of the IPCC concluded that failure to put complainants at the heart of procedures placed at risk the statutory duty of the IPCC to increase public confidence in the complaints system.

Public confidence in the police was seriously undermined by a number of revelations around this time, including: publication of evidence that South Yorkshire Police officers had concealed evidence that police negligence contributed to the death of 96 Liverpool Football Club supporters at the Hillsborough Football Stadium in 1989 (Hillsborough Independent Panel 2012); appointment of an independent panel to inquire into the unsolved murder of Daniel Morgan in 1987 following an apology by the Met that police corruption had thwarted the murder investigation (Morgan and Jukes 2017) and appointment of a judicial inquiry into undercover policing after acknowledgement by the Met that, dating back to the 1960s, undercover officers had infiltrated civil society organisations that were engaged in lawful activities (Lewis and Evans 2013). The HAC (2013) soon returned to the subject of police complaints, and the government acted on their recommendation to transfer funds from police services to the IPCC for the purpose of increasing the Commission's capacity to conduct independent investigations. A flurry of Home Office activity followed with publication of reviews of the police disciplinary system (Chapman 2014); Triennial Review of the IPCC (Home Office 2015); and IPCC governance arrangements (Drew Smith 2015). Under

Section 33 of the Policing and Crime Act 2017 the IPCC was renamed the Independent Office for Police Conduct with a reformed governance structure. The IPCC Chairperson was replaced by a Director General of the IOPC and Commissioners were replaced by non-executive and employee members.

Despite the move towards independent investigation in recent years, police forces continue to handle the vast majority of complaints and the IOPC investigates only serious and sensitive cases, including deaths and serious injury in compliance with Articles 2 (the right to life), and 3 (prohibition of torture and ill-treatment) of the European Convention on Human Rights. The latest statistics published by the IOPC, which presents figures of police and IOPC complaints investigations separately, reveal that in 2018/19 police forces received a total of 31,097 complaint cases comprising 58,478 allegations,[7] and 21,764 allegations were finalised by investigation (IOPC 2019c). The same year, 4097 complaints cases were referred by police forces to the IOPC (2019a), and the IOPC started 687 investigations and completed 717; of the 2969 appeals against police decisions completed, 96% were found to be valid.

To conclude this brief overview of police complaints reform since the 1960s, research on public satisfaction with procedures conducted since the 1980s, covering the years when each of the four independent oversight bodies referred to above have been operational, has consistently shown that the majority of people with grievances against the police do not complain (Bucke 1995; Smith 2009a). The Crime Survey for England and Wales has routinely found that more than 80% of people that were annoyed or dissatisfied with the police in the previous five years did not complain: of those that did, over 75% were dissatisfied with how their complaint was handled (Office for National Statistics 2010, 2019).

It is all too easy to lose sight of the fact that the police complaints system is fundamentally concerned with the accountability of officers for their conduct. Burgeoning legislation and regulations have resulted in an increasingly complex complaints system with an expanded remit that now includes all expressions of dissatisfaction with the police.[8] Yet, complaining is the principal means by which the victim of police misconduct may seek to hold the officer responsible to account. Nomenclature is important, and the noun *misconduct* refers here to all forms of wrongdoing by a police officer, including criminal offences; tortious conduct; disciplinary offences; poor work performance; and incivility or showing disrespect to a member of the public. All of these types of misbehaviour when reported to police by a member of the public in the form of a complaint are within scope of the complaints system, and under current procedures 'special requirements' have to be adhered to where the allegation is that a criminal or disciplinary offence may have been committed (IPCC 2015). Of course, an officer may be held to account out with the complaints system, for example when an officer is reported by a senior officer or colleague for misconduct or as the result of evidence obtained by a criminal investigation. In these instances, in the absence of a complaint being made by a member of the public the criminal justice and internal disciplinary processes serve to hold officers to account. Private remedies at common law out with the complaints system are also available. A victim may seek to bring criminal proceedings against a police officer by applying to a magistrate for a summons or, as noted above, claim damages from the chief officer of police in civil proceedings, referred to by practitioners in the field as a *police action*. Available in principle, private prosecutions are impractical today, partly because the prosecutor carries the risk of having to defend a claim for malicious prosecution, and are primarily of historical significance, as will be shown in the pages below. Whereas police actions have proved to be an effective remedy in recent years, and play a prominent role in exposing the inadequacies of the complaints system, the financial risks involved for claimants together with the difficulties they face obtaining legal aid leaves complaining as the only practical means by which the vast majority of victims may seek to hold a police officer accountable for misconduct. Continuing for a moment with the importance of language, discourse on accountability as an essential normative component of democratic governance arrangements only emerged as recently as the last quarter of the twentieth century (Marshall 1978; Mulgan 2003; Smith 2009b). A situational concept, accountability is often used as a form of shorthand for a range of complex socio-legal encounters, interactions and relationships in an attempt to focus attention on whether or not power has been exercised fairly and effectively, either by an institution as a matter of policy or by an individual in practice. Underpinning accountability discourse the acts, omissions and decisions of state agents are conceptualised in terms of the authority and powers vested in them, derived from common and statute law, for the purpose of performing their duties and responsibilities which, in the case of police officers is to enforce the law. Throughout the history of modern police, state authorities have always upheld that an officer alleged to have acted unlawfully is answerable to the law in the same way as any other member of the public, which is a normative claim that fails to stand up to close empirical inspection and has always been considered with scepticism by the public at large.

Writing shortly after operationalisation of the IPCC, Smith (2006) observed the existence of a police complaints reform cycle comprising four stages—mounting public concern, appointment of government inquiries, legislative reform and inception of the new regime. In addition to illustrating the slow and incremental trend towards independent investigation of the police over the course of four overlapping cycles, the cyclical heuristic highlighted two constant and interdependent features of complaints reform. Firstly, in the face of public dissatisfaction with the effectiveness of police investigations of police and the resultant damage to trust and confidence, the cycles clearly demonstrated the capacity of the police to retain control of complaints procedures and successfully resist widespread demands for independent investigation. Secondly, in each completed cycle there was under-representation and marginalisation of the interests of complainants, key stakeholders in the reform process, at every stage and particularly during the final inception stage of the cycle. This was when the fine detail of new arrangements was agreed by Home Office civil servants, senior police officers and newly appointed overseers. The police complaints reform cycle captured the reality that policy was going round and round in circles, and it was apparent that having peaked in the late 1990s, exemplified by six-figure awards of damages against the Met Commissioner and Macpherson finding that police forces were institutionally racist, the public interest in addressing police misconduct was significantly diminished by the time the IPCC commenced operations.

Smith's study focused on changes to the complaints system ushered in by legislative reform, and therefore commenced with events leading up to when first codified under the Police Act 1964, and ended before IPCC records were available for analysis. In the mid-2000s it was already evident that the cycle was entering its fifth iteration, which concluded with launch of the IOPC, and it is apparent at the time of writing, 15 years later, that a sixth reform cycle is underway. In July 2019, as part of their 'Macpherson Report: Twenty Years On' inquiry, the HAC (2019a) subjected Director General Michael Lockwood to a gruelling examination on IOPC monitoring of the ethnicity of police officers subjected to complaints investigations. Later in the year, after criticism was directed at the IOPC for finding that there was no evidence of misconduct on the part of Met officers engaged in the Operation Midland child sexual abuse investigation (IOPC 2019b),[9] the HAC (2019b) announced that it was holding an inquiry into the work of the new body and invited written submissions of evidence.[10]

This book is the first of a two-volume study of complaints against Metropolitan Police officers. The study aims to take forward Smith's (2006) analysis and improve understanding of the dilemmas that impede the design and implementation of a fair and effective complaints system. Beginning with formation of the first and by far the largest police force in England and Wales, and ending with codification of the complaints system in 1964 the purpose of this first volume is to explore the antecedents of the present system and attempt to unpick the nexus between police and public that is central to police complaints discourse. The historical examination will, then, serve as the foundation of a second volume that will bring developments up to date.

Standpoint is essential to understanding accountability. The police officer accountability conundrum rests on disputes between two actors that are metaphorically speaking on the wrong side of the law, yet, depending on standpoint, are also likely to believe themselves to be on the right side. From the outset the dispute is defined by asymmetrical power. Irrespective of whether or not the victim is known to police or suspected of committing a criminal offence, by purporting to have acted under the cloak of authority it is open to the officer to seek to justify their conduct, including the use of physical force, by reference to their duty to enforce the law. The victim appears to be on the wrong side of the law not for having acted unlawfully but because they have suffered as a consequence of the behaviour of a police officer who belongs to an institution that represents and symbolises 'the law'. For the majority of victims that is the end of the matter as they believe it is not worthwhile to complain. For the victim that decides to make a stand and formally complain, in objecting to police ill-treatment and seeking to achieve a remedy they take what is for many a major step in attempting to address their victimisation by becoming an active complainant. The police officer complained against appears to be on the wrong side of the law having been accused of acting unlawfully, whether alleged to have committed a criminal offence, a tort or a breach of police discipline. Believing that they are on the right side of the law the complainant that fails to achieve satisfaction is left harbouring a deep sense of injustice against the police. Reassured by the solidarity and support shown by colleagues, the officer believes that they have done nothing wrong and is also likely to feel aggrieved by the experience.

Complainants, including family and friends and those that campaign for accountable policing are all too often dismissed as anti-police. This has the effect of closing down opportunities for dialogue, and the unfortunate tendency for those with policing and oversight responsibilities to reject the experiences and perspectives of people with intimate and invaluable knowledge of police practice. The invisibilisation and disempowerment of victims of misconduct, which have been constant in police history, are countered here by development of a complainant-centred rather than victim-centred standpoint to police officer accountability. Self-evidently, adherence to a complainant-centred standpoint involves examination of the complaints system from below, or bottom up, and priority is given in the chapters below to the public interest in holding officers to account for their conduct. This approach contrasts with the vast majority of studies of policing which focus on the law enforcement functions of police or administrative structures which facilitate law enforcement, where effective law enforcement is widely upheld as the primary public interest. In this study the capacity of police to enforce the law serves as important context, and it is held that in examining the emergence of police as gatekeepers to the criminal justice system and the doctrine of constabulary independence by reference to the experiences of complainants, understanding will be enhanced not only of officer accountability but also of operational law enforcement more generally.

The complainant-centred standpoint developed in this study is under-pinned by personal experiences of victimisation and civil society activism. Arrested with a black gay friend when out one evening in 1983 in Manchester, I was taken unconscious from the police station to hospital where sutures were applied to a head wound. Charged with drunk and disorderly behaviour the following morning, I was told that I was so drunk when I arrived at the station that I fell down a flight of steps. I did not see a doctor and like many others in my position did not consider for one moment that I should complain or speak to a solicitor. I returned to work after spending several days walking the streets in an effort to gather my thoughts and let my stiff and heavily bruised body heal. At work I received an unsympathetic hearing when telling a colleague what had happened, and did not speak about the subject again. I pleaded guilty to the offence, left my job and moved to London.

After finding work and settling in Stoke Newington in the north east London Borough of Hackney, a friend insisted that I complain when a police officer threatened me with arrest and locked me in the back of a patrol car. Although I had done nothing wrong, I froze when spoken to by the officer. Since my experiences at the hands of Manchester officers I had avoided contact with the police and on this occasion I stoically submitted to authority in the hope that I could remove myself from the situation quickly and with the minimum of fuss. Satisfied that I had not committed an offence the officer released me from the car after about three-quarters of an hour. I was upset, but resigned to the fact that the police could, and would, treat me like that. To my friend, this amounted to an unwarranted interference with my rights and was cause enough to complain. Complaining was not a positive experience and whenever in the company of an officer I felt that I was wasting valuable police time. Several weeks after recording my complaint at the local police station two officers visited my home to tell me that after speaking to the officer concerned they were satisfied that his conduct was justified. I subsequently received written notification that my complaint had been resolved.

Early in 1987 graphic posters showing a young man of African Caribbean heritage on a life support machine after he had been detained in Stoke Newington police station were stuck up all over Hackney (Kirby 1987). Determined to address my fear of the police I joined the Family and Friends of Trevor Monerville Campaign. Two further incidents involving the local constabulary attracted national media attention that year. In June, Tunay Hassan died following his arrest by Stoke Newington officers (*The Guardian*, 15 January 1988), and in October Gary Stretch was assaulted by seven off-duty City Road officers (Rose 1987). The following year Hackney Community Defence Association (HCDA), which described itself as a self-help group comprising victims of police crime, was formed. At the Hackney Town Hall launch many were sceptical that HCDA would be able to make a difference. That they were proved wrong was due to the commitment and drive of a core of volunteers with personal experience of police misconduct. As victims and complainants we knew what it was like to be criminalised and feel alone, abandoned and fearful for the future. In truth, many of us were dealing with our own post-traumatic stress disorder when spending time together and offering mutual support. Fiercely independent of political parties and ideologies HCDA's work was uninformed by police theories and academic research. This was not down to a crude form of anti-intellectualism, more a belief that in order to challenge a power many considered insuperable new and radical perspectives had to be explored and developed. HCDA investigated cases and referred directly and provocatively to police crime. Police violence and injustice were directly addressed in terms of the inequality between powerful offenders and powerless victims. Evidence led, HCDA provided a collective voice to complainants and sought to turn the table on the frontline police officers that were responsible for their suffering. In the five years between January 1989 and December 1993, 381 cases of alleged misconduct by Hackney, including City Road, and Stoke Newington police officers were recorded: over half (n = 200) of complainants were of African Caribbean heritage. Assault cases were the highest category investigated (n = 131), and 79.3% of the victims had to defend themselves against criminal charges (HCDA 1994). On learning of allegations that members of Stoke Newington drug squad had been involved in the supply of crack cocaine (Campbell 1992), HCDA conducted a parallel investigation to the Metropolitan Police Operation Jackpot counter-corruption investigation (HCDA 1992; Smith 1999). A total of 90 allegations against Stoke Newington CID officers between December 1988 and November 1992, primarily fabrication of evidence associated with the planting of drugs, were investigated. Of 77 drugs related prosecutions, 70% (*n* = 54) were unsuccessful either as a result of no evidence offered, jury acquittal or appeal against conviction. Eschewing the complaints process, HCDA worked closely with specialist solicitors and supported 83 claimants in police actions against the Met Commissioner.[11]

There are good epistemological reasons for a case study of complaints against officers serving with the Metropolitan Police, which has been known as the Metropolitan Police Service since 1989 (Mawby and Worthington 2002). Mention has already been made of the force's prominent role in national policing affairs, including the modelling of the 1964 statutory complaints system on Met procedures. The governance arrangements for the Met, with the Metropolitan Police Act 1829 providing for the Home Secretary to serve as the Police Authority for the Metropolitan Police District, are of particular importance to the historical examination undertaken in this book.[12] Members of Parliament would regularly table petitions and raise complaints against Met officers on behalf of their constituents in House of Commons debates and written questions, and on several occasions government inquiries were appointed to examine Met officer conduct. A significant amount of research material is available in the shape of reports of Parliamentary debates, written answers, Royal Commissions, and committees of inquiry (including written submissions and minutes of oral evidence).[13] Augmented by press reports and internal records and correspondence between the Met and the Home Office stored in the National Archives, these data sources are interrogated, or re-interrogated, from a complainant-centred standpoint in the chapters below.

Having set out the purpose and standpoint of this book, before providing an outline of chapter contents explanation of some of the limitations of the study will hopefully be of assistance to the reader. Inevitably, there are many omissions and gaps. Primarily concerned with the opportunities available to a member of the public that has fallen victim to police abuse of power to hold the perpetrator to account, it follows that some forms of police offending fall outside the scope of this study. Allegations of bribery and corruption, whether associated with police involvement in professional crime or failure to enforce the law against persons suspected of having committed a criminal offence, in relation to prostitution, gambling, alcohol licensing or drug markets, for example, have been a constant feature of police history (Dixon 1991; McLagan 2003; Morton 1993). Although local knowledge of the impunity enjoyed by a corrupt constable may reinforce asymmetric power between police and community and deter a person from making a complaint, police corruption is not central to the narrative developed here and is only given passing mention in the chapters below. The same applies to police misconduct in the shape of fabrication of evidence associated with miscarriages of justice. Unfortunately there is not the space in this short volume to do justice to what is a distinct and extensive area of study which straddles law enforcement and officer accountability paradigms (McConville et al. 1991; Nobles and Schiff 2000; Walker and Starmer 1999). Another aspect of policing that may appear neglected in the following pages are disputes surrounding political environments in which the police operate (Reiner 1992): whether in the form of allegations of police interference in politics; or arguments that political parties have interfered in police affairs; or disagreement over the activities of police bodies formed to represent the interests of their members like the Police Federation or the Association of Chief Police Officers.[14] The principal reason for the absence of a political commentary is to avoid engaging in a discourse that is of little material consequence to a bottom-up complainant-centred approach to officer misconduct. Exception is made, however, in regard to the politicisation of policing that occurred following a complaint by Irene Savidge about the conduct of Scotland Yard detectives in 1928. It will be argued below that the significance of the Savidge complaint, including appointment of a committee of inquiry and the Royal Commission on Police Powers and Procedure (1928/29 Commission), to the development of the doctrine of constabulary has been overlooked in the literature.

Outline of Chapters

There was much public opposition to creation of a civil force with coercive powers under Sir Robert Peel's Metropolitan Police Act 1829. Retention of the office of constable under the Act and appointment of two *ex officio* justices of the peace commonly known as Commissioners to run the Met were intended to reassure the public that reorganisation of the policing of London was in the interest of administrative efficiency and did not pose a threat to civil liberties. It took a century for what were referred to as the *new police* to establish themselves as gatekeepers to the criminal justice system and assume control of the pre-trial stages of the criminal process. Development of police powers to investigate crime and bring criminal proceedings at common law in the first part of the twentieth century provides important context for the first chapter of this book.

From the outset Met policing was, by all accounts, brutal. The press routinely reported, not always censoriously of police, on violent clashes between police and public with constables invariably resorting to their truncheons. A correspondent of *The Times* captured the violence that preceded the fatal stabbing of a constable at a banned political meeting at Cold Bath Fields in 1833.

> The police furiously attacked the multitude with their staves, felling every person indiscriminately before them; even the females did not escape the blows from their batons—men and boys were lying in every direction weltering in their blood and calling for mercy. The inhabitants from their windows and balconies cried "Shame, shame, mercy, mercy," but the officers still continued the attack, which they kept up for several minutes. A large space of ground within our view was strewed with the wounded, besides others who were less injured who were able to crawl to a surgeon's. (*The Times*, 14 May 1833)

Home Secretary Lord Melbourne had declared the meeting illegal and directed the first Met Commissioners, Lieutenant-Colonel Sir Charles Rowan and Richard Mayne, to prevent the assembly from taking place. With successive home secretaries taking a hands-on approach to operational policing, and the first Commissioners resorting to a strict disciplinary strategy in order to win public support and approval, Chap. 2 examines the evidence relevant to the accountability of Met officers in the nineteenth century. Many constables were dismissed from the force in the early years and it was not uncommon for officers to have to answer for their conduct in criminal proceedings before magistrates in London's police courts. Particular attention is paid to the criminalisation of officer misconduct under Section 14 of the Metropolitan Police Act 1839, which fell into disuse in the latter part of the century as the numbers of officers dismissed and prosecuted declined. Met returns to Parliament giving details of proceedings against officers, supplemented by newspaper reports of proceedings in the police courts, serve as important data sources for examination of officer accountability in the nineteenth century.

At the same time as police were developing their capacity to investigate crime and prepare prosecutions, leading eventually to recognition of their position as gatekeepers to the criminal justice system, reduced numbers of constables prosecuted and convicted in the police courts is taken to indicate that officer accountability was declining in the second half of the nineteenth century. The available statistical data reveal that police assumption of responsibility for preparing criminal prosecutions did not extend to cases where the alleged offender was a constable, and victims of police misconduct, particularly in cases alleging unlawful use of force, were obliged to prosecute privately if they wished to see the officer account for their conduct in a criminal court. A little known Home Office instruction issued in 1868, which required the Met to refer complainants who alleged an officer had committed a criminal offence and the evidence was conflicting to a police court magistrate, had the practical effect of compelling a victim to bring proceedings privately if they wished to achieve a remedy.

Conforming to the first two stages of the police complaints reform cycle, mounting public concern with the conduct of Met officers in the late Victorian early Edwardian era was to lead to the appointment of the 1906–08 Royal Commission upon the Duties of the Metropolitan Police (1906–08 Commission). In Chap. 3 emphasis is placed on the role nascent civil society activism played in supporting victims of misconduct hold officers to account. Much overlooked in the policing literature, the work of the little-known Police and Public Vigilance Society (PPVS) is highlighted.[15] Secretary and Chairman of the Society, James Timewell and Earl Russell, respectively, served as the agent of the 1906–08 Commission, communicating with complainants and arranging the attendance of witnesses at evidence hearings, and counsel for the PPVS in Commission proceedings. The chapter includes narratives of the experiences of three PPVS supported complainants who sought to hold officers to account for their conduct in criminal proceedings, a police action and written complaint to the Met Commissioner. After hearing the evidence in the three cases, the 1906–08 Commission concluded that officers were guilty of misconduct and reached the same findings against a total of one sergeant and eight constables arising from eight cases brought before them by complainants.

The 1906–08 Commission represented an important moment in the history of police complaints reform as the result of failure on the part of the Met to implement their proposals for reform. Close interrogation of their *Report* (1906–08 Commission 1908) along with the minutes of evidence and appendices reveals that the Commissioners examined the same officer accountability problematic considered by the 1960–62 Commission. The conclusions and recommendations of two Royal Commissions held 50 years apart, the first forensically scrutinising complaints procedures in the Metropolitan Police and the second generally considering practice around the United Kingdom, bear close comparison. Accepting that police should investigate police, the 1906–08 Commission recommended that victims of officer misconduct should have access to quasi-judicial internal complaints procedures in addition to criminal and civil law remedies. Contrary to the wishes of government, however, the Met did not introduce the proposed quasi-judicial complaints system, and it was another 50 years before police complaints procedures featured as prominently in public discourse as was the case in the first decade of the century.

Research on the accountability of Met officers for their conduct is restricted by the lack of openness and transparency associated with the operation of internal police complaints systems. In Chap. 4 the complainant-centred narrative continues in the context of the development of police as gatekeepers to the criminal justice system, which is taken to have been established in the late 1920s (1928/29 Commission 1929). Judged on their capacity to enforce the law, and criticised if considered to have failed to deliver fair and effective criminal justice, the reputation of the Met was damaged in the 1920s by a series of high-profile complainants that alleged officers had abused their powers and failed to respect their rights. The complaints gave rise to public concern, which the Home Secretary responded to by appointing a series of public and quasi-judicial inquiries. Reports of parliamentary debates and inquiries, together with internal Met and Home Office documents, provide rare and important insights into police misconduct and officer accountability in this period. The primary purpose of the inquiries was to identify flaws in criminal procedure and make recommendations on how they may be remedied, and in the course of some inquiry proceedings evidence was also obtained of officer misconduct. The pattern of complaints reflected a crisis in policing as the Met tried to keep step with the changing criminal justice landscape, and whether fault was found with law enforcement policy, police regulations or officer conduct the conclusions and recommendation of these inquiries required the attention of the Home Secretary and Met Commissioner.

Once again mounting public concern was to lead to the appointment of a Royal Commission. The 1928/29 Commission was triggered by allegations that Irene Savidge had been subjected to 'third degree' methods when interrogated as a potential witness by Met detectives investigating whether there was a *prima facie* case for charging two constables with perjury. The intention of government was for a specific inquiry with limited terms of reference to examine the Savidge case (Inquiry in Regard to the Interrogation by the Police of Miss Savidge 1928) and, then, for a general inquiry to examine police criminal investigations and the prosecution of offences (1928/29 Commission 1929). Events were to take a different direction. Having divided on party political lines the Savidge Inquiry was inconclusive and the press were highly critical of government for meddling in police affairs. In contrast to the political fall-out that accompanied the Savidge scandal, the impact of the 1928/29 Commission on the police and criminal justice system was limited. The 1920s controversies had exposed tensions in the working relationship between the Home Secretary and Met Commissioner, on which governance arrangements for the Met were based. It is held that after the Savidge case there was a behind the scenes reappraisal of the responsibilities of these two high office holders that was to result in the withdrawal of the Home Secretary from a prominent role in police affairs, and which coincided with the development of the doctrine of constabulary independence.

Chapter 5 steps aside from the historical narrative to discuss a constitutional convention that has been of fundamental importance to the development of internal police complaints systems. The doctrine of constabulary independence is re-imagined in the context of the turmoil arising from the Savidge case and adjustment of the responsibilities of the Home Secretary and Met Commissioner. The origin of the constitutional convention is traced back to a claim for false imprisonment in the case of *Fisher* v. *Oldham Corporation* [1930] 2 K.B. 364, and judgment that when performing their law enforcement duties a police officer exercises an original authority and the local police authority was not liable for the damages incurred. The effect of *Fisher* was that in the performance of their law enforcement function police were protected from political interference, which left forces under the operational control of the chief constable in provincial forces, and policing scholars are agreed that this transfer of responsibility took place in the 1930s (Keith-Lucas 1960; Marshall 1965).

Mr. Fisher's claim and judgment in the case are reconsidered in Chap. 5 by reference to firstly, recalibration of the Home Secretary and Met Commissioner's responsibilities which preceded changes to the relations between police authorities and chief constables in other forces across the country and, secondly, a public discourse on police authority and responsibility which had been prompted by events in the Met. Senior Home Office civil servants with responsibilities for policing were prominent participants in the discourse on police governance, and their propositions on the responsibilities of police authorities for policy, their exclusion from matters concerning operational law enforcement and the original authority exercised by a constable were expressed in remarkably similar language by the 1928/29 Commission and McCardie J in the *Fisher* judgment. A consequence of police operational independence which was not raised in debate was that in protecting the police from political interference, operational independence was also to protect the police from democratic scrutiny.

If the first three decades of the twentieth century were witness to the police consolidating their status as gatekeepers to the criminal justice system, the next three were to see police forces at the peak of their powers as the convention of constabulary independence took centre stage. Chapter 6 resumes the historical narrative and is largely devoted to examination of the centralised internal complaints system developed in the early 1930s by A-1 Branch located in the Met Commissioner's Office at Scotland Yard, believed to be the first in the United Kingdom. Discussion on the pre-war years focuses on annual complaints summaries comprising statistical data sets that were internally disseminated within the Met, and not shared with the public. Emphasis is placed on types of data recorded and the quality of collection methods; police prioritisation of the circumstances and characters of complainants rather than allegations of misconduct against officers; disparities in substantiation rates between categories of complaints that corresponds with the seriousness of allegations. The volume of complaints recorded dropped during the war years and it was the late 1950s before pre-war figures were matched. With A-1 Branch attributing the increase in complaints to a growing awareness among members of the public of their civil liberties and individual rights, notes included in their annual summaries on complaints which involved *ex gratia* payments or settlements of civil claims serve to illustrate aspects of the developing system. The chapter concludes with a discussion of the evidence on complaints submitted to the 1960–62 Commission by the Met, along with evidence presented by the National Council for Civil Liberties, Justice and legal associations in support of independent oversight of the police.

Notes

1. S. 33 (3) (a) of the Police Act 1964 provided for the police authority to serve as disciplinary authority for the chief constable, deputy chief constable and assistant chief constables, and the chief constable was the disciplinary authority for all other ranks under s. 33 (3) (b).
2. Under the Police (Appeals) Act 1927, and Police (Appeals) Act 1943.
3. National Archives MEPO 2/11196, Police Advisory Boards working party on investigation of complaints against police officers report.
4. The Royal Commission on Criminal Procedure was also instrumental to prosecution reform and creation of the Crown Prosecution Service under the Prosecution of Offences Act 1985.

5. The DPP voluntarily relinquished responsibility for decision making in police cases pending the outcome of an independent inquiry (Butler 1999).
6. In parallel with the Home Office funded KPMG research, Liberty obtained research funding from the Nuffield Foundation (Harrison and Cunneen 2000).
7. Each complaint case may comprise one or more allegation.
8. Under s. 14 (2) of the Policing and Crime Act 2017.
9. *Hansard*, Parl Debs HC 7 October 2019, cols. 1553–1562. See also: three chapters of Sir Richard Henriques (2016) review of Met investigations into non-recent sexual abuse offences published online on 4 October 2019 with introduction; Henriques (2019), Lockwood (2019).
10. The inquiry was delayed as a result of the dissolution of Parliament on 5 November 2019.
11. The work of HCDA will be examined in Volume Two of this study.
12. This was a different arrangement to the one introduced in the rest of England and Wales. Watch committees were appointed, which comprised elected councillors and representatives of local justices, in borough police forces, and similarly constituted joint standing committees governed county forces in accordance with rules drafted by the Home Secretary. The Home Secretary was replaced as the Police Authority for the Metropolitan Police District by the Metropolitan Police Authority under Section 312 of the Greater London Authority Act 1999; and the Metropolitan Police Authority was replaced by the Mayor's Office for Policing and Crime under Section 3 of the Police Reform and Social Responsibility Act 2011.
13. Now provided by ProQuest Parliamentary Papers Online at https://www.proquest.com/products-services/House-of-Commons-Parliamentary-Papers.html.
14. Replaced by the National Police Chiefs' Council on 1 April 2015.
15. With the notable exception of Johansen (2011, 2013) the PPVS has largely escaped the attention of policing scholars.

References

1906–08 Commission, see Royal Commission upon the Duties of the Metropolitan Police.
1928/29 Commission, see Royal Commission on Police Powers and Procedure.

1960–62 Commission, see Royal Commission on the Police.

Benn, M., & Warpole, K. (1986). *Death in the City*. London: Canary Press.

Bucke, T. (1995). *Policing and the Public: Findings from the 1994 British Crime Survey*. Home Office Research and Statistics Department Research Findings No. 28. London: HMSO.

Butler, G. (1999). *Inquiry into Crown Prosecution Service Decision-making in Relation to Deaths in Custody and Related Matters*. London: TSO.

Campbell, D. (1992, January 31). Police Suspected of Drug Dealing. *The Guardian*, p. 1.

Chapman, C. (2014). *An Independent Review of the Police Disciplinary System in England and Wales*. London: Home Office Retrieved from https://www.gov.uk/government/publications/the-police-disciplinary-system-in-england-and-wales.

Chief Inspector of Constabulary. (1964). *Report of Her Majesty's Chief Inspector of Constabulary for the Year 1963*, 1963–64 HC 259. ProQuest Parliamentary Papers Online.

Commissioner of Police of the Metropolis. (1965). *Report of the Commissioner of Police of the Metropolis for the Year 1964*, 1964–65 Cmnd. 2710. ProQuest Parliamentary Papers Online.

Commissioner of Police of the Metropolis. (1997). *Report of the Commissioner of Police of the Metropolis for the Year 1996/97*. London: Metropolitan Police Service.

Council of Europe Committee for the Prevention of Torture. (2000). *Report to the United Kingdom Government on the Visit to the United Kingdom and the Isle of Man Carried Out by the European Committee for the Prevention of Torture and Inhuman or Degrading Treatment or Punishment (CPT) from 8 to 17 September 1997*, CPT/Inf (2000) 1. Strasbourg: Council of Europe.

Demuth, C. (1978). *'Sus', a report on the Vagrancy Act 1824*. London: Runnymede Trust.

Dixon, D. (1991). *From Prohibition to Regulation: Bookmaking, Anti-gambling, and the Law*. Oxford: Oxford University Press.

Drew Smith, S. (2015). *An Independent Review of the Governance Arrangements of the Independent Police Complaints Commission*. London: Home Office Retrieved from https://www.gov.uk/government/publications/governance-of-the-independent-police-complaints-commission.

Fisher, H. A. P. (1977). *Report of an Inquiry by the Hon. Sir Henry Fisher into the Circumstances Leading to the Trial of Three Persons on Charges Arising Out of the Death of Maxwell Confait and the Fire at 27 Doggett Road, London SE6*, 1977–78 HC 90. ProQuest Parliamentary Papers Online.

HAC, see Home Affairs Committee.

Hackney Community Defence Association. (1992). *A Crime is a Crime is a Crime: A Short Report on Police Crime in Hackney*. London: HCDA.

Hackney Community Defence Association. (1994). *Who Killed Patrick Quinn? The Framing of Malcolm Kennedy*. London: HCDA.

Harrison, J., & Cunneen, M. (2000). *An Independent Police Complaints Commission*. London: Liberty.

HCDA, see Hackney Community Defence Association.

Henriques, R. (2016). *An Independent Review of the Metropolitan Police Service's Handling of Non-recent Sexual Offence Investigations Alleged against Persons of Public Prominence*. Metropolitan Police Service Online Publication. Retrieved January 4, 2020, from https://www.met.police.uk/henriques.

Henriques, R. (2019, October 7). Lamentable. Inadequate. Inexcusable: Sir Richard Henriques Blasts the Police Watchdog Who Ruled Not One Officer Should Be Punished over the 'Nick the Fantasist' Scandal. *Mail Online*. Retrieved from https://www.dailymail.co.uk/news/article-7544207/Sir-Richard-Henriques-blasts-police-watchdog-ruled-not-one-officer-punished.html.

Hewitt, P. (1982). *A Fair Cop*. London: National Council for Civil Liberties.

Hillsborough Independent Panel. (2012). *The Report of the Hillsborough Panel*. Retrieved from http://hillsborough.independent.gov.uk/report/.

Home Affairs Committee. (1982). *Fourth Report from the Home Affairs Committee, Police Complaints Procedures*, 1981–82 HC 91-I. ProQuest Parliamentary Papers Online.

Home Affairs Committee. (1998). *First Report, Police Disciplinary and Complaints Procedures*, 1997–98 HC 258-I. ProQuest Parliamentary Papers Online.

Home Affairs Committee. (2010). *The Work of the Independent Police Complaints Commission: Eleventh Report of Session 2009–10*, HC 366. Retrieved from http://www.publications.parliament.uk/pa/cm200910/cmselect/cmhaff/366/366.pdf.

Home Affairs Committee. (2013). *Independent Police Complaints Commission: Eleventh Report of Session 2012–13*, HC 494. Retrieved from https://publications.parliament.uk/pa/cm201213/cmselect/cmhaff/494/494.pdf.

Home Affairs Committee. (2019a). Oral Evidence: The Macpherson Report: Twenty Years On, HC 1829, Tuesday 9 July 2019. Retrieved from http://data.parliament.uk/writtenevidence/committeeevidence.svc/evidencedocument/home-affairs-committee/the-macpherson-report-twenty-years-on/oral/103657.html.

Home Affairs Committee. (2019b). *The Home Affairs Committee Launches an Inquiry into Police Conduct and Complaints.* Retrieved from https://www. parliament.uk/business/committees/committees-a-z/commons-select/home-affairs-committee/news-parliament-2017/police-conduct-and-complaints-launch-19-20/.

Home Office. (2015). *Triennial Review of the Independent Police Complaints Commission (IPCC).* London: Home Office Retrieved from https://assets. publishing.service.gov.uk/government/uploads/system/uploads/attachment_ data/file/411566/IPCC_Triennial_Review.pdf.

Humphry, D., & John, G. (1971). *Because They're Black.* Harmondsworth: Penguin.

Hunte, J. A. (1966). *Nigger Hunting in England?* London: West Indian Standing Conference.

Independent Office for Police Conduct. (2019a). *Annual Report and Statement of Accounts 2018/19.* London: IOPC Retrieved from https://www.policecon-duct.gov.uk/sites/default/files/Documents/Who-we-are/accountability-per-formance/IOPC_annual_report_and_accounts_2018-19.pdf.

Independent Office for Police Conduct. (2019b). *Operation Kentia: A Report Concerning Matters Related to the Metropolitan Police Service's Operation Midland and Operation Vincente.* London: IOPC Retrieved from https://www. policeconduct.gov.uk/sites/default/files/Operation_Kentia_Report.pdf.

Independent Office for Police Conduct. (2019c). *Police Complaints: Statistics for England and Wales 2018/19.* London: IOPC Retrieved from https://www. policeconduct.gov.uk/sites/default/files/Documents/statistics/coplaints_ statistics_2018_19_v2.pdf.

Independent Police Complaints Commission. (2005). *Annual Report and Accounts 2004/05,* HC 608. London: TSO. Retrieved from https://assets. publishing.service.gov.uk/government/uploads/system/uploads/attachment_ data/file/235247/0608.pdf.

Independent Police Complaints Commission. (2008). *Annual Report and Accounts 2007/08,* HC 898. London: TSO. Retrieved from https://assets. publishing.service.gov.uk/government/uploads/system/uploads/attachment_ data/file/248451/0898.pdf.

Independent Police Complaints Commission. (2015). *Statutory Guidance to the Police Service on the Handling of Complaints.* London: IPCC Retrieved from https://www.policeconduct.gov.uk/sites/default/files/Documents/statuto-ryguidance/2015_statutory_guidance_english.pdf.

Inquiry in Regard to the Interrogation by the Police of Miss Savidge. (1928). *Report of the Tribunal Appointed under the Tribunals of Inquiry (Evidence) Act, 1921,* Cmd. 3147. ProQuest Parliamentary Papers Online.

IOPC, see Independent Office for Police Conduct.

IPCC, see Independent Police Complaints Commission.

Johansen, A. (2011). Keeping Up Appearances: Police Rhetoric, Public Trust and "Police Scandal" in London and Berlin, 1880–1914. *Crime, History & Societies, 15*(1), 59–83.

Johansen, A. (2013). Defending the Individual: the Personal Rights Association and the Ligue des droits de l'homme, 1871–1916. *European Review of History, 20*(4), 559–579.

Keith-Lucas, B. (1960). The Independence of Chief Constables. *Public Administration, 38*(1), 1–15.

Kirby, T. (1987, January 23). Police 'Forcibly Took Man's Prints'. *Independent*, p. 2.

KPMG. (2000). *Feasibility of an Independent System for Investigating Complaints against the Police*. Police Research Series Paper No. 124. London: Home Office Policing and Reducing Crime Unit.

Lambert, J. R. (1970). *Crime, Police, and Race Relations: A Study in Birmingham*. London: Oxford University Press.

Lewis, P., & Evans, P. (2013). *Undercover: The True Story of Britain's Secret Police*. London: Faber and Faber.

Lockwood, M. (2019, October 8). Operation Midland made Mistakes, but the Presumption of Innocence Must Prevail. *The Guardian*. Retrieved from https://www.theguardian.com/commentisfree/2019/oct/08/mistakes-operation-midland-iopc-investigation-carl-beech.

Macpherson, W. (1999). *The Stephen Lawrence Inquiry: Report of an Inquiry by Sir William Macpherson of Cluny*, 1998–99 Cm 4262. ProQuest Parliamentary Papers Online.

Marshall, G. (1965). *Police and Government: The Status and Accountability of the English Constable*. London: Methuen.

Marshall, G. (1978). Police Accountability Revisited. In D. Butler & A. H. Halsey (Eds.), *Policy and Politics* (pp. 51–65). London: Methuen.

Mawby, R. C., & Worthington, S. (2002). Marketing the Police—From a Force to a Service. *Journal of Marketing Management, 18*(9–10), 857–876.

McConville, M., Sanders, A., & Leng, R. (1991). *The Case for the Prosecution: Police Suspects and the Construction of Criminality*. London: Routledge.

McLagan, G. (2003). *Bent Coppers: The Inside Story of Scotland Yard's Battle against Police Corruption*. London: Orion Publishing.

Met Commissioner, see Commissioner of Police of the Metropolis.

Morgan, A., & Jukes, P. (2017). *Untold: The Daniel Morgan Murder Exposed*. London: Blink.

Morton, J. (1993). *Bent Coppers: A Survey of Police Corruption*. London: Little, Brown.

Mulgan, R. (2003). *Holding Power to Account: Accountability in Modern Democracies*. Basingstoke: Palgrave.

National Audit Office. (2008). *The Independent Police Complaints Commission: Report by the Comptroller and Auditor General*. NAO. Retrieved from http://www.nao.org.uk/publications/0708/police_complaints_commission.aspx.

Nobles, R., & Schiff, D. (2000). *Understanding Miscarriages of Justice: Law, the Media and the Inevitability of Crisis*. Oxford: Clarendon.

Office for National Statistics. (2010). Table S28: Perceptions of Police Contact and Complaints Process, Year Ending March 2004 to March 2010, Crime Survey for England and Wales. Retrieved August 12, from https://www.ons.gov.uk/peoplepopulationandcommunity/crimeandjustice/adhocs/005773tables28perceptionsofpolicecontactandcomplaintsprocessyearsending-march2004tomarch2010csew.

Office for National Statistics. (2019). Table S27: Perceptions of Police Contact and Complaints Process, Year Ending March 2011 to March 2018. Retrieved August 12, 2019, from https://www.ons.gov.uk/peoplepopulationandcommunity/crimeandjustice/datasets/crimeinenglandandwalesannualsupplementarytables.

Plowden, P. (1981). *The Establishment of an Independent Element in the Investigation of Complaints against the Police: Report of a Working Party Appointed by the Home Secretary*, Cmnd. 8193. ProQuest Parliamentary Papers Online.

Povey, D., & Cotton, J. (2001). *Police Complaints and Discipline England and Wales, 12 Months to March 2001*. London: Home Office Research Development and Statistics Directorate.

Prenzler, T., & Ronken, C. (2001). Models of Police Oversight: A Critique. *Policing and Society: An International Journal, 11*(2), 151–180.

Reiner, R. (1992). *The Politics of the Police*. Hemel Hempstead: Harvester Wheatsheaf.

Rose, D. (1987, November 11). Off-duty Policeman in Pub Beating Claim: Investigation Launched as Wounded Man Seeks Damages for Savage Beer Glass Attack. *The Guardian*.

Royal Commission on Criminal Procedure. (1981). *Report*, 1980–81 Cmnd 8092. ProQuest Parliamentary Papers Online.

Royal Commission on Police Powers and Procedure. (1929). *Report of the Royal Commission on Police Powers and Procedure*, Cmd. 3297. ProQuest Parliamentary Papers Online.

Royal Commission on the Police. (1962). *Final Report of the Royal Commission on the Police*, Cmnd. 1728. ProQuest Parliamentary Papers Online.

Royal Commission upon the Duties of the Metropolitan Police. (1908). *Report of the Royal Commission upon the Duties of the Metropolitan Police Along with Appendices, Vol. I*, Cd. 4156. ProQuest Parliamentary Papers Online.

Savage, S. (2007). *Police Reform: Forces for Change*. Oxford: Oxford University Press.

Scarman, L. G. (1981). *The Brixton Disorders 10–12 April 1981: Report of an Inquiry by the Rt. Hon. The Lord Scarman, OBE*, Cmnd. 8427. ProQuest Parliamentary Papers Online.

Scraton, P., & Chadwick, K. (1986). *In the Arms of the Law*. London: Pluto Press.

Select Committee on Race Relations. (1972). *Police/Immigrant Relations Report*, 1971–72 HC 471-I. ProQuest Parliamentary Papers Online.

Sivanandan, A. (1982). *A Different Hunger: Writings on Black Resistance*. London: Pluto Press.

Smith, G. (1997). The DPP and Prosecutions of Police Officers. *New Law Journal, 147*(6804), 1108.

Smith, G. (1999). The Legacy of the Stoke Newington Scandal. *International Journal of Police Science & Management, 2*(2), 156–163.

Smith, G. (2001). Police Complaints and Criminal Prosecutions. *Modern Law Review, 64*(3), 372–392.

Smith, G. (2006). A Most Enduring Problem: Police Complaints Reform in England and Wales. *Journal of Social Policy, 35*(1), 121–141.

Smith, G. (2009a). Why Don't More People Complain against the Police? *European Journal of Criminology, 6*(3), 249–266.

Smith, G. (2009b). Citizen Oversight of Independent Police Services: Bifurcated Accountability, Regulation Creep, and Lesson Learning. *Regulation & Governance, 3*(4), 421–441.

Trew, W. N. (2015). *Black for a Cause… Not Just Because…: The Case of the 'Oval 4' and the Story it Tells of Black Power in 1970s Britain*. London: Trew Books.

Walker, C., & Starmer, K. (Eds.). (1999). *Miscarriages of Justice: A Review of Justice in Error*. Oxford: Oxford University Press.

2

Disciplined Force

Formation of the Metropolitan Police (Met) is attributed to the political acumen of Sir Robert Peel. As Chief Secretary of Ireland he was responsible for creation of the Peace Preservation Force, precursor of the Royal Irish Constabulary, and following his appointment as Home Secretary in 1822 he quickly established his credentials for criminal justice reform.[1] That Peel should be remembered more as the founder of police forces in the English speaking world, rather than principal architect of the modern criminal justice system is unsurprising. The police established themselves as gatekeepers to the criminal process, gained a reputation for fair and effective law enforcement and flourished as a powerful symbol of liberal democratic Britain.

A network of police forces was established by statute across England and Wales in the quarter-century or so following the Metropolitan Police Act 1829. The Lighting and Watching Act 1833 allowed for the appointment of serjeants of the watch and watchmen to serve as constables in provincial towns. The Municipal Corporations Act 1835 enabled the first local authorities to set up borough police forces, the County Police Act 1839 allowed provincial counties to do the same and the City of London Police Act 1839 protected the independence of a small force surrounded

© The Author(s) 2020
G. Smith, *On the Wrong Side of The Law*, Palgrave's Critical Policing Studies,
https://doi.org/10.1007/978-3-030-48222-0_2

by the Met. The Town Police Clauses Act 1847 clarified police powers and, finally, the County and Borough Police Act 1856 required all local councils to establish forces.

The historical backdrop to the emergence of modern police forces, referred to as the *new police*, was of a country deep in the throes of revolutionary upheaval. With the economic and political power of the landed aristocracy waning, and industrialisation transforming the geographical landscape, society changed beyond recognition within a single generation. Until the 1830s the main unit of organisation was the parish, and the Justice of the Peace, or magistrate, was at the hub of local administration. The Reform Act 1832 extended the franchise to the industrial middle class, and elected local authorities were established by the Municipal Corporations Act 1835.

The constable was, and remains to this day, the basic building block of police organisations in the United Kingdom.[2] The origin of the office is often traced back to the thirteenth century, and there are references to the constable serving as a senior officer of the court. Yet, there was little resemblance between the high constable and the lowly parish or petty constable, an office that did not appear in statute until the end of the fifteenth century (Critchley 1967; Simpson 1895). With little mention in statute or case law until the eighteenth century, it is widely accepted that the custom of local parishes appointing constables to keep the peace was acknowledged by parliament in legislation. An executive officer who was subordinate to the Justice of the Peace, the parish constable had few powers that separated him from the citizen.

Continuation of the subordination of Met constables to the authority of a magistrate was maintained under the Metropolitan Police 1829 Act by appointment of two *ex-officio* Justices with joint responsibility for administration of the Force. The first two, Lieutenant-Colonel Sir Charles Rowan and Richard Mayne, a barrister, were commonly referred to as Commissioners and their duties were restricted to preserving the peace, preventing crime, and the detection and committal of offenders.[3] Section 1 of the Act laid down that the Commissioners would direct and control constables they commanded under the immediate authority of the Secretary of State for the Home Department, thereby establishing the Home Secretary as the Police Authority for the Metropolitan Police District with express powers to issue directions 'from time to time' to the Commissioners.[4]

Controversy surrounded the new police from the outset, and two parliamentary select committees were appointed in 1833. The Select Committee on Cold Bath Fields Meeting (1833) was set up to inquire into police use of force at a meeting of the National Political Union of the Working Classes. Home Secretary Lord Melbourne, with the government fearful of revolutionary turmoil, declared the meeting illegal and directed the Met Commissioners to prevent the event from taking place. Government trepidation in the face of popular dissent was a recurring theme throughout the nineteenth century, and *The Times* (14 May 1833) graphically described the brutality of the police at Cold Bath Fields. Three police officers were stabbed in the melee, PC Robert Culley fatally, and the jury at the coroner's inquest into the cause of his death returned a verdict of justifiable homicide. Under bizarre circumstances the Solicitor-General applied for judicial review and four judges sitting in the Court of the King's Bench unanimously quashed the verdict for having no validity in law (*The Times*, 31 May 1833). In response, the jurors petitioned parliament to complain that their integrity and the authority of juries generally had been undermined. The lawfulness of the banning order was discussed in the House of Commons,[5] before the Select Committee exonerated the police in a two-page *Report* (Select Committee on Cold Bath Fields Meeting 1833).

Shortly before announcement of the Cold Bath Fields inquiry, another select committee was appointed to inquire into an allegation of spying (Select Committee on the Petition of Frederick Young and Others 1833). William Cobbett MP presented a petition to the House of Commons by Frederick Young and other members of the Southwark and Wallworth Union of the Working Classes complaining that Police Sergeant William Popay joined the Union under the guise of an artist.[6] The Select Committee found that Popay had exceeded his instructions and had not been supervised as closely as he should have been. They condemned the use of spies as 'most alien to the spirit of the Constitution' (Select Committee on the Petition of Frederick Young and Others 1833: 3) and Popay was dismissed from the Metropolitan Police.[7]

With the first Met Commissioners and their supporters in favour of increasing police powers in the interest of improving the prevention and detection of crime, their opponents warned of the risk of damage to constitutional rights as a result of expansion of state power.[8] One occasion when a constable could justify interfering with the constitutional rights of a citizen was after an allegation that a criminal offence had been committed (*Samuel* v. *Payne* (1780) 1 Dougl. 39; *Beckwith* v. *Philby* (1827) 6 B. & C. 635). A corollary of the common law power of the constable to arrest on grounds of reasonable suspicion for the purpose of taking a suspect before a magistrate for questioning was that the new police were steered in the direction of law enforcement, rather than crime prevention, from their very formation. The permissiveness of the common law allowed the police to assume responsibility for criminal investigations and prosecutions and emerge as gatekeepers to the criminal process.

In the wake of the Popay scandal there was reluctance on the part of the Commissioners to develop the capacity of the Met to investigate crime, commonly attributed to their cautious approach to winning public approval (Ascoli 1979). Nine years later public pressure arising from failure to arrest a murder suspect persuaded Rowan and Mayne to ask the Home Secretary for permission to establish a small detective force comprising two inspectors and six sergeants.[9] Some 25 years later in his first year as Met Commissioner (1870), Lieutenant-Colonel Sir Edmund Henderson reported that he inherited 15 detectives, all stationed at Scotland Yard, and 180 detectives were appointed later the same year to serve across the divisions of the Metropolitan Police. Further scandal hit the detective department in 1877 when three senior officers were convicted of turf fraud, which triggered extensive reorganisation and creation of the renowned Criminal Investigation Department (CID) (Commissioner of Police of the Metropolis 1878). Thus, it was close to half-a-century before public opposition to criminal investigation by police was sufficiently neutralised, and an elite squad of officers was established with their own administrative structure.[10]

Alongside their evolving criminal investigation capacity police assumption of responsibility for criminal prosecutions illustrated the proactive character of policing. The quality of justice left much to be desired in the early to mid-nineteenth century and prosecutions were conducted privately at great expense to victims (Hay and Snyder 1989). Proceedings were often long drawn out affairs which required the services of a solicitor, and for many people the time, expense and emotional considerations discouraged them from prosecuting offenders.[11] As early as 1837 Commissioner Mayne gave evidence to the Commission on Criminal Law (1837) that police officers were responsible for many prosecutions in London, a pronouncement that was critically received by members of the legal profession.[12] The Commission on Criminal Law (1845) shortly returned to the issue and, with no end in sight of the controversy over whether prosecutions should be conducted privately or by police a select committee was eventually appointed (Select Committee on Public Prosecutors 1855, 1856). Fiercely contested debates took place between supporters of the police and members of the legal profession: favourable reports of police marshalling prosecution witnesses and liaising with court clerks were countered by allegations of corrupt and over-zealous police. The Select Committee's recommendation that salaried public prosecutors should be appointed to each county court district was not acted on by government, and over the course of the next two decades the tide of opinion turned. When the subject was next debated in parliament, leading up to creation of the Director of Public Prosecutions (DPP) under the Prosecution of Offences Act 1879, disagreement about the responsibilities of the police for criminal prosecutions had been largely settled. After the 1879 Act police continued to rely on their common law powers to prepare the vast majority of prosecutions and difficult cases, previously referred to the Treasury Solicitor, were passed to the DPP[13] (Edwards 1964; Hetherington 1989).

Expansion of police powers into investigation and prosecution required recalibration of the administration of criminal justice in the lower courts. In his *History of Criminal Law in England*, the celebrated late nineteenth-century jurist Sir James Fitzjames Stephen (1883) outlined the change when observing that the Justice's responsibilities for the detection and apprehension of offenders passed to the police.[14] In an often quoted passage of his book, Stephen (1883: 493–494) introduced the idea of the police officer serving as a citizen in uniform:

The police in their different grades are no doubt officers appointed by law for the purpose of arresting criminals; but they possess for this purpose no powers which are not also possessed by private persons. They are, indeed, protected in arresting innocent persons upon a reasonable suspicion that they have committed felony, whether in fact felony has been committed or not.… A policeman has no other right as to asking questions or compelling the attendance of witnesses than a private person has; in a word, with some few exceptions, he may be described as a private person paid to perform as a matter of duty acts which, if so minded, he might have done voluntarily.

Staggered introduction of police forces around England and Wales in the mid-nineteenth century inevitably resulted in uneven development of criminal justice procedures. As the first and largest force it is generally held that the Met served as pioneers of best practice, and police prosecutions became the norm in the police courts of London earlier than elsewhere in the country (Churchill 2014; Gattrell 1990; Godfrey 2008). In developing their position as gatekeepers to the criminal process it is evident that the quality of criminal justice improved with introduction of the new police, and the status of the constable as an independent law enforcement officer rests at the heart of official police narratives. It is equally apparent that the concentration of power in an executive body, absent appropriate checks and balances, created immense difficulties for aggrieved citizens who sought to hold police officers to account for any wrongs they may have suffered. This is a narrative seldom heard, and close interrogation of nineteenth-century records is required to discover evidence of the realities faced by victims of police abuse.

Early Complaints Mechanisms

Citizens commonly raised grievances by petitioning the House of Commons in the nineteenth century, and Members of Parliament would regularly ask questions of the Home Secretary about the conduct of Metropolitan Police officers on the floor of the House.[15] A general inquiry into the efficiency of the new police was postponed pending the conclusion of the two 1833 select committees appointed to consider the petitions to parliament referred to above. The 1834 Select Committee on the Police of the Metropolis (1834 Select Committee 1834: 21) concluded that the force was 'one of the most valuable of modern institutions'.

Evidence to the 1834 Select Committee was not entirely uncritical of the police, and questions were raised about the problems citizens faced if they wished to hold officers accountable for their conduct. Robert Broughton, a magistrate in East London, testified to the difficulties facing magistrates when dealing with allegations against police—'if they are charged with an assault or any offence, for which as citizens they are liable, we grant a warrant, or more generally a summons; but there are many little misdemeanours and misconduct on the part of the constable' (1834 Select Committee 1834: 141). John Hardwick, another East London magistrate, captured the powerlessness of victims of police misconduct in his evidence:

> one of the new police was brought to the office on a warrant… I thought it was a gross case; but as this officer was on duty at the time, and knowing that the Commissioners had the power of punishing him, I thought it would be more advisable to direct the superintendent to report all the circumstances that had occurred, in order that the Commissioner should inquire into them; and I confess I was a little struck at the memorandum that was made upon the back of that report, in the handwriting of one of the Commissioners, that 'the offence was so gross that he could not believe that a police constable would be guilty of it,' and no further inquiry took place. (1834 Select Committee 1834: 178)

Although he believed it to be his duty to report such conduct, Hardwick admitted that he had not done so again as a result of this experience.[16] Hardwick was appointed stipendiary magistrate at Marylebone Street Police Court in 1841, and heard cases arising out of a disturbance in Hyde Park in July 1855 (see further, below).

Asked about the liability of officers in actions for false imprisonment and assault, Queen Square magistrate William White answered 'what damages could a police constable give to a man so imprisoned, or what kind of action could a poor labourer, who has been locked up all night and got his head broken, bring against the police?' He added, 'I think there is no security to the poor, because I think they are very much ill-treated by the police' (1834 Select Committee 1834: 150) White was of the opinion that criminal justice had improved with creation of the police and, along with other magistrates, had not resorted to complaining because he did not wish to 'be looked upon as an enemy of the Police force' (1834 Select Committee 1834: 151).

Consistent with the evidence to the 1834 Select Committee, few references to civil or criminal proceedings and complaints are to be found in official documents, including parliamentary and law reports, of the nineteenth century. In *Bowditch* v. *Balchi* (1850) 5 Ex. 378, 155 E.R. 165, a rare example of a reported civil claim against a constable, a City of London officer was found liable for assault and false imprisonment after arresting a suspect without a warrant.[17]

Under Section 5 of the Metropolitan Police Act 1829, Commissioners Rowan and Mayne were responsible for force regulations and discipline. There was a turnover of over 80% in force strength in the first 16 months: dismissal for being drunk on duty amounting to 80% of the total (1834 Select Committee 1834: 31–32), and resignations were largely attributed to the low wages of three shillings a day (Radzinowicz 1968). In evidence to the 1834 Select Committee (1834: 420–421), Commissioner Mayne outlined the Met's complaints procedure:

A party may now either write a letter to the Commissioner, upon which he receives an immediate answer that inquiry will be made into the subject of the complaint; his letter is then sent down to the Superintendent of the Police at the place, who makes his inquiries from the parties at times the most convenient to them; he calls upon them, takes down their statement, and hears what the officer accused has to say in answer; or sometimes the parties complaining prefer going to the Superintendent's office on the spot to make their statement; in that case, if the offence be trifling, it is sometimes settled by the officer expressing sorrow and apologising to the party, or some small fine is imposed by the Superintendent, which is afterwards submitted to the Commissioners, as is done in all cases, and they approve of it, or otherwise, as appears fit; or should the party wish to come down to the Commissioners, if it be a case which is likely to require the dismissal of a man, or any other reason makes him wish to come before them, he may

2 Disciplined Force   37

do so, and then a time, the most convenient to him, is appointed for the purpose, and the case is then disposed of; or if the case be of that importance that the Superintendent cannot settle it, and that the parties do not choose to come down to Whitehall, the statements of all are taken down in writing on the spot, and sent to the Commissioners, upon which they have the man before them, and decide the case without requiring the parties to attend. The Commissioners think they can safely say, that they do not believe that any complaint has been withheld from the want of facility in having it heard and decided on the spot.

Three returns to parliament submitted by the Metropolitan Police (1844a, 1849a, 1853) gave numbers of officers who resigned, were dismissed or received other disciplinary sanctions. A total of 2841 officers were dismissed in the 11 years between 1842 and 1852, and a further 6279 received the lesser sanctions of a fine or reduction in rank. The strength of the Metropolitan Police (1844b) was 4393 in 1842, which increased to 5513 in 1848 (Metropolitan Police 1849b). Thus, after the very high turnover of officers in the years immediately following creation of the Met, the annual rate fell to 18.7% by 1842: 6.9% of the total turnover was due to dismissals, which was further reduced to 3.4% in 1848. Publication of annual statistics on police numbers commenced in the first annual report of the Commissioner of Police of the Metropolis (1870). The annual turnover of officers as a consequence of dismissals and requirements to resign (some of which will have been for health reasons) steadily fell from 5.5% in 1862, to 0.9% in each of the last three years of the nineteenth century.[18]

Maintaining discipline was of major concern to the first Met Commissioners, and government intervened early to introduce what may be described as a police criminal code under Section 10 of the Administration of Justice Act 1833:

[If] any Constable appointed and sworn in as herein-before last mentioned, shall be guilty of any disobedience of Orders, Neglect of Duty, or of any Misconduct as such Constable, and shall be convicted thereof before Two Justices of the Peace, he shall forfeit any Sum not exceeding Ten Pounds, and in default of immediate Payment shall suffer Imprisonment, with or without hard Labour, for any Time not exceeding Three Months.

The types of misconduct set out in statute were also offences at common law, and Section 10 was considered to be a pragmatic solution to the inconvenience faced by members of the public who had to travel to Metropolitan Police headquarters in Whitehall in order to make a complaint (1834 Select Committee 1834; Radzinowicz 1968). However, it is evident that the purpose of the code was not limited to making the complaints system accessible to people who lived in the suburbs of London. In evidence to the Select Committee (1834: 339) Commissioner Mayne declared: 'it would be preferable to send complaints much more frequently to magistrates than to us; we conceive it to be less immediately our duty, and I think it would be more satisfactory to the public.' Rather than to simply facilitate complaints it is apparent that the purpose of Section 10 was to criminalise police misconduct. The provision was revised by Section 14 of the Metropolitan Police Act 1839, and throughout England and Wales police neglect of duty and disobedience of lawful orders were criminalised.[19]

The returns to parliament submitted by the Metropolitan Police in 1844, 1849 and 1853 included data on criminal proceedings before magistrates. The returns had been requested by two Members of Parliament who proposed the appointment of select committees to inquire into the financial cost of the Metropolitan Police, Henry Tufnell MP and Lord Dudley Stuart MP, respectively.[20] Covering the years 1842 to 1852, the returns included information on the rank and length of service of each officer charged; nature of each charge; whether brought by one of the Commissioners or a private individual; outcome of proceedings; and whether or not the officer was retained in service. A total of 988 officers were prosecuted, of which 248 were convicted: see Table 2.1 below. Prosecutions brought by private individuals and the Commissioners have been separated out in the Table, and the charges officers faced have been divided into three categories. *Misconduct offences*, although reference is not made in the Returns to Section 14 of the Metropolitan Police Act 1839 the charges described are covered by the offences set out in the statute (including charges of absent without leave, neglect of duty, drunk on duty, abusive language and improper exercise of powers); *offences of violence*, primarily assault and including sexual offences; and *other offences*, including theft and offences of dishonesty.[21]

Table 2.1 Metropolitan police officers charged before magistrates, convicted and not retained in service: 1842–1852

	1842	1843	1844	1845	1846	1847	1848	1849	1850	1851	1852	Total
Total no. charged	132	117	120	105	95	64	71	65	85	73	61	988
Total no. convicted	40	34	29	26	33	22	10	14	13	18	9	248
Not retained in service	42	38	35	30	35	24	7	14	17	16	10	268
Charged privately												
Total no. charged privately	105	102	100	82	74	53	67	57	84	64	57	845
Total no. charged privately convicted	25	21	16	11	15	13	6	8	12	11	5	143
Not retained in service	24	24	19	13	15	13	3	8	16	11	6	152
No. charged with misconduct offences	51	53	61	46	37	28	35	20	28	29	19	407
No. convicted of misconduct offences	5	7	7	3	3	5	4	1	2	5	0	42
Not retained in service	5	7	8	2	2	5	1	0	3	3	0	36
No. charged with offences of violence	42	36	30	28	33	22	23	28	40	31	35	348
No. convicted of offences of violence	15	7	6	7	12	6	2	3	7	6	4	75
Not retained in service	12	10	6	6	12	5	2	4	6	7	4	74
No. charged with other types of offence	12	13	9	8	4	3	9	9	16	4	3	90
No. convicted of other types of offence	5	7	3	1	0	2	0	4	3	0	1	26
Not retained in service	7	7	5	5	1	3	0	4	7	1	2	42
Charged by police												
Total no. charged by police	27	15	20	23	21	11	4	8	1	9	4	143

(continued)

Table 2.1 (continued)

	1842	1843	1844	1845	1846	1847	1848	1849	1850	1851	1852	Total
Total no. charged by police convicted	15	13	13	15	18	9	4	6	1	7	4	105
Not retained in service	18	14	16	17	20	11	4	6	1	5	4	116
No. charged with misconduct offences	17	7	13	12	18	10	2	6	–	7	4	96
No. convicted of misconduct offences	10	7	9	8	17	9	2	5	–	6	4	77
Not retained in service	9	7	12	9	17	10	2	5	–	3	4	78
No. charged with offences of violence	2	3	3	4	–	–	1	1	1	1	–	16
No. convicted of offences of violence	2	2	2	3	–	–	1	0	1	1	–	12
Not retained in service	2	2	2	3	–	–	1	0	1	1	–	12
No. charged with other types of offence	8	5	4	7	3	1	1	1	–	1	–	31
No. convicted of other types of offence	3	4	2	4	1	0	1	1	–	0	–	16
Not retained in service	7	5	2	5	3	1	1	1	–	1	–	26

Source: Parliamentary returns (Metropolitan Police 1844a, 1849a, 1853)

With an overall conviction rate of 25.1%, there was significant divergence between charges brought privately and by the Commissioner in each of the three categories. The conviction rate for privately brought misconduct charges was 10.3%, compared to 80.2% for charges brought by the Commissioners; 21.6% for privately brought charges of violence, compared to 75%; and 28.9% for other charges compared to 51.6%. On these figures it is evident that magistrates were more reluctant to find against police officers in criminal proceedings brought by private individuals than in proceedings brought by the police.

Closer examination of the returns on the nature of some of the charges brought helps understand why criminal proceedings were resorted to on the part of private individuals in comparison to the reasons of the Met Commissioners. Of the 407 prosecutions for misconduct that were brought by private individuals, 101 involved allegations that an officer had unlawfully interfered with the rights of a member of the public: improperly taking a person into custody or making a false charge or accusation, for example. A further 32 related to allegations that police failed to protect a member of the public: by refusing to take a person into custody or take a charge, for example. Taken together, offences of police violence, improper arrest or charge, and failure to protect a member of the public accounted for nearly two-thirds of private prosecutions. It is apparent that in these cases members of the public sought to gain redress for the harms they claimed to have suffered at the hands of the police.

Of charges brought by the Met Commissioners, by way of contrast, none of the officers were prosecuted for interfering with the rights of a member of the public or failure to protect. Of the 16 officers charged with offences of violence, 11 were alleged to have assaulted fellow officers. In these cases it would appear that the primary interest of the Commissioners when turning to the criminal courts was to ensure good police administration.

At this early stage in police history when officers were frequently disciplined, brought before the criminal courts to answer for their conduct and dismissed, a picture emerges of practical inequalities before the law between officers and members of the public. Arguably, police and public were equal before the law, and police accountability should be measured not by the number of officers convicted but by the number charged before magistrates and acquitted on the evidence. Recalling that as early as 1837 Commissioner Mayne had informed the Commission on Criminal Law that Met officers acted as prosecutor in many cases brought before the courts, the figures presented in Table 2.1 suggest that wronged citizens who sought to hold officers to account before the courts did so largely unsupported by police, and were heard unsympathetically by magistrates. In 1844, when proposing a select committee on the Metropolitan Police, Henry Tufnell MP referred to the perception that 'in many instances great negligence, and, in some cases, unfairness, had been evinced by Magistrates in dealing with those cases in which police-men were charged with violating their duty.'[22] Of course, there are several unknowns that prevent full understanding of why this was the case. The strength of evidence and standards to which each case was prepared are not known, nor is it known whether or not the Commissioners sup-ported private prosecutors.

With over 85% of all prosecutions against police officers brought pri-vately, increasing to 98.5% for allegations of unlawful use of violence, it is apparent that the criminal prosecution services the police offered to members of the public did not fully extend to cases where the suspected offender was a police officer. Two decades after formation of the Metropolitan Police, and before police forces had been created in many districts of England and Wales, there were signs that rather than serve as an effective accountability mechanism for victims of police abuse, the criminal sanction was deployed by police managers as a disciplinary measure.[23]

Intervention by the Home Secretary

Further evidence of hesitancy on the part of the police to prosecute offi-cers and reluctance of magistrates to issue summonses is to be found in connection with the policing of a protest held in Hyde Park on 1 July 1855. After police charged protestors and bystanders at a demonstration called in opposition to the Sunday Trading Bill, letters of complaint were published in *The Times* (2, 3 and 4 July 1855). William Stephens com-plained that he suffered serious injury after being assaulted by several officers in nearby Park Street and was refused admission when he attended Marylebone Street Police Court for the purpose of obtaining summonses against officers whose numbers he had noted (*The Times*, 4 July 1855). The magistrate John Hardwick, whose concerns expressed 20 years earlier about remedying police misconduct were noted above, was sitting at the Court on 2 and 3 July. *The Times* reported:

> Mr Hardwick could not admit for a moment that the oath of a constable, because he was a constable, ought to be passed over, or that any motive could operate improperly on the constable to induce him to give false evidence… If the police behaved improperly or displayed an excess of their duty, the course to take was to lodge a complaint before the commissioner, who would refer the matter to a magistrate if the complaint was well founded. (*The Times*, 4 July 1855)

Speaking in the House of Commons three days later, Home Secretary Sir George Grey initially resisted calls to appoint a select committee arguing that there was no need to inquire into petitions about the conduct of the police on account of the 'great facilities afforded individuals who have complaints to make against the police'.[24] Pressed by Tom Duncombe MP, among others, who stressed that an internal police inquiry would be insufficient, the Home Secretary relented and appointed a Royal Commission.

The Commissioners noted that many complainants were reluctant to appear before them, and taking evidence from 179 witnesses they examined 46 cases, many of which involved multiple complaints (Royal Commission on the Alleged Disturbance of the Public Peace in Hyde Park on Sunday, July 1st, 1855 (1855 Commission) 1856). These included allegations of misconduct by victims and witnesses against identified and unidentified police officers, conditions of the cells in Vine Street police station and refusal to grant bail to nine defendants eventually acquitted at Marylebone Street Police Court. The Commissioners found that 12 identified officers resorted to unjustifiable force, and 6 unidentified officers probably resorted to unwarranted violence. The Commissioners believed four of the nine arrests were probably unwarranted and regretted that all defendants were denied bail; they condemned the oppressive conditions under which they were held (1855 Commission 1856). Superintendent Hughes, who ordered officers to use their truncheons to clear an area of Hyde Park, was singled out and severely censured for failure to give proper consideration to the safety of people who were not offending against the law.

On receiving the Commission Report, the Home Secretary wrote to Met Commissioner Mayne (*The Times*, 22 November 1855). He directed that Mayne convey to Superintendent Hughes the disapproval of the Home Secretary and left it to the Met Commissioner to take appropriate disciplinary action in all but three cases. He directed that three officers— Sergeant William Bewlay, and PCs William Gearing and Charles Madgett—should be indicted. Bewlay and Gearing were acquitted of assault charges at the Old Bailey on 7 January 1856, and Madgett received a nine months prison sentence for assaulting William Stephens.[25] That was more than six months after Stephens unsuccessfully attempted to obtain summonses in person at Marylebone Street Police Court.

In his letter, published in *The Times* (22 November 1855), instructing the Met Commissioner to convey his disapproval to the superintendent censured in the Report, the Home Secretary's reasons that dismissal from the force would be 'harsh and uncalled for' were set out in detail. Determining that dismissal from the force would be insufficient punishment for three officers whose alleged acts of violence the Home Secretary considered 'gross and unprovoked' if proved, Rowan was instructed to bring criminal proceedings. In several other cases the Home Secretary trusted the Met Commissioner to act on his own authority, although parameters were laid down: 'in the exercise of the power vested in you by law, you will award in each case such punishment, either by suspension or dismissal, as you shall think right.'

In contrast to the openness with which Grey instructed Mayne on how to proceed with allegations against named officers, a general instruction which was to have lasting significance for Met complaints policy was quietly issued in 1868 and only revealed by Home Secretary Henry Bruce the following year. The case of John Poyndestre, George Bennett and Arthur Boutell was raised in the House of Commons after Marlborough Street Police Court Magistrate Mr. Knox dismissed charges of assaulting police in the execution of their duty against the three young bank clerks.

Evidence given by several independent witnesses was consistent with the defendants' counter allegations that they had been assaulted by police, and the Magistrate concluded by commenting that the police evidence was improbable and he 'had no other course than to disbelieve them' (*The Daily Telegraph*, 16 July 1869). Asked in the House if he intended to issue directions in regard to proceedings in the case, the Home Secretary replied:

> The rule established by the Home Office, after much experience in such matters for the guidance of the Chief Commissioner of Police, has been that, in all charges against members of the force where the evidence is conflicting, and is supported on either side by witnesses who are not members of the force, the case should be left to the decision of a magistrate. The Chief Commissioner of Police has no means of conducting a judicial inquiry, without which no decision affecting the character and interests of the members of the force could be properly made. The proper course, therefore, in the present case would seem to be that the gentlemen aggrieved should either summon the policemen for assault before a magistrate, or should proceed against them by way of indictment. Should the result of either of these proceedings be unfavourable to the policemen, it would be the duty of the Chief Commissioner to inflict such punishment by dismissal or otherwise, as might seem adequate to the offence.[26]

Giving evidence 40 years later to the Royal Commission upon the Duties of the Metropolitan Police (1908) Assistant Secretary of State in the Home Office Edward Troup[27] gave a little background to the instruction. The general rule that a magistrate should hear charges against constables where there was conflicting evidence was apparently issued on the recommendation of the Under Secretary of State in the Home Office after concluding that an inquiry he held into a case at the Home Office, to which all witnesses attended, was an unsatisfactory mechanism for addressing disputed evidence. Although it was open to the Met Commissioner under the rule to make preliminary enquiries prior to legal proceedings, the expectation was that the victim would apply for a summons, as was suggested by the Home Secretary in the case of the three bank clerks.

It has not been possible to trace details of the 1868 case that gave rise to the instruction,[28] and there is no record of Poyndestre, Bennett or

Boutell bringing proceedings against the officers. Widely reported in the press, five experienced officers including an Inspector and three sergeants gave evidence at the police court, and the Magistrate singled out PS Houlton, alleged to have kicked Bennett, for criticism for the manner in which he gave evidence and conducted himself in court (*Sunday Times*, 18 July 1869). The London Recorder Russell Gurney MP, the senior circuit judge of England and Wales, spoke forthrightly on the case when contributing to an unsuccessful attempt to persuade Home Secretary Bruce to reconsider his decision not to intervene. Pointing out that the 'real decision' of the magistrate was that the police officers were guilty, it was not for the three young men pronounced innocent, and with their good names vindicated, to privately carry the burden of ensuring that further inquiry was made in the public interest. The Home Secretary 'could easily direct proceedings to be taken, which could leave no doubt as to which party was really to blame'[29] (*The Daily Telegraph*, 5 August 1869).

1888 Snapshot

London was in turmoil in the late 1880s, and once again government expected the Met to police protest. Under the Representation of the People Acts of 1867 and 1884 (known as the second and third reform acts) the franchise was extended to include unpropertied and working-class men. With the expansion of democracy a nascent civil society, including socialist societies and pressure groups, grew in influence alongside a free and critical press (Petrow 1994; Johansen 2013).

Commissioner Henderson resigned in February 1886 following the failure of the Met to police a demonstration which culminated in rioting and looting (Committee to Inquire and Report as the Origin and Character of the Disturbances Which Took Place in the Metropolis 1886). His replacement, Major-General Sir Charles Warren, and Home Secretary Henry Matthews faced much criticism from freedom of expression lobbyists for banning public meetings in Trafalgar Square. *The Times* (14 November 1887) supported Commissioner Warren and the deployment of military tactics to prevent a demonstration in support of Irish

Home Rule being held at Trafalgar Square on 13 November 1887,[30] remembered as Bloody Sunday. It was reported in the press that as many as 200 civilians required hospital treatment after some 2000 officers backed up by troops and cavalry prevented 250,000 people from partici- pating in the protest, and the Metropolitan Police (1888a) later reported that 77 officers were injured on the day. Further injuries were reported the following Sunday when mounted police dispersed a crowd of people from the streets surrounding Trafalgar Square (*The Times*, 21 November 1887).

Days before the demonstration, which became a focal point for radical opponents of government, the Law and Liberty League was established (*Pall Mall Gazette*, 10 and 11 November 1887). In addition to support- ing a radical political agenda, the League was set up for the purpose of providing bail and legal advice to people arrested for exercising their right to protest, and 'the prosecution for false imprisonment and assault of every police constable who is proved to have wrongfully arrested and falsely accused men guilty of no crime' (*Pall Mall Gazette*, 10 November 1887).

Questioning the Home Secretary in the House of Commons about two allegations of assault against Met officers which did not proceed to trial, including an incident connected with the Trafalgar Square protests, Charles Bradlaugh MP requested information on assaults by officers and criminal proceedings.[31] Covering 24 April 1887 to 24 April 1888, differ- ent information was given in the Metropolitan Police (1888b) Return[32] that had been provided to parliament some 40 years earlier. The Return gave dates, names of individual complainants and defendants, and details of proceedings and costs. A total of 50 charges were listed,[33] which involved 46 complainants and 45 accused officers, 6 of whom were con- victed (not including 4 convictions which were quashed on appeal). Seven police officers brought charges of assault against eight officers, resulting in the conviction of one officer; and two officers successfully brought charges of misconduct (withdrawal from duty) against two offi- cers.[34] Thirty-three members of the public brought charges of assault against 34 officers, resulting in the conviction of 3 officers; 5 unsuccess- fully brought charges of perjury against 3 officers and 3 other types of charge against 4 officers were also unsuccessful. In regard to costs, the

Receiver of Police covered prosecution and defence costs in five charges of violence against three officers accused by four colleagues; and one officer convicted of misconduct was ordered to pay two shillings in costs. In proceedings where individual members of the public were named as complainants, one officer convicted of assault was ordered to pay costs and the Metropolitan Police Fund covered the defence costs in one case of perjury. Eleven complainants who alleged they were the victims of police violence were ordered to pay costs, including three complainants who also unsuccessfully charged an officer with perjury.

All but 1 of the 35 officers charged with an offence of violence against a member of the public in 1887/88 was prosecuted privately.[35] Six of the complainants had been accused of assaulting police. Convicting PC Frederick Broad of assaulting Maurice Gooding, the Westminster Police Court Magistrate Mr. Partridge said that there was no doubt that the constable had 'trumped up a false charge against an innocent man' (*The Times*, 6 January 1888). At the same court, this time before Mr. d'Eyncourt, PC David Howells was convicted of an assault on John Watts. The constable's attempt to take his victim into custody had been thwarted by a passer-by, and in his evidence Watts explained that when he reported the assault at the police station the inspector on duty sought to discourage him from charging the constable (*The Times*, 17 April 1888).

Some of the cases in the 1888 Return arose from the Trafalgar Square disturbances. Four charges of assault against three officers, one identified only by his number, were listed at Bow Street Police Court for Saturday, 10 December 1887 (*The Times*, 12 December 1887). John Coleman summonsed PC Harry Greenwood for an alleged assault at Bow Street Police Station on 13 November. Coleman did not attend the court hearing because he was serving a one-year prison sentence for assaulting PC Greenwood in the execution of his duty, which was the reason for his arrest and detention at the police station (*Standard*, 10 December 1887). Dennis White and John Crawford summonsed PC Frederick Goodwin for assaulting them at the same police station on the same day, and Fergus O'Connor summonsed PC 98 A for assaulting him with a truncheon in Northumberland Avenue on 20 November (*Pall Mall Gazette*, 8 December 1887). The Court was informed that PC 98 A was not on duty in the vicinity of Trafalgar Square on the day in question, and the cases were adjourned for one week for the purpose of arranging the attendance of Coleman and making further enquiries into the unidentified officer. On hearing the following week that the situation was unchanged, and the complainants wished to withdraw the summonses, the Magistrate ordered each to pay costs of 10 guineas (*Standard*, 19 December 1887). O'Connor unsuccessfully challenged the order (*The Times*, 24 January 1887), and several months later, with the Treasury having issued summonses for non-payment, Charles Bradlaugh MP raised the subject in Parliament[36] (*The Times*, 7 July 1888). The obstacles placed in the way of citizens who sought to bring police officers before the courts were described in the House of Commons debate. Bradlaugh referred to the excessive costs imposed in the Trafalgar Square cases, and James Stuart MP said that it seemed the police authorities were 'determined to teach a very heavy lesson to any person who should have the effrontery to prosecute [the police]'.[37] In regard to the difficulties O'Connor faced, James Rowland MP accused the police of failing to help the complainant identify the officer accused of assault.[38]

The unsuccessful attempts to charge three police officers for assault appear to be the only prosecutions supported by the Law and Liberty League, which existed for a little more than a year. Newspaper reports (see *Pall Mall Gazette*, 23 November and 15 December 1887) indicate that the League provided legal support to defendants arrested on 13 and 20 November 1887, and financial assistance to dependants of imprisoned protestors. One case taken up by the League was the death of Alfred Linnell, who died in Charing Cross Hospital two weeks after having been injured on Northumberland Avenue on 20 November. A dozen police officers gave evidence to the coroner's inquest into the cause of his death, and all stated that police did not charge the crowd and that they did not see anyone lying on the ground. His sister and a friend, both of whom visited him in hospital, said that he had told them that he and several other people were knocked over and trampled on by mounted police before a group of people carried him to hospital (*Pall Mall Gazette*, 5 and 6 December 1887). The unanimous verdict of the jury was that Linnell died from pyaemia as a result of a fractured thigh, and the foreman of the jury went on to say that 'the lack of evidence by witnesses in this case was inexplicable' (*The Times*, 13 December 1887). Celebrated as a martyr,

Linnell was laid to rest after what the *Pall Mall Gazette* (19 December 1887) described as the largest funeral procession through the streets of London since the 1852 funeral of the Duke of Wellington.

Cass v. Endacott

Included in the 1888 Return was the Old Bailey acquittal of PC Bowen Endacott[39] for perjury arising from the acquittal of Elizabeth Cass at Marlborough Street Police Court on a charge of solicitation and common prostitution (Petrow 1992; Taylor 2015; Walkowitz 1998). On the evening of 28 June 1887 Endacott arrested Cass, whom he claimed to have seen on Regent Street on three occasions in the previous six weeks, after a man complained to him that she had repeatedly taken hold of his arm. Cass had only moved to London from Teeside three weeks before her arrest, and she maintained that she did not touch or speak to anybody when out on her own. Dismissing the charge the Magistrate, Robert Newton, expressed the view that Cass was in Regent Street for an improper purpose, advised her not to walk there on her own at night and warned that he would convict if she came before him again. Following the hearing Cass's employer, Mrs. Bowman, wrote a letter of complaint to the Met Commissioner, and Llewellyn Atherley-Jones MP, a member of the Personal Rights Association, raised the case in Parliament.[40] Home Secretary Henry Matthews initially refused to institute an inquiry into the case, arguing that he did not have the power to do so. Unaware that Bowman had made a complaint, he informed the House of Commons that if Cass had been wronged by Endacott legal remedies were available to her and it would be for the Met Commissioner to act on any complaint. In the ensuing adjournment debate much criticism was levelled at the Metropolitan Police, including an allegation that letters of complaint were deliberately ignored, and William Caine MP accused officers of blackmail. He said that he had spoken to 30 girls on Clapham Common who told him that officers demanded a nightly payment of sixpence for plying their trade.[41]

Having lost the adjournment vote, with senior members of the Government speaking in favour of an inquiry, the Met Commissioner was directed to conduct an inquiry into the allegation of perjury against PC Endacott and the Lord Chancellor sought an explanation from Newton on the proceedings in the Police Court.[42] Surprisingly, no mention was made to the general rule laid down by the Home Office 20 years earlier that cases of precisely this type should be heard by a magistrate. In consequence, perhaps, there was much confusion as to the purpose of the four-day Met inquiry, to which representatives of the press were invited and witnesses gave their evidence on a voluntary basis.[43] The Home Secretary subsequently reported to Parliament that, after the Law Officers of the Crown had considered the report of the inquiry, the DPP had been instructed to prosecute PC Endacott for perjury. In regard to the review of proceedings before the Magistrate, the Home Secretary reported the disapproval of the Lord Chancellor on the way in which they had been conducted.[44]

By the time the DPP had been instructed to prefer charges against Endacott, Cass had already applied for a summons against the constable and opted to continue to prosecute privately with the Treasury agreeing to cover the costs. Following PC Endacott's acquittal, the Home Secretary determined that only £150 of his defence costs, totalling £717: 6 shillings, would be paid out of the police fund on account that he was not entirely without blame.[45] The outstanding sum was covered by colleagues across the Met who contributed to a subscription fund set up on his behalf.[46]

Rosa Parton and Annie Coverdale were two women whose encounters with police were also raised in parliament in this period (Taylor 2015). Edward Pickersgill MP described at length how Parton, supported by the Society for the Protection of Women and Children, unsuccessfully attempted to bring a charge of assault against PC James Butler at Clerkenwell and Bow Street Police Courts. Following an internal inquiry, PC Butler was reprimanded and transferred to other duties.[47] PC Bloy was accused of dishonesty by West Ham Police Court Magistrate Ernest Baggallay when dismissing a charge of drunk and disorderly against Annie Coverdale in January 1888 (*The Times*, 26 January 1888). Commissioner Warren swiftly conducted an internal police inquiry and, although PC Bloy was transferred to duties elsewhere in London, the Commissioner issued a memorandum to officers which exonerated the officer. The Met informed the press of the memorandum (*Pall Mall Gazette*, 31 January 1888), and Baggallay expressed his displeasure at how the matter had been handled (*The Times*, 2 February 1888) before the subject was raised by Pickersgill in the House of Commons.[48]

An internal Met inquiry was also conducted into the allegations of corruption made by William Caine MP during the adjournment debate on Cass. Commissioner Warren reported to the Home Secretary that an investigation by Assistant Commissioner James Monro, in charge of the CID, found that there was not a 'tittle of proof' in the claim by Caine that officers from W Division were systematically levying blackmail from prostitutes on Clapham Common (*The Times*, 6 February 1888). In a letter to *The Times* (8 February 1888) Caine responded to criticism that he failed to assist the inquiry, and questioned how a 'careful and exhaustive inquiry' could be conducted by police on behalf of others in the same force.

Diminishing Officer Accountability

Retention of the common law office of constable had been intended to assuage public opposition to the creation of a civil force with coercive powers, yet the first Commissioners faced an uphill task defending the Metropolitan Police against their detractors. They were not helped by the politically charged climate associated with extension of the franchise under the 1832 Reform Act and the jostling for power that ensued. Although the impact of Chartism, campaigning for universal suffrage in the late 1830s and 1840s, was not felt as greatly in London as the rest of the country, the political unions posed a considerable threat (Miller 1987). The circumstances under which government ministers banned the 1833 Cold Bath Fields meeting and, then, the way in which the jury verdict that PC Culley was justifiably killed was overturned, did not help the Commissioners as they set out to gain public trust and confidence. Legitimacy was undermined further in the same year by the Popay spying affair: self-inflicted damage caused by a Met initiative against the Political Union of the Working Classes.

The cautious approach of the first Met Commissioners to winning public approval is evident in their reluctance to develop criminal investigation capacity: reversed a decade later in response to the Daniel Good scandal. The dismissal of Popay, along with many other officers, and the number the Commissioners brought before magistrates charged with misconduct, points to a determination to maintain a disciplined force and regulate officer conduct. As the functions, structure and culture of the new police gradually established the institutional character of the Metropolitan Police, force strength increased and the number of dismissals steadily declined. The difficulties encountered establishing the legitimacy of the new police and the acclaimed policing by consent ethos, to the extent that it was achieved (Churchill 2014; Gattrell 1990), was due in no small part to adherence to a strict self-regulatory command and control-type organisational structure. The proactivity of the new police in gradually asserting their authority as gatekeepers to the criminal process was of major importance to securing public support. A consequence of the growing influence of police over the pre-trial investigation and criminal process, whether intended or unintended, was to have repercussions for victims of abuse and the opportunities available to them to hold the individual officer to account for his conduct.

The claim that the officer was accountable to the law in like manner as the citizen, as maintained under the office of constable, did not stand up to close scrutiny. The Constables Protection Act 1750 and the development of reasonable suspicion at common law shielded officers from claims in the tort of false imprisonment (Smith 2002). The power of the constable to arrest a suspect on grounds of reasonable probable cause even if an offence had not been committed, which has never been available to the citizen, was further protected by introduction of the criminal offence of resisting an officer in the execution of his duty in the mid-nineteenth-century police statutes.[49] Justification for this separation of the constable from the citizen has always rested on the public interest argument that a police officer has to be provided with the authority and powers, including the use of physical force, to independently and impartially enforce the law.

The right of the citizen to prosecute a constable was another limb of the officer's accountability to the law. Despite frequent press reports alerting to the brutality of the new police, and although more Met officers were brought before the courts in the nineteenth century than they have in subsequent years, prosecutions were relatively rare. As long as victims were perceived to be confined to the massed ranks of impoverished, powerless and uneducated slum dwellers, variously described as the 'dangerous classes', 'residuum' and 'sub-proletariat', the newspaper reading public would instinctively turn a blind eye. The returns to parliament on prosecutions of officers between 1842 and 1852, and again in 1887–88 allow for a rare insight into the effectiveness of the criminal sanction as an accountability measure, although opportunities for analysis are limited on account of the numbers being small. Starting with a low baseline 13 years after formation of the Met, the clear impression is of diminishing accountability over the course of the nineteenth century. Undoubtedly, the instruction issued by the Home Office in 1868 that had the practical effect of requiring victims of police misconduct to privately bring criminal proceedings will have contributed to this trend. Whereas in the mid-nineteenth century criminalisation of misconduct under Section 14 of the Metropolitan Police Act 1839 assisted members of the public bring officers before the courts, some 40 years later there were no privately brought prosecutions for misconduct and only two brought by police for withdrawal from duty. One interpretation of this trend would emphasise that the reduction was a consequence of improving standards and greater police professionalism. Another interpretation would assert, to the contrary, that citizens were increasingly denied the opportunity to hear officers account for their conduct in court.

In regard to prosecutions of officers for offences of violence the figures were remarkably constant. Breaking down the 1842–52 figures an average of 33 officers were charged annually, compared with 35 in 1887–88 and the same percentage of prosecutions were brought privately: 95.6% and 97.1%, respectively. The same is not the case for convictions. Whereas 75% of officers charged by the Commissioners were convicted between 1842 and 1852, 12.5% were convicted in 1887–88. For private prosecutions, the 33.3% conviction rate in the mid-eighteenth century dropped to 9.1% in 1887–88. Contrary to the claim that police had assumed responsibility for prosecutions, it is apparent that private citizens continued to carry the burden of prosecuting police officers for offences of violence in the late 1880s (and well into the twentieth century as will be shown in subsequent chapters), and magistrates were increasingly reluctant to convict officers brought before them. Given that there was not a realistic prospect of gaining a conviction, it is not unreasonable to presume that victims of police violence, either of their own motion or on receiving legal advice, elected not to bring proceedings as would appear to have happened in the case of the three bank clerks cleared of assaulting police in the execution of their duty in 1869.

The figures that are available for prosecutions of police officers in the nineteenth century give rise to important questions concerning the rule of law. The principle of equality before the law, as propounded by Dicey (1959) at a time of increasing bureaucratisation and the imposition of executive discretion in the late Victorian era, could not be said to apply if the constable was not subject to the same standards and procedures as applied to the ordinary citizen. These were the very same concerns raised by politicians in regard to the difficulties faced by citizens in obtaining access to justice when alleging misconduct on the part of constables. The evidence suggests that a police culture of impunity, if not already in existence, was developing by the end of the century. Important safeguards against impunity were the free press, which routinely reported proceedings in the police courts, the radical press, which facilitated critical discourse on state power, and a civil society that supported victims of abuse in their struggles for justice. Partly due to an agitation organised by a small civil society organisation called the Police and Public Vigilance Society, which made a significant contribution to the 1906–08 Royal Commission upon the duties of the Metropolitan Police, attempts by the Met and Home Office to curtail public scrutiny of police misconduct in the wake of the Cass scandal were delayed into the twentieth century.

Notes

1. Peel ushered in a raft of legislation on punishment, public order, criminal procedure and substantive offences: Gaols Act 1823; Judgment of Death Act 1823; Transportation Act 1824; Vagrancy Act 1824; Stealing from Gardens Act 1826; Criminal Law Act 1826, and 1827; Larceny Act 1827; Indemnity Act 1827; Offences Against the Person Act 1828.

2. 'The history of the police is the history of the office of constable and, notwithstanding that present day police forces are the creation of statute and that the police have numerous statutory powers and duties, in essence a police force is neither more nor less than a number of individual constables, whose status derives from the common law, organised together in the interests of efficiency.' Halsbury's Laws of England > Police and Investigatory Powers (Volume 84 (2013), paras 1–431; Volume 84A (2013), paras 432–800) > 1. The Office of Constable > (1) Development of the Office of Constable > 1. The common law constable.

3. S. 4 of the Metropolitan Police Act 1839 re-styled the *ex-officio* justices Commissioners of Police of the Metropolis; S. 1 of the Metropolitan Police Act 1856 allowed for only one Commissioner, and it was not until S. 1 (9) of the Administration of Justice Act 1973 that the Commissioner was derecognised as a justice.

4. It was 170 years before a locally elected Metropolitan Police Authority was established under S. 312 of the Greater London Authority Act 1999.

5. *Hansard*, Parl Debs, HC: 13 June 1833 cols 679–698; 14 June 1833 cols 797–811.

6. *Hansard*, Parl Debs, HC: 27 June 1833 cols 1254–1263; 1 July 1833 cols 1359–1361; 15 July 1833 cols 646–649; 7 August 1833 cols 404–408 and 834–839. The member of the Political Union that confronted Popay about his spying was George Fursey (or Furzey), who was charged with unlawfully wounding two police officers at Cold Bath Fields on 13 May 1833 (*The Times* 14 May 1833). Fursey was in custody when Cobbett presented the petition in the House of Commons, and later acquitted at the Old Bailey on 4 July 1833: *Old Bailey Proceedings Online* (www.oldbaileyonline.org, version 7.2, 30 March 2015), July 1833, trial of George Fursey (t18330704-5).

7. *Hansard*, Parl Debs, HC: 22 August 1833 cols 834–839.

8. In the 1838 Select Committee on Metropolitan Police Offices (1838), Commissioners Rowan and Mayne defended the force against criticism that there had been little improvement in crime detection and argued that police effectiveness was restricted by the limited legal authority available. Police powers were significantly strengthened following the government's acceptance of recommendations by the Select Committee in the Metropolitan Police Act 1839 and the Metropolitan Police Courts Act 1839.

9. Discovery of the body of a murdered girl in Roehampton on 6 April 1842 was followed by a public outcry for failing to arrest Daniel Good, who was eventually convicted and publicly hanged (Ascoli 1979).

10. For the history of criminal investigation in the Metropolitan Police see Hobbs (1988). With regard to the deployment of detectives in provincial forces, no mention is made in early inspectors of constabulary annual reports of when introduced or their early development. Major General William Cartwright, Inspector for No. 1 District, suggests appointment of detectives in county forces so that they can liaise with borough detectives in the first Annual Report (Inspectors of Constabulary 1858). Cartwright was succeeded by Lieutenant C. A. Cobbe in 1869, and he regularly reported that approximately 50 detectives served the boroughs in No. 1 District throughout the 1870s increasing to 60–65 in the mid-1880s. The Inspectors for the other two regions did not report on detective strengths throughout this period.

11. Eighteenth-century legislation provided for the recovery of some prosecution costs following conviction in felony cases. The Criminal Justice Act 1826, part of Peel's reforms, extended this provision to cover all witnesses and included some misdemeanours, notably assaults.

12. It is apparent that police involvement in prosecutions had the approval of Home Secretary Peel. In his 1826 House of Commons speech proposing the Criminal Law Act 1826 he voiced his support for the Procurator Fiscal in Scotland and his preference for moving from private to public prosecutions in England and Wales (*Hansard*, Parl Debs, HC: 9 March 1826 cols 1214–1244).

13. Practice that continued until creation of the Crown Prosecution Service under the Prosecution of Offences Act 1985.

14. The shift in the balance of power between the police and magistracy in criminal procedure was reflected in local government statutes in the 1880s. The power of Justices to suspend and dismiss borough police officers were limited to suspension under s. 191 (4) of the Municipal Corporations Act 1882. Justices' administrative responsibilities for county forces were reduced by creation of joint standing committees consisting of county councillors and magistrates under s. 9 of the Local Government Act 1888; see Critchley (1967).

15. See, for example, *Hansard*, Parl Debs, HC: 15 June 1830 cols 356–364; HL: 15 Nov 1830 cols 493–500; HC: 18 Nov 1830 cols 575–582; HL: 25 Nov 1830 col 665; HC: 24 July 1832 col 670.

16. See also evidence of H. M. Dyer and A. S. Laing (1834 Select Committee 1834: 157–158 and 182–183, respectively).

17. In a leading nineteenth-century reasonable suspicion case, *Hogg* v. *Ward* (1853) 3 H. & N. 417, a claim for false imprisonment was brought against a York police officer by a butcher arrested on suspicion of stealing horse traces. The officer made the arrest without warrant on the word of a person claiming that the traces had been stolen from him the previous year. In spite of the butcher giving a full explanation for his possession of the traces, he was detained in custody overnight before the charge was dismissed by the magistrate the following morning. At the hearing, the Judge rejected a submission to enter a verdict for the police officer on grounds of reasonable suspicion and ruled that the question of fact was to be put to the jury along with determination of damages. The officer's appeal was disallowed on grounds that the law allowing arrest without warrant required a reasonable charge and suspicion, which the facts in the case did not support.

18. A similar trend is revealed in the inspectors of constabulary annual reports, which published figures of officers who were dismissed from provincial forces between 1876 and 1899 (figures were not included in reports again until 1928). Officer turnover as a result of dismissals fell from 4.6% in 1876 to 0.7% in each of the last four years of the nineteenth century (numbers of officers required to resign were not included in inspectors of constabulary reports).

19. S. 80 of the Municipal Corporations Act 1835 (which granted magistrates the additional power of dismissal, and revised by s. 194 of the Municipal Corporations Act 1882); s. 12 of the County Police Act 1839; and s. 16 of the Town Police Clauses Act 1847. Only one police misconduct case appears to have been reported. In *Chisholm* v. *Holland* (1886) 50 J.P. 197, a Stafford County police officer's appeal against conviction for neglect of duty under s. 12 of the County Police Act 1839 was dismissed. He had accepted a gratuity of one shilling and sixpence when collecting licensing fees from a publican contrary to rules and regulations drawn up by the County Chief Constable. One year earlier the officer had been disciplined following a similar incident and expressly forbidden to accept gratuities. He was fined 40 shillings plus 15 shillings costs, or a 14 days' prison sentence with hard labour.

20. Tufnell in 1844 (*Hansard*, Parl Debs, HC: 5 March 1844 cols, 592–597); and Stuart in 1849 (*Hansard*, Parl Debs, HC: 3 July 1849 cols,

1258–1268) and 1853 (*Hansard*, Parl Debs, HC: 2 August 1853 cols, 1164–1166).

21. Several of the cases recorded in the returns refer to more than one charge, but only one outcome. To protect against double counting, the more serious charge has only been included in Table 2.1.

22. *Hansard*, Parl Debs, HC: 5 March 1844 col 592.

23. Also included in the 1844, 1849 and 1853 returns to parliament were the number of prosecutions of officers of the smaller City of London Police force. Although proceedings brought by police and private individuals were not separately recorded, the data provided a similar picture. Of the 34 officers charged with misconduct type offences, 15 were convicted and 17 were dismissed from the force; 9 of the 27 charged with offences of violence were convicted and 3 dismissed; and 16 were charged with other types of offences, of which 6 were convicted, and 7 were dismissed.

24. *Hansard*, Parl Debs, HC: 6 July 1855 col 520.

25. *Old Bailey Proceedings Online* (www.oldbaileyonline.org, version 7.2, 30 March 2015), January 1856, trial of William Bewlay (t18560107-195); January 1856, trial of William Gearing (t18560107-194); January 1856, trial of Charles Madgett (t18560107-193).

26. *Hansard*, Parl Debs, HC, 23 July 1869 col 562.

27. Troup went on to serve as Permanent Under Secretary of State in the Home Office between 1908 and 1922, see further Chap. 6, below.

28. Reference was made 80 years later to the instruction 'laid down as long ago as 1868, by the then Home Secretary, as a definite rule', by Home Secretary Jonson-Hicks when defending his decision to refer a complaint to the DPP (see further Chap. 4, below): *Hansard*, Parl Debs, HC, 20 July 1928, col 827.

29. *Hansard*, Parl Debs, HC, 3 August 1868, cols 1223–1224.

30. Criticised for writing an article in *Murray's Magazine*, in which he defended his record as Commissioner, Warren refused to first ask the permission of the Home Secretary if he intended to publish his views on the Metropolitan Police in future and resigned after less than three years in post (*The Times*, 14 November 1888; see further Chap. 6, below).

31. *Hansard*, Parl Debs, HC: 6 March 1888 cols 376–379.

32. Erratic statistics were included in early annual reports of Met Commissioner Lieutenant-Colonel Sir Edmund Henderson after his appointment in 1869. Between 1860 and 1869 a total of 179 officers

were prosecuted, of which 124 were convicted and 135 were not retained in service (Commissioner of Police of the Metropolis 1870).

33. Two cases against officers who were ordered to send their children to school are not included.

34. Two inspectors brought the misconduct charges against two constables; and the one assault conviction resulted from eight charges of violence against seven officers by seven of their colleagues (six of these charges arose from two separate incidents where groups of officers made counter-allegations against each other). Only one of the cases in which an officer was named as the complainant involved a charge brought on behalf of a member of the public.

35. The exception was PC Benjamin Hewlett, charged by an inspector for feloniously wounding the constable's own son: Hewlett was declared insane (*The Times*, 11 February 1888).

36. *Hansard*, Parl debs, HC: 6 July 1888 cols 567–569 and 582–597.

37. *Hansard*, Parl debs, HC: 6 July 1888 col 587. James Thomas was ordered to pay two guineas in costs after his summons for assault against PC Albert Baker was dismissed (*The Times*, 17 August 1887).

38. *Hansard*, Parl debs, HC: 6 July 1888 cols 592–593. In a similar case, witnesses gave Thomas Murphy the numbers of three officers he went on to charge for assault. The Magistrate dismissed the summonses after the officers gave evidence that they were elsewhere when the alleged assaults took place, and Murphy was ordered to pay costs (*The Times*, 7 November 1887).

39. *Old Bailey Proceedings Online* (www.oldbaileyonline.org, version 7.2, 30 March 2015), October 1887, trial of BOWEN ENDACOTT (t18871024-1058).

40. *Hansard*, Parl Debs, HC: 5 July 1887 cols 1796–1825 and 6 July 1887 cols 1826–1830; *Standard*, 7 July 1887; *Lloyd's Illustrated Newspaper*, 10 July 1887.

41. Writing a few days later in the *Pall Mall Gazette* of 9 July 1887, Caine gave fuller details of his allegations and claimed that the Home Office and police must have been aware of the corruption.

42. *Hansard*, Parl Debs, HC, 6 July 1888, col 1827.

43. Reported in full in *The Times* of 12, 13, 23, 26 and 27 July 1887.

44. *Hansard*, Parl Debs, HC: 9 August 1888 cols 1715–1716. Renowned for hearing police evidence uncritically, Marlborough Street Police Court Magistrate Robert Newton faced further calls for a public inquiry after

declaring in Court that had Professor Ray Lankester apologised to two
constables he would not have bound him over for obstructing an officer
in the execution of his duty (*The Times*, 14 October 1995; National
Archives HO 45/9711/A51190).

45. National Archives, MEPO 3/139, letter of 20 June 1888.
46. National Archives, MEPO 3/139, PC Endacott's Defence Fund.
47. *Hansard*, Parl Debs, HC: 1887 28 July 373–375, 22 August 1438–1461;
    Pall Mall Gazette 1 August 1887.
48. *Hansard*, Parl Debs, HC: 10 February 1888 cols 151–152; 13 February
    1888 cols 253–254; 20 March 1888 cols 1848–1868. See, also, the con-
    tribution of Pickersgill to a debate on salaries and expenses of civil
    departments, including the Metropolitan Police, when he referred to
    several complaints: *Hansard*, Parl Debs, HC: 6 April 1888 cols 681–686.
49. S.8 of the Metropolitan Police Act 1829: in provincial forces under s.81
    of the Municipal Corporations Act 1835 and s.18 of the County Police
    Act 1839: retained under s.51(1) of the Police Act 1964 and, currently,
    s.89(1) of the Police Act 1996. The offence of assaulting an officer in the
    execution of his duty, in addition to common assault, has similarly but-
    tressed the authority of the police in statute.

References

1834 Select Committee, see Select Committee on the Police of the
Metropolis (1834).

1855 Commission, see Royal Commission on the Alleged Disturbance of the
Public Peace in Hyde Park on Sunday, July 1st, 1855 (1856).

Ascoli, D. (1979). *The Queen's Peace: The Origins and Development of the
Metropolitan Police, 1829–1979*. London: Hamish Hamilton.

Churchill, D. C. (2014). Rethinking the State Monopolisation Thesis: The
Historiography of Policing and Criminal Justice in Nineteenth-Century
England. *Crime, Histoire & Sociétiés/Crime, History & Societies, 18*(1), 131–152.

Commission on Criminal Law. (1837). *Third Report from the Commission on
Criminal Law (Juvenile Offenders)*, HC 79. ProQuest Parliamentary
Papers Online.

Commission on Criminal Law. (1845). *Eighth Report of Her Majesty's
Commissioners on Criminal Law*, HC 656. ProQuest Parliamentary
Papers Online.

Commissioner of Police of the Metropolis. (1870). *Report of the Commissioner of Police of the Metropolis for the Year 1869*, Cmnd. 150. ProQuest Parliamentary Papers Online.

Commissioner of Police of the Metropolis. (1878). *Report of the Commissioner of Police of the Metropolis for the Year 1877*, Cmnd. 2129. ProQuest Parliamentary Papers Online.

Committee to Inquire and Report as the Origin and Character of the Disturbances Which Took Place in the Metropolis on Monday, The 8th of February…. (1886). *Report of a Committee to Inquire and Report as the Origin and Character of the Disturbances Which Took Place in the Metropolis on Monday, The 8th of February and as to the Conduct of the Police Authorities in Relation to Thereto*, C.4465. ProQuest Parliamentary Papers Online.

Critchley, T. A. (1967). *A History of Police in England and Wales*. London: Constable.

Dicey, A. V. (1959). *Introduction to the Study of the Law of the Constitution*. London: Macmillan.

Edwards, J. L. J. (1964). *Law Officers of the Crown*. London: Sweet and Maxwell.

Gattrell, V. A. C. (1990). Crime, Authority and the Policeman-State. In F. M. L. Thompson (Ed.), *The Cambridge Social History of Britain* (Vol. 3, pp. 243–310). Cambridge: Cambridge University Press.

Godfrey, B. (2008). Changing Prosecution Practices and Their Impact on Crime Figures, 1857–1940. *British Journal of Criminology, 48*(2), 171–189.

Halsbury's Laws of England > Police and Investigatory Powers Volume 84. (2013). London: LexisNexis.

Hansard. ProQuest Parliamentary Papers Online.

Hay, D., & Snyder, F. (Eds.). (1989). *Policing and Prosecution in Britain 1750–1850*. New York: Oxford University Press.

Hetherington, T. (1989). *Prosecution and the Public Interest*. London: Waterlow.

Hobbs, D. (1988). *Doing the Business: Entrepreneurship, the Working Class and Detectives in the East End of London*. Oxford: Oxford University Press.

Inspectors of Constabulary. (1858). *Inspectors of Constabulary Reports for Year Ending 29 September 1857*, HC 20. ProQuest Parliamentary Papers Online.

Johansen, A. (2013). Defending the Individual: the Personal Rights Association and the Ligue des droits de l'homme, 1871–1916. *European Review of History, 20*(4), 559–579.

Met Commissioner, see Commissioner of Police of the Metropolis.

Metropolitan Police. (1844a). *Returns of Metropolitan and City of London Police, 1842–43*, HC 238. ProQuest Parliamentary Papers Online.

Metropolitan Police. (1844b). *A Return of the Number of the Irish Police Force, and of the Metropolitan Police, in Each Year since They Were Established, and the Amount of Public Money Voted for the Same in Each Year*, HC 189. ProQuest Parliamentary Papers Online.

Metropolitan Police. (1849a). *Return of Officers of Metropolitan and City Police Forces Charged with Offences before Magistrates, 1844–48; Number of Robberies, and Number of Persons Taken into Custody, 1844–48*, HC 133. ProQuest Parliamentary Papers Online.

Metropolitan Police. (1849b). *Abstract Return of the Number of Divisions into Which the Metropolitan Police District is Now Divided; and the Letter and Name of Each Division; the Parishes and Places Comprised in Each Division, and Population Thereof, with Number of Police in Each Division; and the Salaries and Allowances of Each Class*, HC 24. ProQuest Parliamentary Papers Online.

Metropolitan Police. (1853). *Return of Officers of Metropolitan and City Police Charged with Offences before Magistrates; Number of Robberies, and Number of Persons Taken into Custody, 1849–52*, HC 544. ProQuest Parliamentary Papers Online.

Metropolitan Police. (1888a). *Return of Policeman Injured on the 13th day of November 1887, Giving the Name, Rank, and Number of the Person Injured, the Nature of the Injury, and the Time and Place at Which it was Sustained*, HC 109. ProQuest Parliamentary Papers Online.

Metropolitan Police. (1888b). *Return of All Cases in Which Metropolitan Police Constables have been Charged before Metropolitan Police Magistrates, or upon Indictment, during the past Twelve Months...*, HC 188. ProQuest Parliamentary Papers Online.

Miller, W. M. (1987). Party Politics, Class Interest and Reform of the Police, 1829–56. *International Review of Police Development, 10*, 42–60.

Old Bailey Proceedings Online (www.oldbaileyonline.org, version 7.2, 27 March 2015).

Petrow, S. (1992). The Legal Enforcement of Morality in Late-Victorian and Edwardian England. *University of Tasmania Law Review, 11*, 59–74.

Petrow, S. (1994). *Policing Morals: The Metropolitan Police and the Home Office 1870–1914*. Oxford: Clarendon Press.

Radzinowicz, L. (1968). *A History of English Criminal Law; Vol IV, Grappling for Control*. London: Stevens & Sons.

Royal Commission on the Alleged Disturbance of the Public Peace in Hyde Park on Sunday, July 1st, 1855. (1856). *Report of Her Majesty's Commissioners*

Appointed to Inquire into the Alleged Disturbance of the Public Peace in Hyde Park on Sunday, July 1st, 1855; and the Conduct of the Metropolitan Police in Connexion with the Same. Together with the Minutes of Evidence, Appendix, and Index, C2016. ProQuest Parliamentary Papers Online.

Royal Commission upon the Duties of the Metropolitan Police. (1908). *Minutes of Evidence Taken before the Royal Commission upon the Duties of the Metropolitan Police Together with Appendices and Index. Vol. III.*, Cd. 4261. ProQuest Parliamentary Papers Online.

Select Committee on Cold Bath Fields Meeting. (1833). *Report from the Select Committee on Cold Bath Fields Meeting*, HC 718. ProQuest Parliamentary Papers Online.

Select Committee on Metropolitan Police Offices. (1838). *Report from the Select Committee on Metropolitan Police Offices, with Minutes of Evidence*, HC 578. ProQuest Parliamentary Papers Online.

Select Committee on Public Prosecutors. (1855). *Report of the Select Committee on Public Prosecutors*, 1854–55 HC 48. ProQuest Parliamentary Papers Online.

Select Committee on Public Prosecutors. (1856). *Report of the Select Committee on Public Prosecutors*, HC 206. ProQuest Parliamentary Papers Online.

Select Committee on the Petition of Frederick Young and Others. (1833). *Report from the Select Committee on the Petition of Frederick Young and Others*, HC 62. ProQuest Parliamentary Papers Online.

Select Committee on the Police of the Metropolis. (1834). *Report from the Select Committee on the Police of the Metropolis, with the Minutes of Evidence, Appendix and Index*, HC 600. ProQuest Parliamentary Papers Online.

Simpson, H. B. (1895). The Office of Constable. *The English Historical Review, 10*(40), 625–641.

Smith, G. (2002). Reasonable Suspicion: Time for a Re-evaluation? *International Journal of the Sociology of Law, 1*(30), 1–16.

Stephen, J. F. (1883). *A History of the Criminal Law of England: Vol I*. London: Macmillan & Co.

Taylor, D. (2015). Cass, Coverdale and Consent: The Metropolitan Police and Working Class Women in Late-Victorian London. *Cultural and Social History, 12*(1), 113–136.

Walkowitz, J. R. (1998). Going Public: Shopping, Street Harassment, and Streetwalking in Late Victorian London. *Representations, 62*, 1–30.

3

The Police and Public Vigilance Society and Royal Commission upon the Duties of the Metropolitan Police

Walking on Newington Causeway, South East London late one autumn night in 1897, Bloomsbury tailor James Timewell witnessed the violent arrest of diminutive 25-year-old wheelwright George Hillman. Timewell followed the police officers and their prisoner to Southwark police station, where Hillman was charged with being drunk and disorderly, to make a complaint. The Southwark Police Court trial of the following day was adjourned after Timewell gave evidence that he saw Hillman savagely manhandled by four constables and subjected to electric shock treatment in the police station. Two days later Timewell wrote a letter to the *Standard* (21 October 1988) appealing for witnesses, and he launched a public subscription to cover Hillman's legal costs. After more than a dozen hearings at Southwark Police Court and a Central Criminal Court trial, at which four police officers were acquitted of assault[1] (*The Times*, 13 January 1989), Hillman was eventually convicted of the drunk and disorderly charge and fined ten shillings (*Daily Mail*, 19 January 1898).

Advised by other witnesses present on the night of the incident not to go to the police station, Timewell was harshly criticised for intervening. It was suggested that he misunderstood the violence of the prisoner for the violence of the police (*Standard*, 3 November 1897) and he was

© The Author(s) 2020
G. Smith, *On the Wrong Side of The Law*, Palgrave's Critical Policing Studies,
https://doi.org/10.1007/978-3-030-48222-0_3

accused of seeking to prejudice proceedings by writing letters to the press (*Standard*, 21 December 1897). During the Old Bailey trial it was alleged that Timewell coached prosecution witnesses,[2] and C. F. Gill Senior Counsel to the Treasury defending the four constables put to the jury that it was entirely due to Timewell's 'anxious labour' that a case of common assault was heard at the Central Criminal Court (Timewell 1898).

The appeal for subscriptions to cover Hillman's legal costs raised £120 from more than 100 donors, and a month after the conclusion of proceedings Timewell (1898) published a pamphlet in which the formation of an association to support victims of police abuse was proposed. Not since the short-lived Law and Liberty League had an organisation existed for the sole purpose of supporting citizens who found themselves in conflict with the police. Whereas the League was formed to support protestors, Timewell wrote of the need for an organisation that would campaign on behalf of the vulnerable and powerless working man or woman who had cause to complain as the result of a routine encounter with the police. The aim of such an organisation would be to support poor people living in bad neighbourhoods who were not deemed respectable, and who were unable to express their grievances or assert their rights when confronted by authority (Johansen 2011). Their powerlessness was in sharp contrast to the privileges enjoyed by the rogue constable who unlawfully resorted to violence safe in the knowledge that he would be backed up by colleagues, and believed in court. For the victim, the most probable outcome would be a conviction for assault or disorderly behaviour and, for the constable, 'in dealing with such prisoners he may, short of actually maiming them, handle them as he likes with impunity' (Timewell 1898: 4). For Timewell the Hillman case demonstrated that casual prosecutions of police officers were futile on their own. What was required was a permanent campaigning association, an agitation, which would both lend practical support to victims and promote reform by challenging unlawful police violence and fabrication of evidence.

The objectives of the Police and Public Vigilance Society (PPVS), formally launched in February 1903 were: 'To assist persons who, after enquiry, may reasonably be supposed to have been wrongfully accused or treated with unnecessary violence by the police' (Timewell 1905a: 2).

Timewell worked closely with Frank Russell, the second Earl Russell, and they served as the secretary and chairman, respectively, of the Society. Allegations of police brutality, fabrication of evidence and corruption continued in the late Victorian and Edwardian era and the press regularly reported on police court hearings in which allegations were made against Metropolitan Police (Met) officers. As the result of an early PPVS case a constable was allowed to resign and another had his pay reduced by three shillings a week after the Magistrate reported that an attempt had been made to induce the victim of a police assault, himself charged with assault, not to give evidence (*Daily Mail*, 11 November 1902). After the *Daily Express* (16 January 1904) ran a story alleging police blackmailed bookmakers, Timewell called for the appointment of a Royal Commission (*Police Review and Parade Gossip*, 29 January 1904).

Royal Commission upon the Duties of the Metropolitan Police

Appointment of the Royal Commission upon the Duties of the Metropolitan Police (1906–08 Commission) was announced by Prime Minister Sir Henry Campbell-Bannerman following controversial arrests by Met officers. On 12 April 1906, Dr. Maurice Gerothwohl wrote to Home Secretary Herbert Gladstone requesting an inquiry into the conduct of police officers following the dismissal of drunk and disorderly charges against him and his friend Henri Lavalette (1906–08 Commission 1908). Rebutting questions about the case in the House of Commons, Gladstone said that it was for the complainants to apply to the courts if they wished to take the matter further.[3] Within weeks the Home Secretary faced further questions about the conduct of officers after a charge of behaving in a riotous and indecent manner against Eva D'Angeley was dismissed.[4] Gladstone consulted Met Commissioner Sir Edward Henry, and confident that the police would be exonerated Henry pressed for the appointment of a Royal Commission.[5] The limited scope of the inquiry, into the policing of drunkenness, disorder and solicitation in the streets excluding cases of assault, was challenged firstly by Lord Robert

Cecil MP in the House of Commons[6] and, then, by PPVS Chairman Earl Russell in the House of Lords.[7]

When deliberating their terms of reference, the four Commissioners, all of which were lawyers and two were MPs, determined that in addition to hearing evidence on the Gerothwohl and D'Angeley cases that triggered the inquiry they would invite members of the public to forward complaints to them. In total about 300 were received and the Commission heard evidence on a further 17 'special cases', involving in total 21 complainants alleging misconduct against numerous Met officers. The process for selection of the special cases was opaque. In their *Report* the Commission stated that 99 of the 300 complaints received contained charges of misconduct against police officers. Without disclosing the selection criteria, the Commission explained that they only heard complaints that clearly came within their terms of reference and which would throw light on the task ahead of them. Criticising this approach, especially in regard to the exclusion of complaints of assault (Timewell 1908, 1909), the PPVS consistently addressed the lawfulness of police conduct independently of the character or behaviour of the victim. Dating back to the Hillman case the unequivocal position of the Society was that the unlawful conduct of a police officer ought not to be justified or excused on account of the unlawfulness of the victim, particularly once taken into custody (Timewell 1905b). In addition to the 19 cases heard by the Commission, the PPVS put forward a further 20 for examination. Three were accepted, but the complainants failed to appear at the arranged hearing time, and the Commission declined to hear 17: 11 of the complainants having been convicted by magistrates.[8] Acknowledging that the PPVS Secretary effectively served as their agent, the 1906–08 Commission (1908a) expressed their gratitude to Timewell for obtaining the addresses of many witnesses, 292 in total, and arranging for their attendance at the 64 evidence hearings; held at the Middlesex Sessions court in Westminster Guildhall. With 16 of the 21 complainants supported by the PPVS, which raised funds by public subscription[9] and provided representation in the quasi-judicial hearings, it is evident that the Society ensured that the voices of victims of police abuse were heard.

With over half of the special cases having been reported in the press, a criticism levelled at the Commission was that the hearings served as a court of appeal at which the Met could challenge the decisions of magistrates that went against them. Much time was devoted to the high-profile Gerothwohl and D'Angeley cases, with the Commission concluding that there had been no police misconduct in either case. French citizen Madame D'Angeley remained in Paris throughout the hearings and did not participate in proceedings in any way. Writing many years later in his autobiography, *My apprenticeship to crime*, Harding (circa 1970: 140), whose complaint of police persecution was not upheld, regretted his participation: 'for a man in my position to jeopardise his future by going against the police at a public inquiry was very silly and about the daftest thing a man could do.' In a further four cases in which magistrates had dismissed charges against the complainant the Commission found that there was no misconduct on the part of the police. Yet, in eight of the cases the Commission found that there had been misconduct on the part of eight constables and one sergeant, and three inspectors had made errors of judgment. In regard to one case, which involved allegations of corruption over a period of 20 years made by bookmaker Alfred Platt, and which had been the source of the *Daily Express* blackmail story mentioned above, the Commission found there was insufficient evidence of systemic misconduct on the part of officers (Dixon 1991).

Key details of the cases heard by the 1906–08 Commission which resulted in misconduct findings are provided below in Table 3.1. In the first three columns are the details of each complaint in chronological order including date of incident, complainant name, occupation and type of allegation. There were four main types—assault, false imprisonment (arising from an unlawful arrest), perjury and malicious prosecution (arising from the fabrication of evidence). In the remaining four columns are details of the outcomes of proceedings in the police courts, by the Commission and the Metropolitan Police, and recorded attempts by the complainant to achieve a legal remedy.

The Commissioners did not disagree with decisions made by magistrates in any of the cases they heard, including where they found police guilty of misconduct; the case of James Clinch, for example. Having

Table 3.1 Special cases heard by the Royal Commission upon the Duties of the Metropolitan Police that resulted in a misconduct finding

Complaint details			Police Court verdict against complainant	Royal Commission finding	Metropolitan Police internal inquiry finding	Legal action outcome
Date	Complainant	Allegation				
5/12/1902	Albert Dubery: Cab yard hand	Assault	Charge of assault refused at police station	PC Murray misconduct	PC allowed to resign: Request for ex-gratia payment unsuccessful	Witnesses declined to support civil claim
6/6/1903	Louise Braham: Wife of managing clerk	Assault; FI; perjury; MP	Disorderly behaviour charge dismissed	PC Atkinson misconduct Insp Billson error of judgment	PC & Insp strictly cautioned; CPM partial apology	n/a
3/8/1904	George Wilson: builder's labourer	Assault	Attempted rescue of prisoner, violently resisting arrest and drunkenness charges dismissed	PC Worsley misconduct	PC fined £5 and transferred at his own expense	*Wilson v. Worsley:* Awarded £20 + £5 costs for assault (covered by police fund)
16/10/1905	James Clinch: Post office porter	Assault	Not charged	PC Gibbard misconduct Insp Gadd improper act	No action reported following acquittal of PC	PC Gibbard acquitted of assault

Date	Complainant	Allegations	Charges	Finding	Inquiry result	Outcome
21/8/1906	George Gamble: painter's labourer	Assault	Not charged	PC Ashford misconduct PS Sheedy misconduct	PC suspended pending trial: Both officers dismissed	PC Ashford convicted of actual bodily harm
9/9/1906	George Mullins: market porter	Assault; FI; perjury; MP	Drunkenness, riotous and disorderly behaviour charges dismissed	PC Morgan misconduct Insp wheeler error of judgment	No misconduct	n/a
30/9/1906	James Baker: ironmonger's assistant	FI; perjury; MP	Drunk and disorderly charge dismissed	PC Pittuck misconduct Insp Mason error of judgment	No record of inquiry	n/a
13/10/1906	Edward Wells: gents outfitter	FI; perjury; MP	Drunk and disorderly charge dismissed	PC Dunham misconduct	No record of inquiry	n/a

FI false imprisonment, *MP* malicious prosecution
Source: Royal Commission upon the duties of the Metropolitan Police (1908a, b, c)

disbelieved Clinch's evidence regarding an alleged assault by PC Walter Gibbard the Commission relied on evidence provided by two independent witnesses in support of Clinch's claim that the constable had sexual intercourse with a woman while on duty. Clinch also complained that Inspector Gadd visited him at work and tried to discourage him from bringing charges against Gibbard. The Commission found that the Inspector had not attempted to obstruct proceedings, but he had acted improperly in interviewing a witness (1906–08 Commission 1908a).

In only one of the complaints upheld, made by Albert Dubery, did the Commission concur fully with the outcome of the internal police inquiry. Late at night in the cab yard where he worked, Dubery was struck with a truncheon by PC John Murray after he discovered the drunken constable with a woman in a cab. The duty Inspector at Hunter Street police station realised the police officer was drunk and refused to accept a charge of assault against Dubery. A former soldier with excellent service record and only seven weeks' experience as a constable, Murray was allowed to resign from the Met. Supported by the PPVS, a solicitor took a statement from Dubery and advised that he could claim damages for his injuries and loss of wages. His witnesses, one of whom was applying to the Met for a cab licence, declined to support the civil claim for fear of drawing the attention of the police to themselves. A letter was also written to the Met seeking an *ex gratia* payment: Dubery informed the Commission that he left the police to deal with the matter after failing to receive an answer.[10]

Of the eight cases listed in Table 3.1, three are particularly helpful to understanding police misconduct in the early twentieth century and the obstacles facing complainants who sought to hold the officers responsible to account. George Wilson was the victim of a police assault who, with the assistance of the PPVS, was successful in his claim for damages against PC Worsley. Louise Braham's husband applied for a summons for assault and perjury against PC Atkinson and was advised by the Magistrate to complain to the Commissioner. PC Ashford was convicted of assault occasioning actual bodily harm to George Gamble following a PPVS investigation.

Wilson v. *Worsley*

George Wilson was having a drink in a public house on Kensal Road, West London one summer evening when he noticed two constables outside of the pub talking to his friend Frederick Mallows.[11] According to Wilson, he walked over to speak to Mallows with the intention of advising him not to argue with the police. As soon as he spoke to Mallows, one of the policemen set about him with his truncheon. Wilson used his arm to block several blows to the head before one landed and caused him to fall to the ground unconscious. When he regained consciousness he was some 300 yards away from where he fell, and he then walked the short distance to Harrow Road police station. According to PC Iven Worsley, he had been called to deal with an incident in a rough neighbourhood involving half a dozen men. While he was struggling with Mallows, Wilson ran towards them shouting and launched a running kick at him and, with others, continued to aim blows and kicks striking him on the leg. Worsley took out his truncheon and avoided hitting Wilson once or twice before striking him on the arm and head causing him to fall to the ground. He denied hitting Wilson with his truncheon when he was on the ground.

Bailed from the police station later that evening, Wilson attended St Mary's Hospital where his injuries were noted: a cut and bruising on the left arm, sprains at the elbow and a 1½ inches long scalp wound at the back of his head with a great deal of bleeding. Local newspaper, *The Indicator*, reported that Wilson appeared before the Marylebone Police Court Magistrate the following morning with his head heavily bandaged and left arm in a sling giving the appearance of a 'wounded soldier returned from the war' (cited in Timewell 1905a). Dismissing charges of attempting to rescue a prisoner and violently resisting lawful apprehension, the Magistrate explained that Wilson had been punished enough.

With the approval of the Home Secretary, the Met defended Wilson's claim for damages and Commissioner Henry decided that any disciplinary action would wait until after the outcome of proceedings.[12] The action was heard by Stoner J at Marylebone County Court on 9 December, with judgment reserved until 21 December 1904.[13] Several witnesses gave evidence corroborating Wilson's evidence and, crucially, John Oakway, who volunteered to give evidence at the request of PC Worsley some three weeks after the incident, testified that he saw the constable use his truncheon twice when Wilson was on the ground. Judgment was that use of the truncheon by the defendant was justifiable in the first instance, but the blow to the head was excessive and use of the truncheon against the claimant when on the ground was without justification. Damages of £20 were awarded with £5 costs. A rare example of a civil action against a police officer,[14] the PPVS published a pamphlet on the case (Timewell 1905a).

In January 1905 the Met Commissioner wrote to inform the Home Secretary of the County Court judgment and his recommendations for disciplinary action against Worsley. Commissioner Henry's letter provides a unique insight into the police approach to managing conduct which had been censured in a court of law. Questioning whether a civil action could properly take into account all of the circumstances that had a bearing on the incident, he set out what amounted to five grounds justifying the decision to retain the services of PC Worsley. Firstly, the officer was acting in the execution of his duty. Called to deal with a fracas outside a rowdy public house where drunken men were quarrelling and using obscene language, the constable could have omitted to take action but determined it was his duty to intervene single handed and disperse the men. Secondly, with good reason to fear for his personal safety when confronted by a man with seven convictions for drunkenness and assault[15] the constable, who was of a nervous disposition, drew his truncheon to protect himself. Thirdly, the officer was disadvantaged at trial by the absence of independent witnesses to support his denial that he struck a helpless man. Ignoring that one witness called for the defence gave evidence that the claimant was struck when on the ground, the Commissioner explained that constables could not rely on the support of bystanders in rough neighbourhoods. Fourthly, although police regulations on use of the truncheon cautioned against blows to the head, experience showed that in the context of a struggle it was not possible for a constable to take careful aim and avoid striking the head. If use of the truncheon was justifiable, as it was found to be at trial, the constable could not then be blamed for landing a blow to the head of the claimant. Finally, in the interest of law enforcement it was essential that constables were supported, and understood that they would be supported, when exercising their duty. Otherwise, for fear of facing legal or disciplinary proceedings constables could not be relied upon to take prompt action, including resort to extreme measures when faced with disorder.

Commissioner Henry recommended that the damages and costs awarded should be paid out of the police fund, and PC Worsley should be disciplined for using his truncheon unnecessarily. The constable was fined £5 and transferred to another police district at his own expense. Neither Wilson nor the press were informed of the disciplinary outcome. The details only came to light when Commissioner Henry read out his letter to the Home Secretary in full when giving evidence to the 1906–08 Commission some two and a half years later.[16] The Commission robustly examined Henry on the adequacy of the punishment, with the Met Commissioner insisting that the expense and disruption to private life as a result of the transfer was not unduly lenient, and that he and senior colleagues were best placed to determine how to manage police misconduct.

Braham Complaint Against PC Atkinson

Similar exchanges between the Commission and Met Commissioner took place with regard to the Braham case, which provides a useful insight into how the complaints system operated in the early 1900s.[17]

Rushing to catch a tram car home just after midnight on 6 June 1903, Mrs. Louise Braham complained that a police constable suddenly came up and took hold of her in an offensive manner. After she requested assistance from a bystander and asked for his name and number, the constable took her into custody. PC Walter Atkinson denied assaulting Mrs. Braham and, attributing her behaviour to drunkenness, arrested her when she would not stop shouting. At Larkhall Lane police station Inspector William Billson took PC Atkinson into his office, so that Mrs. Braham could not hear their conversation, and informed him that he did not accept the charge that Mrs. Braham was drunk, and she was charged with disorderly behaviour. Bailed to appear at Westminster Police Court later that same Saturday morning, the hearing was adjourned until the afternoon to allow for Inspector Billson to attend and give evidence. On learning that the Inspector was on holiday, the Magistrate dismissed the charge. In response to a request by Mrs. Braham's husband, Philip Braham, for a summons for assault and perjury against PC Atkinson, the Magistrate told him to complain to the Met Commissioner.

Widely reported in the press, the case exposed the Met to unwanted publicity.[18] The Inspector on duty at the police court immediately submitted a report to Superintendent Charles Doyle, in charge of W Division, and on Monday 8 June Hornsey Licence Watch Committee and PPVS member James Crabb wrote to the Met Commissioner to draw his attention to the case. The following day Commissioner Henry directed Superintendent Doyle to report on the case to Assistant Commissioner (Administration) Major Frederick Wodehouse.

PC Atkinson and four other officers submitted written reports testifying that they did not hear Mrs. Braham make a complaint in the police station. In the absence of a formal complaint the Sub-divisional Inspector, Divisional Superintendent and District Chief Constable noted Crabb was anti-police and recommended ignoring his letter and waiting until Inspector Billson returned from leave before enquiring further. By this time Mr. Braham's letter of complaint had been received, and Assistant Commissioner Wodehouse forwarded a file containing all internal and external documents to Acting Superintendent James Taylor, covering for Superintendent Doyle, directing him to conduct an inquiry into the complaint.

Taylor arranged for all witnesses to attend Brixton police station on 16 June, and he presided over the inquiry. In attendance were Mr. and Mrs. Braham, Miss Marion Young (Mrs. Braham's friend), PC Atkinson, Inspector Billson and two other constables present in the police station during the period Mrs. Braham was in custody. The Acting Superintendent took down in writing Mrs. Braham's complaint and, then, put to Mrs. Braham four questions asked by Atkinson before recording her answers in writing. Atkinson, Billson (who made a written report of the incident on the same day as the inquiry) and the two other constables did not wish to add anything to the written reports they had already submitted. In accordance with Met policy, as set out in the *Instruction Book for the*

Government and Guidance of the Metropolitan Police Force, known as the *White Book*, (1906–08 Commission 1908a: 52–53) the Brahams were not asked if they wished to put questions to Atkinson or the other police witnesses. Nor did the Acting Superintendent ask the officers any questions about their written reports.

The 'Special Report' of the internal inquiry into the complaint comprised three documents: the delayed report of Inspector Billson; Mrs. Braham's statement of complaint together with PC Atkinson's questions and her answers; and the Acting Superintendent's overview of the case. Taylor reported that Miss Young informed the inquiry that Mrs. Braham left her home at about midnight, and Mr. Braham said that his primary concern was whether Mrs. Braham was suspected of soliciting: the Acting Superintendent reassuring Mr. Braham that there was no such suggestion. In regard to Mrs. Braham's complaint, Taylor wrote that there was no corroboration and it was her word against PC Atkinson's, adding that it was a pity Billson had not attended the court to give evidence.

Two days after the inquiry, Mr. Braham wrote a second letter to the Met Commissioner declaring that he and his wife had no complaint against the police in general. A clerk replied to Mr. Braham on behalf of Commissioner Henry explaining that the inquiry did not throw fresh light on the case and he expressed the Commissioner's regret that the Inspector did not attend the hearing. Mr. Braham wrote two days later accepting the Commissioner's apology and entrusting him to suitably deal with PC Atkinson. There was no further correspondence between Mr. Braham and the Met Commissioner on the matter.

Learning the lessons from the complaint, on the direction of Assistant Commissioner Wodehouse a circular to the Divisions was included in the *General Orders* of 25 June 1903 requiring that before charging a respectable lady of the middle or upper class with being drunk or disorderly, the Divisional Superintendent or Chief Inspector should be consulted and a special report submitted.

District Chief Constable Major W. E. Griffiths interviewed Inspector Billson and PC Atkinson on 30 June and reported to Assistant Commissioner Wodehouse. In the opinion of the Chief Constable, Atkinson made a mistake arresting Mrs. Braham and Billson made an error of judgment in preferring the disorder charge, and ought to have attended the police court. Assistant Commissioner Wodehouse decided that Billson would be strictly cautioned for failing to properly exercise his discretion in dealing with the charge and showing negligence in not attending the court. Atkinson would also be strictly cautioned. In his judgment the constable may initially have made an error of judgment in approaching Mrs. Braham, and it appeared that he then sought to make the case stronger by preferring the charge of drunkenness. Commissioner Henry confirmed the sanctions and Divisional Superintendent Doyle strictly cautioned the two officers on 4 July 1903. The final outcome of the complaint inquiry was not communicated to Mr. and Mrs. Braham or the press.

Appearing before the 1906–08 Commission over three years later, Mr. Braham was surprised to learn that PC Atkinson had only been cautioned, and remarked that what he had considered an apology proved to have been an insult. The Commission were similarly unimpressed with the way in which the Met handled the complaint: in regard to both the effectiveness of the inquiry and adequacy of the sanction. The ineffectiveness of the Met complaint investigation was exposed when, on examination by the Commission Chairman, PC Atkinson volunteered that he suspected Mrs. Braham of soliciting when he first approached her in the street. The Commission concluded the constable did not assault Mrs. Braham, but that he gave a false account of her arrest and said something to her which aroused her indignation. Atkinson went on to wrongly charge her with being drunk and disorderly, and when Inspector Billson refused the disorder charge he charged her with disorder knowing that his own conduct had provoked her behaviour. Further, at the police court (and in his evidence to the internal inquiry) he did not disclose all of the relevant facts to the Magistrate. The Commission found that Inspector Billson was guilty of an error of judgment on two counts: for speaking to Atkinson in his office, out of the hearing of Mrs. Braham, and for accepting the disorderly behaviour charge. Having examined Commissioner Henry on the case, the Commission disagreed with his assessment of the seriousness of the case and found that a mere caution, which would not be kept on record, was an inadequate punishment. The Commission went on to address the Met complaints regulations and the effectiveness of the complaints system in their recommendations (see further below).

Complaints by Dubery, Braham, Wilson and Clinch were concluded before the 1906–08 Commission started hearing evidence. This meant that in these four cases disciplinary outcomes of internal investigations that the Met had kept out of the public domain were subjected to scrutiny and placed on public record. Arrested on 9 September 1906, George Mullins's case was heard over three days by the Commission a couple of months later in late November/early December of the same year. Mullins was supported by the PPVS, with Timewell taking statements from witnesses, and the police court hearing was reported in the press (*Daily Mail*, 11 September 1906). Met documents disclosed to the Commission revealed that the internal police investigation into Mullins's complaint that he was assaulted by PC John Morgan in Kennington Road police station while in custody was concluded within three days of the incident. Finding in favour of the constable, the Divisional Superintendent determined that Mullins had been untruthful and was fortunate not to have been convicted by the Magistrate. The Commission reached a different conclusion. Finding PC Morgan an unsatisfactory witness who often declined to answer their questions, they were of the opinion that two constables gave false evidence in order to shield their colleague from the charge of striking a helpless prisoner (1906–08 Commission 1908a: 317–319). In regard to Inspector Thomas Wheeler, the Commission found that he made an error of judgment in accepting PC Morgan's charge at Kennington Road police station that Mullins was drunk.

The Met did not present any details to the Commission of internal investigations into two other complaints made by James Baker and Edward Wells, in September and October 1906 respectively, which the Commission upheld. It would appear that neither of these complaints, which did not attract the attention of the press, were investigated by the Met.

R v. Ashford

It is evident that inadequate police investigation of complaints impeded justice in some of the cases heard by the 1906–08 Commission, a sorry state of affairs that was perfectly illustrated by the last case the Commission agreed to hear. After a brutal assault by a police constable on 21 September 1906, George Gamble was treated in hospital for two months and then spent three weeks in a convalescent home.[19] The case was investigated by the PPVS, and following publication of the Commission Report PC Edwin Ashford was convicted of assault occasioning actual bodily harm.

Walking home to a lodging house near Brick Lane, East London in the early hours of the morning Gamble stopped to talk to a woman he knew by her first name, Ethel, who worked as a prostitute. He did not know the name or number of the constable who came up and interrupted their conversation. Gamble walked away and was shortly joined by Ethel who informed him that she had refused the constable's request to have sexual intercourse. The constable soon caught up with both of them and started harassing Gamble, eventually pushing him to the ground and repeatedly kicking him between the legs. A police sergeant at the scene intervened, and Gamble was able to escape briefly by running away, before the constable caught up with him and kicked him again. When the constable finally stopped kicking him, Gamble managed to walk to his lodgings where Ethel and a young man found him leaning against a wall. With his groin swelling up, the two helped him to the London Hospital where a ruptured urethra was diagnosed which required emergency surgery and two further operations.

In intense pain and confused, Gamble was registered in the name of Pearce. He could only attribute this to his informing hospital staff that his injury had been caused by the police, and they had recorded the wrong name by mistake. A patient told him about the PPVS, and ten days after the assault Timewell attended the hospital and took a statement shortly before he underwent surgery for the third time. The PPVS had little to go on. From Lincolnshire, Gamble had moved to London to find work and did not know the names of the side streets where he had walked. The constable was a complete stranger to him and he did not see the face of the sergeant, nor could he describe the young man who accompanied him to the hospital. Moreover, his recollection of the times he gave for his movements were inaccurate. All Gamble could help Timewell with were descriptions of streets, the appearance of the constable—aged about 30 years old with a ginger moustache and a description of Ethel.

Within a few weeks of the assault, the PPVS managed to trace and take witness statements from Ethel Griffiths and Joseph Wiltshire, the young man who witnessed the assault and accompanied Gamble and Griffiths to the hospital. The effectiveness of the investigation indicates support for the victim and the efforts of the PPVS to bring the offending officer to justice.[20] Griffiths and Wiltshire had noted the constable's number, PC 207 H, and Wiltshire had made a note of the sergeant's number, PS 5 H. Statements were taken from several other witnesses, including William Hughes, Annie Franks, Isaac Rubenstein, James Hartnett and George Bager, each of whom got out of bed to witness the incident from a window of their bedrooms. Apart from different recollections of the time when the incident took place the witnesses confirmed where a police officer kicked a man on the ground in the presence of another officer, and where an officer kicked a man on the ground without another officer present.

Instructed by Timewell, solicitors wrote to the Met Commissioner on 23 November requesting an investigation into an alleged assault by a constable. The letter explained that proceedings would be issued as soon as George Gamble, having just left hospital, was able to attend. Ethel Griffiths was named as a witness and the assault was stated to have taken place in Spellman Street at 4.00 a.m. (which was the incorrect time); also included in the letter was the number of the constable along with his description. An internal investigation into the complaint was quickly conducted by Sub-divisional Inspector Joseph Hewison. Within two days, PC Ashford submitted a written report stating that he was on night duty in the area of Spellman Street on the day in question, and he denied any knowledge of the alleged assault. Inspector Hewison visited Spellman Street and spoke to four or five shopkeepers who told him that they had not heard anything said of an assault. He then went to the London Hospital and searched their records and was unable to find a patient registered in the name of Gamble. He also drew a blank searching for Ethel Griffiths; none of the local people or constables he spoke to knew of her. On 29 November the Inspector reported the outcome of his enquiries to the Divisional Superintendent, and suggested that the solicitors should be asked for the address of Gamble. His suggestion was not acted upon, and on 8 December a Met clerk wrote to the solicitors informing them that the constable denied knowing or assaulting Gamble and the police knew nothing of the incident.

The 1906–08 Commission heard the case over five days in February and March 1907, and Commissioner Henry was separately examined on 31 July. The five witnesses traced by the PPVS gave evidence on the kicking, and PC Ashford 207 H and PS Thomas Sheedy 5 H were positively identified. In the opinion of the surgeon who treated Gamble at the London Hospital, his injuries were consistent with kicking. Ashford and Sheedy told the Commission that nothing unusual happened on duty that night. Ashford denied meeting Gamble and Griffiths and the alleged assault, and Sheedy denied that he was present at the first assault. Police scepticism of the complaint was apparent throughout proceedings and the Commission considered whether there had been a conspiracy to fabricate evidence and falsely charge the police. Notwithstanding that several of the witnesses may have been biased and hostile to police, the Commissioners determined that the evidence did not support the existence of a conspiracy. PC Ashford was found to have assaulted Gamble as alleged, and PS Sheedy was found to have failed to stop the violence or report what he witnessed.

Dissatisfied with the effectiveness of the Met investigation into Gamble's complaint, the Commission had difficulty understanding why the investigating officer's suggestion to ask for additional information was not acted upon. Examining the Met Commissioner on the adequacy of the investigation the Commissioners were surprised to hear of the 1868 Home Office instruction (see above Chap. 2, and further, below), which prevented police from conducting an internal investigation into a complaint if the complainant was contemplating legal proceedings.

Convicted of assault occasioning actual bodily harm at the Central Criminal Court, PC Ashford was sentenced to nine months' imprisonment with hard labour on 27 October 1908.[21] His application for leave to appeal against conviction on grounds that he had not been properly identified was dismissed (*R* v. *Ashford* (1909) 1 Cr. App. R. 185).

Endgame

The 1906–08 Commission evidential hearings commenced with examination of Met Commissioner Henry. At the conclusion of the first day he was asked to submit a return providing details of police officers accused of misconduct over the previous 20 years. That request was not complied with. Eight returns, not published in the public interest, were submitted which included details of complaints of corruption against officers over the previous ten years. Seeking clarification of the data provided in the unpublished returns and more generally on the handling of complaints the Commissioners recalled Henry for further examination after all of the evidence on the special cases had been heard.[22] Expressly asked how many investigations were held into complaints of misconduct made by members of the public during the year, the Met Commissioner was unable to answer and stated that there were 'about 1800 disciplinary inquiries a year altogether' (1906–08 Commission 1908c: 1228). Unfortunately, the Commissioners did not pursue Henry on his ignorance of the volume of complaints and it is evident that failure to comply with the request for 20 years of complaints data was because records were not kept. An omission that suggests the Met were less interested in addressing the grievances of members of the public and more interested in complaints as a means of maintaining discipline. From a complainant centred standpoint it is apparent that the priority was to manage complaints rather than resolve them.

Following publication of the 1906–08 Commission *Report* Llewellyn Atherley-Jones MP,[23] who had raised the 1887 Cass case in the House of Commons (see Chap. 2, above), filled in some details of the unpublished returns on corruption.[24] Approximately 1000 allegations of misconduct were made over 10 years, including 548 complaints by members of the public of improper relations between police and bookmakers, of which 20 were substantiated together with all 12 complaints made by senior police officers. Ninety-two public complaints related to prostitutes and brothels, of which an unspecified number were substantiated along with all 13 complaints by senior officers. Two hundred and fifteen public complaints were made of improper relations between police and publicans, also without a figure for substantiations and all 19 complaints reported by police were substantiated.[25] These data point to the Met being less than meticulous in recording the outcomes of investigations into public complaints, and the lack of openness and transparency went largely unchallenged by the 1906–08 Commission.

In the interest of completeness, Met statistical returns to the 1906–08 Commission (1908: Appendix xviii; 1908c: Appendix 117) revealed that in the four years between 1903 and 1906, 16 officers were charged with a criminal offence arising from an arrest, of which one was convicted. Although not directly comparable with the Return to Parliament (Metropolitan Police 1888) which contained details of all 50 charges brought against Met officers and six convictions in one year between April 1887 and April 1888 (see above, Chap. 2), the figures indicate that there had been a significant reduction in the frequency of proceedings. Met figures on civil actions and complaints provided to the 1906–08 Commission were the first occasion that these types of data were placed in the public domain. Three out of four civil claims pursued between 1903 and 1906 were successful. One of the successful claims was in *Wilson* v. *Worsley*, and the two others resulted in awards of one shilling and one farthing, respectively (1906–08 Commission 1908c: Appendix xviii). In the same period, following investigation of 123 complaints involving 139 officers where the evidence indicated that persons had been improperly charged, the Met provided particulars of each complaint and the sanction. Six officers were dismissed from the force; two were permitted to resign; 65 were reduced in rank/salary or fined; and 55 were cautioned, reprimanded, stopped leave or transferred to other duties; and no further action was taken against 11 officers (1906–08 Commission 1908c: Appendix 109–122). These data suggest an exceptionally high substantiation rate of over 90%, although the figures need to be treated with caution given the low volume of 30 complaints recorded on average each year.

Although the PPVS may not have been responsible for appointment of the 1906–08 Commission, the Society clearly reflected mounting public concern with police abuses of power and played a crucial role in subjecting the Metropolitan Police to scrutiny. It was entirely due to the efforts of the PPVS that an inquiry appointed to examine police treatment of three respectable individuals was required to consider the violence and brutality of police as experienced by people living in poor and disadvantaged communities. Operating on two fronts the PPVS provided practical support to complainants and, as a prolific letter writer and pamphleteer, Timewell championed a campaign for police reform. Legal representation was arranged and funded for complainants and para-legal work was undertaken in the form of investigating allegations, tracing witnesses and taking down statements. In addition to defending complainants charged with criminal offences the Society also supported claims for damages and prosecutions of constables, as in the cases of Wilson and Gamble described above. That either complainant would have achieved success in the courts is highly improbable if it had not been for the PPVS. The prosecution of PC Ashford, having been initially investigated by the PPVS, was taken over by the police after the 1906–08 Commission reported and an application for a summons against PS Sheedy was refused. In addition to supporting Clinch bring charges against PC Gibbard (see above) the PPVS also supported William Andrews, whose complaint was not upheld by the Commission, bring charges against three officers for alleged assaults which were also unsuccessful. Whether PPVS cases were won or lost they were reported in the press and often accompanied by a commentary written by Timewell. Unafraid of engaging in debate with their opponents the Society regularly featured in the *Police Review and Parade Gossip*, and critical editorial notes would distance newspapers from the content of pieces written by Timewell. There were clear synergies between Timewell's (1905b) study of police work in London and Gamon's (1907) examination of the London police courts. Both authors wrote of the realities working-class Londoners faced of police brutality, corruption and drunkenness which went largely ignored by upper- and middle-class Londoners. Gamon attributed the existence of the PPVS, which he was no friend of, to the scandals that were a routine feature of proceedings in police courts. Irrespective of the unpopularity of the Society among the newspaper reading public, and despite the disrespect shown to Timewell by counsel for the Metropolitan Police and Commissioners (Johansen 2011), the 1906–08 Commission were unable to ignore the evidence on special cases that had been co-ordinated by the PPVS. The weight of evidence was of a public avoiding contact with police and reluctance on the part of victims and witnesses to complain. Among the reasons given were that their busy working lives did not leave them with time to complain; it was unlikely to make any difference; and they did not wish to draw the attention of police to themselves.

The PPVS quickly disintegrated after the 1906–08 Commission reported. Within days Russell announced his resignation and a public spat with Timewell ensued on the letters pages of *The Times* (26 June, 9 and 17 July 1908). Writing several years later in his autobiography Russell (1923) distanced himself from the PPVS when recalling his days at the 1906–08 Commission and referred to Timewell as a fanatic. George Bernard Shaw, who was authoritatively credited with Timewell's 1898 pamphlet on the Hillman case (Petrow 1994), wrote more charitably of his tireless work and the achievements of the PPVS (Shaw 1931). Written out of history, activism of the type practised by the PPVS did not re-emerge to drive reform until the 1970s when defence campaigns organised by black and Asian communities provided complainants with voice.

The 1906–08 Commission (1908a: 144) concluded that the Met were 'entitled to the confidence of all classes of the community'. Finding in favour of the police in the cases that triggered the inquiry, and showing much understanding of the difficulties faced by management to regulate officer corruption and drunkenness, the Commission *Report* was welcomed in Parliament[26] and the mainstream press as full vindication of the police (*The Times*, 1 July 1908).

Met Commissioner Henry evidently did not share these sentiments and he made no reference to the 1906–08 Commission in his annual reports. Could his petulance have been as a result of the criticisms the Commission levelled at the Met and their recommendations for reform of complaints procedures, which Commissioner Henry considered to amount to unwarranted interference in police affairs? Whereas the first Met Commissioners, Rowan and Mayne, informed the Select Committee on the Police of the Metropolis (1834) of their preference for magistrates to hear complaints of misconduct, Commissioner Henry robustly asserted in evidence to the 1906–08 Commission, when countering the suggestion that PC Worsley was treated leniently, for example, that he and senior colleague were best placed to manage misconduct. Much had changed over the course of 70 odd years. There was no mention, for example, of Section 14 of the Metropolitan Police Act 1839 in the 1906–08 Commission *Report*. Complaints against officers that may have once been the subject of publicly held legal proceedings were by the end of the nineteenth century secretly disposed of by way of internal police procedures. The falling into disuse of Section 14, which was eventually repealed under Schedule 10 of the Police Act 1964 along with other obsolete nineteenth-century statutes, coincided with the development of police as gatekeepers to the criminal process.

Impact: Operational Policing and Officer Accountability

Referring back, briefly, to the clamour leading up to appointment of the 1906–08 Commission, it will be recalled that Gerothwohl wrote a letter of complaint to Home Secretary Gladstone. As the Police Authority for the Metropolitan Police District the Home Secretary regularly received complaints which he forwarded to the Commissioner who would, in turn, make enquiries before reporting back. Refusing Gerothwohl's request for an inquiry, Gladstone informed the House of Commons that if Gerothwohl or Lavalette wished to take the matter further it was for them to apply to the courts. It transpired that an inquiry was appointed, and the 1906–08 Commission (1908a: 142) were satisfied that complaints by the two men were adequately investigated by the Home Secretary.[27] The Commissioners arrived at a different conclusion in the Gamble case. In response to their concerns that the Met had only conducted a cursory investigation, Commissioner Henry explained that a full enquiry had not been made because solicitors acting for the PPVS in their letter informing the Met of the case said that proceedings would be issued. The 1906–08 Commission were referred by Henry to Assistant Secretary of State in the Home Office Edward Troup's evidence that it was policy, dating back to the 1868 Home Office instruction, not to investigate allegations where legal proceedings were contemplated. Yet, Henry and Troup clearly did not have the same understanding of the policy. Troup said in evidence that it was 'not a very rigid rule, and I think certainly exceptions to it would be found', and there was nothing to pre-vent the Met Commissioner from conducting a preliminary investigation and bringing proceedings if there was a *prima facie* case (1906–08 Commission 1908c: 1130). The Met Commissioner, on the other hand, interpreted the rule strictly to mean that if a complaint involved an alle-gation that may be pursued in the courts it was not to be investigated. Pressed by the Chairman of the 1906–08 Commission (1908c: 1234) on the importance of discovering the truth if proceedings were to be brought, Henry rather cryptically replied there was a difficulty 'reconciling the directions given by the Home Office and actual practice'. Whether or not an application was to be made to the courts by a complainant the policy, particularly as understood by the Met Commissioner, significantly disad-vantaged complainants. In the expectation that police witnesses would be unwilling to give evidence against a fellow officer, the complainant who applied to a magistrate for a summons against a constable would have to rely solely on evidence that they had been able to obtain from non-police witnesses. For the complainant who decided not to bring legal proceed-ings, much damage will have been caused to their attempt to achieve justice as a result of failure on the part of the police to conduct a prompt and thorough investigation.

Criticism of the Met complaints system by the 1906–08 Commission was made in the context of the effectiveness of the remedies available to the citizen for officer misconduct. Singled out for criticism was the prac-tice of requiring officers to submit written reports, on which complaints investigations depended. With many constables possessing limited writ-ing skills these reports were often written by supervising officers and a statement on the constable's good character and professionalism would normally be appended to the report. The Commissioners were of the opinion that these reports lacked independence and were inadequate for impartial determination of the facts. The Commission were also troubled by the practice of appointing a superior officer, usually the Divisional Superintendent, of the constable complained against to investigate com-plaints, which carried the risk of a conflict of interest. Referring to the way in which the Braham complaint was handled, with the Commissioners clearly at a loss to understand Met Commissioner Henry's refusal to issue an apology for the officer's conduct, the regulations adhered to were described as 'unduly cumbrous and inelastic' (1906–08 Commission 1908: 142).

The 1906–08 Commission proposed formalisation of the complaints process. They did not consider codification necessary and suggested the redrafting of regulations in order to create a quasi-judicial internal process. The Commissioners recommended appointment of a legally qualified Met Assistant Commissioner with responsibility for the investigation of all complaints across the force whether made to the Home Secretary or Met Commissioner. In their conclusions the 1906–08 Commission accepted that the Met were not obliged to investigate Gamble's complaint on policy grounds.[28] Evidently concerned that this disadvantaged complainants in their search for a remedy the Commissioners recommended that a formal inquiry attended by the complainant, officer complained against and any witnesses should be held irrespective of whether legal proceedings were anticipated. Complainants and officers complained against were to be provided with the opportunity to ask direct questions of witnesses. If there was evidence suggesting that a criminal offence had been committed investigation of the complaint would be suspended pending a decision by the Director of Public Prosecutions (DPP), and in the event that proceedings did not follow the investigation would be resumed and completed.

In the face of much of the evidence presented by complainants of and witnesses to police misconduct along with their own conclusions on the ineffectiveness of internal Met investigations, the 1906–08 Commission accepted that complaints were an internal affair and endorsed the practice that had developed in the last part of the nineteenth century of police investigating police. The rationale for their proposals to reform internal procedures, worth presenting here in detail, was in recognition of difficulties complainants faced holding officers to account for their misconduct.

In cases where the misconduct complained of amounts to misbehaviour for which there is no remedy at law, the only course that the aggrieved person can take is to appeal to the Home Office or to the Chief Commissioner, and in such a case we think it is plain that he ought to have the right to obtain full investigation of his complaint. We do not think that the mere fact that the complainant may take legal proceedings if he chooses should be a bar to his complaint being fully inquired into and its truth decided by a Police Inquiry. The remedy by civil action against one in the position of an ordinary constable is not effective, and the application for summons in a Police Court entails expense, trouble and delay from which people naturally shrink. It seems to us, seeing that the police are invested with large powers which may cause great injury to private persons unless exercised properly and in good faith, that anyone who thinks himself aggrieved by an abuse of those powers ought to have the right without embarking on litigation in the Courts to have such alleged misuse of power fully inquired into by the Chief Commissioner or a competent officer acting on his behalf. (1906–08 Commission 1908a: 143)

Recognising the difficulties complainants faced going to law the Commission reasoned that a more effective internal system was better for aggrieved citizens than no remedy at all. This may have gone too far for the Met Commissioner, but not far enough for those that had long spoken out on behalf of victims of police. Addressing the House of Commons following publication of the 1906–08 Commission *Report*, Atherley-Jones averred that justice would be more effectively served by creation of an independent body with powers to investigate complaints.[29] In reply, the Home Secretary informed the House that the government was minded to carry out the recommendation to appoint a fourth Met Assistant Commissioner, provided for the following year under Section 3 of the Police Act 1909, and was giving careful consideration to the Commission's other proposals.[30]

The Met did not implement the recommendations of the 1906–08 Commission as accepted by the Home Secretary.[31] The principal sticking points were firstly, the proposal that complaints enquiries should be conducted by a legally qualified Assistant Commissioner and not the Divisional Superintendent of the officer complained against. Secondly, that the complainant should be able to directly cross-examine police officers at the inquiry held into their complaint instead of having their questions put by the officer conducting the proceedings.[32] Following discussion between Home Office and Met representatives a form of words were agreed which addressed the impasse that had developed. New complaints regulations eventually set out in *General Orders* on 25 June 1910[33] laid down that the Divisional Superintendent was 'primarily' responsible for the 'preliminary' investigation of a complaint, although no mention was made of any requirement to conduct another investigation. The Superintendent was required to submit a serious complaint to the Assistant Commissioner for directions and it was at the discretion of the officer holding the inquiry, normally the Superintendent, to allow the complainant or officer complained against to ask direct questions. The policy dating back to 1868 that complaints should not be investigated if there was a possibility that legal proceedings would be brought was not provided for in the revised regulations. However, despite the reservations of the 1906–08 Commission, the policy remained in force and reference was made to it by Home Secretary Joynson-Hicks in the House of Commons in the summer of 1928 (see below, Chap. 4).

A legally qualified Assistant Commissioner at the helm of a quasi-judicial complaints system did not align with police operational priorities, and within a decade of the 1909 legislation the Assistant Commissioner appointed to the position was transferred to other duties.[34] Complaints investigations were conceived to be part of a wider management duty to determine whether officer conduct met the standards required of a constable. Allegations of misconduct were reported by supervisory officers as well as members of the public, and rather than create a separate system for public complaints it was held that a combined discipline and complaints system more effectively and efficiently met operational requirements. Operational and leadership experience were considered essential for performing these management duties, whereas legal qualifications which may serve to reassure a complainant that their attempt to hold an officer to account would be conducted in accordance with relevant judicial standards were not.[35]

Met complaints policy was clandestinely developed in the early part of the twentieth century outside of the statutory arrangements for democratic oversight by the Home Secretary. Internal police documents reveal that a Royal Commission appointed by the Home Secretary and whose recommendations he accepted had little impact on Met operations.[36] In consequence, the problems associated with officer accountability identified by the 1906–08 Commission in regard to criminal proceedings, officer reports and the conduct of inquiries remained. Proceedings were rarely brought against officers by the DPP[37] and complainants continued to prosecute privately with little success up until the 1960s. In 1937 the Met solicitor brought the Commissioner's attention to the unreliability of officer reports, which prompted an instruction to sub-divisional inspectors to inform officers that it was in officers' own interest to provide a 'full and true account' when required to write a report in response to a complaint (see below, Chap. 6).[38] Finally, shortly after the 1960–62 Royal Commission on the Police was announced, an Acting Deputy District Commander proposed that quasi-judicial complaints hearings of the same type recommended by the 1906–08 Commission should be held in the interest of more effectively establishing the truth, improving public confidence in the complaints system and to deter officer misconduct (see further in Chap. 6). Discussed by command officers for some six months, the proposal was rejected on grounds that if complaints were substantiated and sufficiently serious to result in disciplinary proceedings, then, there would be an opportunity for the complainant to attend before a disciplinary board and hear the officer answer for their conduct.[39]

Notes

1. *Old Bailey Proceedings Online* (www.oldbaileyonline.org, version 7.2, 30 March 2015), January 1898, trial of JOHN FERRIS FREDERICK CORPS RICHARD SANDS CHARLES WOODRIDGE (t18980110112).
2. *Old Bailey Proceedings Online* (www.oldbaileyonline.org, version 7.2, 30 March 2015), January 1898, trial of JOHN FERRIS FREDERICK CORPS RICHARD SANDS CHARLES WOODRIDGE (t18980110112).
3. *Hansard,* Parl Debs, HC: 26 April 1906 col 25.
4. *Hansard,* Parl Debs, HC: 7 May 1906 col 978.
5. *Hansard,* Parl Debs, HC: 29 July 1908 col 1603.
6. *Hansard,* Parl Debs, HC: 14 May 1906 cols 182–187.
7. *Hansard,* Parl Debs, HL: 19 June 1906 cols 7–16 (See also, Timewell 1911). Russell also made specific reference to the conviction of PC William Rolls for perjury, an alleged miscarriage of justice taken up by

the editor of the *Police Review and Parade Gossip* (Kempster 1904), which would not be examined under the terms of reference of the 1906–08 Commission.

8. Despite his persistence, including winning over the Labour Party (Labour History Archive LP/PA/07/1/283–322, Timewell correspondence with Keir Hardie and Ramsay MacDonald), Timewell failed in his attempts to extend the 1906–08 Commission terms of reference.

9. *Police Review and Parade Gossip*, 29 June 1906.

10. For evidence in the Dubery case, see 1906–08 Royal Commission (1908b: 197–203).

11. The narrative of the Wilson case has been compiled from various sources, including *Police Review and Parade Gossip,* 16 and 30 December 1904; *The Times,* 22 December 1904; Timewell (1905b); 1906–08 Royal Commission (1908a: 285–292, 1908b: 347–57, 1908c: 1221–1224).

12. The Met practice of seeking the Home Secretary's approval to cover the cost of defending constables is traced back, at least, to an 1872 General Order. 'If police are proceeded against in respect of matters connected with public duty, and it is subsequently proved that no blame attached to them, the Commissioner may, if he thinks fit, recommend to the Secretary of State that the legal costs of defence should be paid out of the police fund.' National Archives MEPO 2/6037, Legal proceedings against police officers.

13. *The Times* and *Daily Mail,* 22 December 1904; *Police Review and Parade Gossip,* 30 December 1904. The written judgment in *Wilson* v. *Worsley* was placed in the public domain when read out by Henry Schultess Young, counsel for Wilson, nearly two years later during a hearing of the 1906–08 Commission.

14. The Met reported that there had been three between 1903 and 1905 (1906–08 Commission 1908c: Appendix xviii).

15. In the civil hearing Wilson took exception to police evidence that he had a string of convictions, including assaults on police, claiming mistaken identity.

16. For a view from the Home Office on the case, see Assistant Secretary of State in the Home Office Edward Troup's evidence to the 1906–08 Commission (1908c: 1132).

17. The narrative of the Braham case has been compiled from: 1906–08 Commission (1908a: 262–69, 1908b: 217–256, 1908c: 1224–1228; Appendices and Index, 25–32).

18. See, for example, *Lloyd's Weekly News*, 7 June 1903; *Daily Mail* and *Daily Telegraph*, 8 June 1903.
19. The narrative of the Gamble case has been compiled from: 1906–08 Commission (1908a: 388–410, 1908b: 752–852, 1908c: 1223–1224; Appendices and Index, 50–51).
20. Interviewed many years later, Arthur Harding said he assisted with the investigation and passed information to Timewell and the police (Samuel 1981).
21. *The Times*, 28 November 1908: Old Bailey Proceedings Online (www.oldbaileyonline.org, version 6.0, 11 March 2015), October 1908, trial of ASHFORD, Edwin (t19081020-49).
22. Evidence was also heard from eight magistrates who sat in police courts across London, and the Met Commissioner was given the opportunity to respond to concerns raised by Old Street Police Court Magistrate Albert Cluer.
23. Atherley-Jones K. C., appointed the Recorder of Newcastle in 1905 and Commissioner of the Central Criminal Court in 1913, continued to speak out against police injustices and *The Times* (11 June 1928) reported his criticisms of police conduct in the Major Graham Bell Murray and Irene Savidge cases (see below, Chap. 4)
24. No record of the returns were discovered when researching the National Archives, and it has not been possible to examine the original documents for this study.
25. *Hansard*, Parl Debs, HC: 29 July 1908 col 1593.
26. *Hansard*, Parl Debs HC: 6 July 1908 cols 1245–1257; 29 July 1908 cols 1597–1605.
27. In addition to receiving a report on the complaint from the Met Commissioner, which was standard practice as the Home Office did not investigate complaints, Gladstone also received a report from the Magistrate that heard the case.
28. The 1906–08 Commission (1908a: 142) confused evidence given by Commissioner Henry and civil servant Troup in their conclusions. Henry referred to the trial judge in *Cass* v. *Endacott* (1887) unreported (see above, Chap. 2), in support of his claim that the Met were excused from investigating Gamble's complaint (1906–08 Commission 1908c: 1234, Q.52411), whereas Troup referred to the rule laid down by the Home Office 20 years earlier to which exception could be made (1906–08 Commission 1908c: 1130, QQ.48181-2).

29. *Hansard*, Parl Debs HC: 29 July 1908 cols 1592–1598.
30. *Hansard*, Parl Debs HC: 29 July 1908 cols 1602–1604.
31. National Archives, MEPO 3/192, W. P. Byrns letter of 13 May 1910.
32. National Archives, MEPO 3/192, No. 566106/3: G. O. Sec IV—Complaints against the police.
33. National Archives, MEPO 3/192, 25 June 1910 G.O. Complaints against police.
34. Met Commissioner General Sir Nevil Macready evidence to the Committee on the Police Service (Desborough Committee) (1920: 10).
35. National Archives, MEPO 2/1902, Royal Commission on Police Powers and Procedure.
36. National Archives, MEPO 3/192, for example, was not opened to the public until 1986.
37. In evidence to the 1928/29 Royal Commission on Police Powers and Procedure (1929), DPP Sir Archibald Bodkin gave details of only 5 cases, involving proceedings against 10 officers, in the 20 years since the 1906–08 Commission (National Archives, HO 73/121, Royal Commission on Police Powers and Procedure minutes of evidence, p.84).
38. National Archives, MEPO 3/2460, Complaints against police—reports.
39. National Archives, MEPO 2/9846, Commissioner's Office, A3 Branch, 26 July 1960.

References

1906–08 Commission. (1908). See Royal Commission upon the Duties of the Metropolitan Police.

Committee on the Police Service. (1920). *Minutes of Evidence of the Committee Appointed to Consider and Report Whether Any and What Changes Should be Made in the Method of Recruiting for, the Conditions of Service of, and the Rates of Pay, Pensions, and Allowances of the Police Forces of England, Wales and Scotland*, Cmd. 874, Pro-Quest Parliamentary Papers Online.

Dixon, D. (1991). *From Prohibition to Regulation*. Oxford: Clarendon Press.

Gamon, H. P. F. (1907). *The London Police Court Today and Tomorrow*. London: Dent.

Hansard. ProQuest Parliamentary Papers Online.

Harding, A. (c1970). *My Apprenticeship in Crime*. Bishopsgate Institute. Retrieved June 4, 2019, from https://www.bishopsgate.org.uk/content/1413/My-Apprenticeship-to-Crime.

Johansen, A. (2011). Keeping Up Appearances: Police Rhetoric, Public Trust and "Police Scandal" in London and Berlin, 1880–1914. *Crime, History & Societies, 15*(1), 59–83.

Kempster, J. (1904). *The Dalston Perjury Case.* London: Police Review Office.

Metropolitan Police. (1888). *Return of All Cases in Which Metropolitan Police Constables Have Been Charged Before Metropolitan Police Magistrates, or Upon Indictment, During the Past Twelve Months…'.* HC 188. ProQuest Parliamentary Papers Online.

Old Bailey Proceedings Online. (2015, March 27). Retrieved from www.oldbaileyonline.org, version 7.2.

Petrow, S. (1994). *Policing Morals: The Metropolitan Police and the Home Office 1870–1914.* Oxford: Clarendon Press.

Royal Commission on Police Powers and Procedure. (1929). *Report of the Royal Commission on Police Powers and Procedure.* 1928–29 Cmd. 3297. Pro-Quest Parliamentary Papers Online.

Royal Commission upon the Duties of the Metropolitan Police. (1908a). *Report of the Royal Commission Upon the Duties of the Metropolitan Police Along with Appendices, Vol. I.* Cd. 4156. ProQuest Parliamentary Papers Online.

Royal Commission upon the Duties of the Metropolitan Police. (1908b). *Minutes of Evidence taken Before the Royal Commission Upon the Duties of the Metropolitan Police Together with Appendices and Index. Vol. II.* Cd. 4260. ProQuest Parliamentary Papers Online.

Royal Commission upon the Duties of the Metropolitan Police (1908c). *Minutes of Evidence Taken Before the Royal Commission Upon the Duties of the Metropolitan Police Together with Appendices and Index. Vol. III.* Cd. 4261. ProQuest Parliamentary Papers Online.

Russell, E. (1923). *My Life and Adventures.* London: Cassell & Co.

Samuel, R. (1981). *East End Underworld: Chapters in the Life of Arthur Harding.* London: Routledge & Kegan Paul.

Select Committee on the Police of the Metropolis. (1834). *Report from the Select Committee on the Police of the Metropolis, with the Minutes of Evidence, Appendix and Index.* H. C. 600. ProQuest Parliamentary Papers Online.

Shaw, G. B. (1931). *Doctors' Delusions, Crude Criminology and Sham Education.* London: Constable & Co.

Timewell, J. (1898). *The Police and the Public: The Southwark Police Case and Its Moral.* London: James Timewell.

Timewell, J. (1905a). *The Police and the Public: A Marylebone Case.* London: James Timewell.

Timewell, J. (1905b). *Police Work in London*. London: James Timewell.
Timewell, J. (1908). *A Complete List of the Cases Submitted for Investigation to The Royal Commission on the Metropolitan Police by the Police and Public Vigilance Society, with the Charges, Results of Proceedings in Court, Dates, Nature of Complaints Made to the Commission, and Observations Thereon*. London: James Timewell.
Timewell, J. (1909). *The Royal Commission on the Metropolitan Police: The Truth About the Enquiry*. London: James Timewell.
Timewell, J. (1911). *Royal Commission upon the Duties of the Metropolitan Police: Suppressed Evidence*. London: James Timewell.

4

Resort to the Home Secretary

If they achieved nothing else, more than 1200 pages published in three volumes by the Royal Commission upon the Duties of the Metropolitan Police (1906–08 Commission) (1908a, b, c) placed evidence relevant to complaints against Metropolitan Police (Met) officers on public record. Acknowledging that complainants were denied opportunities to hear officers account for their conduct, the Commission proposed changes to internal procedures that were intended to create a more level playing field. However, in the fanfare that accompanied vindication of the Met as a police force that all citizens could have confidence in little attention was paid to the Commissioners' concerns.

The impact of the 1906–08 Commission on the Met was minimal, and public complaints were a low operational priority for many years to come. A corollary of police investigation of police was a complaints system which lacked openness and transparency and, with criminal and civil proceedings rarely brought, as envisaged by the 1906–08 Commission, the Met were left alone to address officer misconduct away from the scrutiny of the press. Scarcely any information was placed in the public domain by the Met, and what is known is contained in reports of parliamentary debates, public inquiries and the press. It is known that in the

© The Author(s) 2020
G. Smith, *On the Wrong Side of The Law*, Palgrave's Critical Policing Studies,
https://doi.org/10.1007/978-3-030-48222-0_4

20 years after the 1906–08 Commission recommended referral of complaints to the Director of Public Prosecutions (DPP) that involved allegations that a criminal offence may have been committed, the DPP was involved in a total of five Met cases in which proceedings were brought against 10 officers.[1] Not all were the result of complaints, and the press reported on two Central Criminal Court trials that arose from complaints and resulted in the conviction of five constables.[2] PCs Albert Brookes, Maurice Weatherill and William Smithe based at Old Street police station were prosecuted in December 1912 for assaulting Mr. George Chapman and his wife Ellen when off-duty (*The Times*, 12, 13 and 14 February 1913).[3] Sixteen years later PCs John Clayton and Charles Stephens, based at Caledonian Road police station, were prosecuted for conspiring to pervert the course of justice by agreeing to prefer false charges against Helene Adele in July 1928 (Wood 2014; Shore 2013). In both cases constables sought to discredit their victims by charging them with criminal offences. George Chapman was acquitted of a charge of assault brought by PC Wetherill at Old Street Police Court, and Adele was acquitted of using threatening words or behaviour at Clerkenwell Police Court. After their conviction on two charges of assaulting Mr. and Mrs. Chapman, PCs Weatherill and Smithe withdrew their not-guilty pleas to charges of perjury and were sentenced to 12 months' hard labour in respect of each offence, to run concurrently; PC Brooks, who played a more peripheral part in the assaults was sentenced to four months' hard labour. PCs Clayton and Stephens were sentenced to 18 months imprisonment without hard labour, and an acting police sergeant who gave evidence on behalf of the two officers was subsequently dismissed following a disciplinary hearing (*Daily Telegraph*, 2 October 1928).

With police powers to enforce the law continuing to expand, the fair and effective administration of criminal justice was a pressing public policy issue in the first decades of the twentieth century.[4] Transfer of responsibility for questioning suspects from magistrates to police, which developed unevenly around the country, inevitably resulted in confusion. In 1906 the Lord Chief Justice responded to a request for advice from the Chief Constable of Birmingham after constables had been chastised by judges on the same court circuit. One constable was criticised for failing to question his prisoner under caution and another for having done so.

Following further requests for advice from police around the country, in 1912 the Judges of the King's Bench Division drafted four rules which were supplemented by another five in 1918 before nation-wide circulation to police and courts (Royal Commission on Police Powers and Procedure (1928/29 Commission) 1929). In providing guidance to police on the questioning of suspects under caution, the Judges' Rules were administrative directions without the force of law which, if not observed, may have resulted in the exclusion of evidence in criminal proceedings. The Rules were never far from controversy and Members of Parliament often raised complaints alleging police abuse of power on behalf of their constituents in the House of Commons. Often in regard to cases involving the Met the MP asking a question would prompt the Home Secretary to appoint an inquiry in his capacity as the Police Authority for the Metropolitan Police District. Of course, the 1906–08 Commission was one such inquiry and in the following two decades a further two were appointed: one regarding the denial of rights to a suspect while detained in custody (Rawlinson 1925) and the other on the denial of rights to a witness taken by car to Scotland Yard for interview (Inquiry in regard to the interrogation by the police of Miss Savidge (Savidge Inquiry) 1928). In addition, a sub-committee of the Street Offences Committee was appointed to investigate the conduct of Met officers following successful appeals against conviction by Major Graham Bell Murray and schoolmaster Francis Champain (*The Times*, 6 October 1927). At the same time as Home Secretary Joynson Hicks agreed to appoint the inquiry into the interrogation of Irene Savidge, he also announced that a Royal Commission would be appointed to examine police powers and criminal investigation methods, including the Judges' Rules.[5]

Resort to the Home Secretary to appoint an inquiry to examine allegations that police had exceeded their powers was arguably the most effective means by which a complainant could hope to have their grievance addressed following the 1906–08 Commission. In addition to the inquiries into complaints relating to police powers to enforce the law mentioned above, this chapter discusses two public order policing incidents where the Home Secretary was asked by complainants to appoint public inquiries, unsuccessfully in the first instance and successfully in the second.

Public Order Policing Complaints: Suffragettes and Striking Dock Workers

Home Secretary Winston Churchill resolutely withstood demands for a public inquiry into allegations of police brutality and indecent assault at three protests organised by the Women's Social and Political Union (WSPU) in November 1910 (Bearman 2010; Morrell 1981).[6] *The Manchester Guardian* (19 November 1910) reported that 119 arrests were made during six hours of disorder and violence on 18 November, remembered as Black Friday, when suffragette deputations repeatedly attempted to breach the lines of police which prevented their entry to the House of Commons. The following morning at Bow Street Police Court no evidence was offered against the women and a handful of men arrested for public order offences on the instruction of the Home Secretary, and they were duly discharged by the Magistrate (*The Times*, 21 November 1910). On Tuesday 22 November the protesters were out again, this time targeting the Prime Minister's residence in Downing Street and there were a further 159 arrests for public order offences, assaults on police and wilful damage, largely resulting from stones thrown at the windows of government buildings (*The Manchester Guardian*, 23 November 1910). At the police court the following morning the instruction of the Home Secretary not to offer evidence was repeated for women charged with obstruction and resisting the police (*The Times*, 24 November 1910), and later the same day 18 women were arrested and charged with obstruction at a third protest. No evidence was offered against these women on 24 November, and 52 defendants remanded from the previous day were convicted of assault police and wilful damage offences and sentenced to a fine or term in prison (*The Times*, 25 November 1910).

In response to questions in the House of Commons, the Home Secretary said the police misunderstood his instruction to arrest as soon as there was lawful reason, having been instructed by his predecessor (Herbert Gladstone) to avoid arresting for obstruction.[7] Three months later the Conciliation Committee for Women's Suffrage, an all-party parliamentary group supporting extension of the franchise to women, forwarded to the Home Secretary a *Memorandum*[8] calling for the appointment of a public inquiry, which was accompanied by 135 statements of complaint (*The Times*, 23 February 1911). Taken by the Secretary of the Conciliation Committee H. N. Brailsford and Dr. Jessie Murray some of the statements of complaint were anonymous, and many contained multiple allegations as complainant and witness to police misconduct. Although accurate determination of the type and number of allegations was difficult, unnecessary use of force by police was alleged in nearly all of the statements. In addition to the manhandling and pushing to the ground that may be expected to occur in a melee there were complaints of unprovoked punches to the face and breasts, arm twisting and pinching, and bending back of thumbs. Indecent conduct in the form of openly handling breasts, placing a knee between the legs and lifting up skirts was also alleged, sometimes aggravated by the use of lewd and improper language. Police officers accused of assault were identified by number or rank in 11 statements.

Dismissing the Conciliation Committee's demand for a public inquiry the Home Secretary informed the House of Commons that the proper course of action would have been for complainants to have preferred charges in a police court.[9] An internal Met analysis of the *Memorandum* and statements was excoriating; rather than investigate the substance of complaints the character of the complainants was questioned.[10] Numbers of named complainants that had been arrested ($n = 73$), discharged ($n = 63$) and convicted ($n = 15$) were highlighted,[11] and mention was made of women who were fit and healthy enough to protest on 22 and 23 November after alleging that they had suffered injury as a consequence of police assaults on Black Friday.

Recalling that quasi-judicial complaints inquiries had only recently been proposed by the 1906–08 Commission, and negotiations on their implementation between the Met and Home Office had concluded only a few months before Black Friday (see Chap. 2, above),[12] the importance of prompt and thorough investigation of allegations of misconduct must have been fresh in the minds of senior police officers. The Home Secretary's assertion that complainants should have brought criminal proceedings indicates that the 1868 rule was still very much in place despite the 1906–08 Commission's reservations, and points to indifference on the part of Churchill to the difficulties faced by complainants.

From the internal police documents it appears that an investigation of some description, presumably without the involvement of the complainant, was conducted into only one of the statements taken by Brailsford and Murray.[13] The complaint was not substantiated.

There has always been what may be described as a shared understanding between police and protesters that police will resort to unlawful violence at political protests, and the WSPU maintained a distance from the Conciliation Committee *Memorandum*.[14] There are, however, limits to the degree of violence resorted to and those that consider the police to have gone beyond what is expected in a civilised society have demanded the appointment of public inquiries. Calls for a public inquiry were acceded to after protests at Cold Bath Fields in 1833 and Hyde Park in 1855, and rejected after Bloody Sunday, November 1887 (see Chap. 1, above). After having dismissed the demand for a public inquiry, Home Secretary Churchill captured the common understanding on the use of violence in answer to a question on Met policy at the November 1910 WSPU protests.

> If a body of four or five hundred men were to endeavour to force their way into the House of Commons, they would, after being duly warned, be dispersed by charges of police. Many would, no doubt, receive blows from police truncheons; the rest would take to their heels, and very few arrests would be made.[15]

Which segues conveniently to use of force by Met officers in an operation to disperse a crowd of striking dock workers at Rotherhithe in 1912. Every day since the start of the strike in May crowds of striking dock workers had hurled abuse at the van drivers, and their police escort, when taking meat from the docks. A larger crowd than normal were throwing missiles at the vans on 11 June and the Superintendent in charge ordered 100 police reinforcements to clear the streets. Complaints of excessive use of force by police followed, especially the use of rolled-up capes as weapons.[16] Few arrests were made and Home Secretary Reginald McKenna appointed Old Street Police Court Magistrate Chester Jones (1912) to hold an inquiry.[17] There was little press interest in the Inquiry: Jones's

Report had been published some two months before the Home Secretary was asked when he would be in a position to publish![18]

Evidence was heard over eight days from 136 police and public witnesses. Finding that the order to clear the streets was justified and many of the complaints unsubstantiated, Jones found that five complaints, corroborated by witnesses, were justified. John Marney was shutting up his shop when he was knocked to the ground having been struck several times by an officer's cape, and another officer struck his wife; Walter Maxwell and George Ings were chased by unidentified officers and struck with capes outside their house; and Frederick Edwards was struck on the face by a sergeant wielding a cape. The names of officers against whom complaints were found to be justified were not included in the Inquiry *Report* on grounds that evidence was not given on oath and rules of evidence were not strictly adhered to.

Jones summed up favourably on the way the police cleared the streets, which was picked up in the few column inches of news following publication of the *Report* (*The Times*, 16 August 1912), with the rider that 'some persons have undoubtedly a right to complain of the treatment they received' (Jones 1912: 6). An internal Met appraisal of the evidence presented by Jones challenged his findings that were unfavourable to the police.[19] It was noted that the officers alleged to have assaulted Maxwell and Ings were not identified and, although on duty in Rotherhithe, the claim by the constable alleged to have assaulted Marney that he was elsewhere at the time of the incident was corroborated by two other constables. The identification evidence against the sergeant alleged to have assaulted Edwards with his cape was said to be conflicting and unreliable. An inspector and constable gave evidence that the sergeant did not have his cape with him, and since giving evidence two of the four witnesses had been dismissed from their jobs because they should have been working on the night of the disturbance. Questioning the Magistrate's approach to the evidence, particularly his reliance on 'irresponsible statements of prejudiced witnesses'[20] the Met analysis questioned the utility of the inquiry as a fact-finding forum.

The Conciliation Committee *Memorandum* and the Jones *Report* are two examples of *prima facie* evidence of police misconduct having been placed on public record. The provenance and authority of the two documents, one drafted by lobbyists and the other a magistrate appointed by government, appear to have made little or no difference to the police. After examination of both reports by Met analysts, the complaints went no further and there are no records of action having been taken against any officer.

Law Enforcement Complaints

The exercise of police discretion when enforcing the law, especially in regard to the policing of public morals, was an area of concern which came to a head in the 1920s (Wood 2010, 2012; Slater 2012). Scandals quickly gathered momentum after respectable people, whose integrity was held to be beyond reproach, were arrested and charged on the evidence of constables. With the veracity of the defendant and constable crucial to the outcome of proceedings, questions would be raised in parliament following an acquittal, or the overturning of a conviction on appeal, about the damage to reputation and financial expenses incurred by the innocent party in seeking to clear their name. Among the issues raised were the arbitrary powers of the police to interfere with the right to liberty of the subject and allegations of misconduct on the part of the officer responsible.

Sir Almeric Fitzroy, K.C.B, K.C.V.O.

Clerk to the Privy Council Sir Almeric Fitzroy was convicted of wilfully interfering and annoying persons using Hyde Park on the evidence of two constables by Marlborough Street Police Court Magistrate Frederick Mead (*Daily Telegraph*, 16 October 1922). The evidence of the constables was that they arrested Fitzroy after seeing him approach Mrs. Dorothy Turner for a second time having already approached two other women, with Turner then accompanying the officers to the police station to provide a statement. During cross-examination by counsel for the defence at the police court hearing, Turner declined to answer several questions about her personal circumstances. The Magistrate eventually intervened when she remained silent after it had been put to her that she had recently provided her name and address to a gentleman who was present in court. Unable to rely on Turner as a witness of truth, the Magistrate determined that the evidence of the constables was untarnished and found that Fitzroy had annoyed the two other women that he had approached in the park. The conviction was overturned on appeal at the London Sessions, the Bench of Justices determining there was no case to answer after hearing the case for the prosecution and the appellant was awarded costs (*Daily Telegraph*, 11 November 1922). Counsel for the defence was careful not to argue that the constables had concocted the offence, but had 'imagined' Fitzroy annoyed the women. Then, when applying for costs, complaint was made that police failed to make basic enquiries about Mrs. Turner, and the defendant had gone to considerable expense, far beyond the reach of most people, to discover that she was a prostitute. There were allegations that police blackmail was involved, and in his concluding remarks the Chairman of the Bench stressed that no blame attached to the two constables (*The Times*, 11 November 1922), which Home Secretary William Bridgeman referred to when summarily dismissing a question in the House of Commons regarding Fitzroy's complaint.[21] Fitzroy had been charged with a similar offence in 1917, which had been dropped at the door of the court with the approval of Met Commissioner Henry on grounds of his social status.[22] Leading counsel for Fitzroy was Sir Henry Curtis Bennet KC, supported by Sir Richard Muir, renowned prosecuting counsel who never took silk and acted for the Met Commissioner at the 1906–08 Commission (1908), neither of whom would have been available or remotely affordable to most defendants in criminal proceedings.

After the Fitzroy appeal, there was a hiatus in solicitation arrests (Slater 2010) amidst concerns within the Met that constables were unlawfully arresting suspects,[23] and reservations by magistrates that they were expected to favour constables as unimpeachable witnesses of truth (Waddy 1925). In a further twist, Turner was convicted of perjury in her real name, Daisy Bainbridge, despite her evidence not having influenced the police court verdict (*Daily Telegraph*, 13 January 1923).

Major Robert Osborne Sheppard, D.S.O., R.A.O.C.

Three years later, controversy of a different kind surrounded the arrest of Major Robert Sheppard when a charge of theft brought by Miss Deltah Dennistoun was withdrawn at the Central Criminal Court on 13 July 1925 (*The Times*, 14 July 1925). Counsel for the prosecution informed the Court that three days before the Grand Jury hearing of the indictment another person of similar appearance to Sheppard had been positively identified by Dennistoun. Counsel for the defence then made a statement to the Court accusing officers of behaving outrageously: for unnecessarily detaining Sheppard in custody; questioning whether he lawfully owned identity documents in his possession; and ordering him around like a dog. Two days later, in response to a question about the case Home Secretary Sir William Joynson-Hicks informed the House of Commons that, at the request of Met Commissioner Brigadier-General Sir William Horwood he had decided to appoint an inquiry which John Rawlinson, KC, MP had agreed to hold.[24]

Along with other national newspapers, *The Times* (4, 5 and 6 July 1925) reported on proceedings held over three days at the High Court of Justice. In forthright exchanges with Sir Patrick Hastings KC, MP acting for Sheppard, Sergeant William Moore, a CID officer based at Vine Street police station, said that he would not have allowed Sheppard to see anyone while in custody and he had known for solicitors to have been denied access to their clients. Sergeant Constantine Woods, also with the CID based at Grays Inn Road police station, who arranged for an identification parade at Vine Street police station and questioned Sheppard while waiting for it to take place stated that he formed the opinion that Sheppard was guilty of the offence. After Sheppard's Counsel complained about the way Woods was speaking to him, Rawlinson advised the experienced officer that he ought to be accustomed to giving evidence and if he could not answer a question he should say so.

Putting to one side the conflicting evidence Rawlinson (1925) relied on the admitted facts in his *Report*, which was highly critical of the police. Sheppard had voluntarily attended Vine Street police station at about 10.00 p.m. on 27 June in the company of Dennistoun after she accused him of stealing property from her rooms. He was transferred to Hunter Street police station to be charged with the theft of property amounting to £18.00, and was released on bail at about 2.30 a.m. Rawlinson found, firstly, that Sheppard had been unnecessarily detained for about four hours. Secondly, PS Woods was in breach of the Judges' Rules when he failed to caution Sheppard before asking him questions relating to the alleged offence. Thirdly, Sheppard was not informed of his right to have someone present at the identification parade, which Rawlinson called a farce and probably illegal. Fourthly, at Hunter Street police station Sheppard was compelled to have his finger prints taken without being informed that he had the right to refuse. Fifthly, officers at both police stations were unaware of the regulations and rights of suspects when detained in custody, and monitoring of adherence to them by supervisory officers was insufficient. Finally, having heard the evidence of the officers Rawlinson expressed serious concern that suspects more vulnerable than Sheppard would also have been mistreated at Vine Street police station.

The Times (17 August 1925) picked up on the arrogance, authoritativeness and ignorance displayed by middle ranking officers in their evidence to the Inquiry, concluding in an editorial that it was necessary for the police authorities and Home Secretary to take action to safeguard the rights of suspects. Home Secretary Joynson-Hicks's letter to Rawlinson setting out in detail action to be taken in response to his *Report* was published in full in *The Times* (28 August 1925). At his direction Met regulations governing the rights of suspects detained in custody, including communicating with a friend, bail arrangements, identification parades and fingerprinting were accordingly revised within weeks.[25]

All of the details of the Sheppard case presented above were reported in the press at the time. Internal Met documents, including correspondence with the Home Office, were opened to the public in 2006 and shed some light on how the Met managed the serious allegations of misconduct raised. In an undated letter, received by the Home Office on 20 August, Commissioner Horwood forwarded his comments on Rawlinson's *Report* to the Home Secretary. He suggested that as soon as possible, in the interest of maintaining public confidence in the Met, there should be an official response to the criticisms contained in the *Report* and the course of action that he as Commissioner would take.[26] Horwood took issue with

Rawlinson's finding that Sergeant Woods was satisfied that Sheppard was guilty and would have to be charged, which in the Commissioner's opinion provided the factual basis for most of Rawlinson's criticisms of the way officers treated Sheppard when in custody. Accepting that Woods did say he had made up his mind about the offence, the Commissioner attributed this to the 'merciless cross-examination' the officer faced which resulted in his being led into stating that he believed the Major was guilty.

Joynson-Hicks shared in advance with the Met Commissioner his letter to Rawlinson in response to the Inquiry *Report*, and it is evident that the Home Secretary did not accept Horwood's suggestion that Rawlinson's criticisms needed to be answered. In a covering letter the Home Secretary informed Horwood that he would be glad if the Commissioner would see that the views he expressed in his letter to Rawlinson on revision of the regulations, published in *The Times*, were carried out. He continued, 'I further leave it to you, as head of the Police, to take such disciplinary measures in regard to the officers affected as you think right.'[27]

Five officers were charged before a Discipline Board which sat over five days: Inspector John Pelling, in charge of Vine Street police station; PS George Dyer, station sergeant in charge of Hunter Street police station; PS Moore; PS Woods; and PC Arthur Davis, based at Grays Inn Road police station.[28] Pelling, Dyer and Davis were acquitted of charges of giving unsatisfactory evidence to the Rawlinson Inquiry; Dyer was also acquitted of making false entries in the Vine Street police station Bail Book; and Davis was also acquitted of failing to inform the Vine Street Inspector of Sheppard's request to contact his friends. Moore and Woods were found guilty of giving unsatisfactory evidence to the Inquiry, and acquitted of failing to inform the Inspector of Sheppard's request to contact his friends. The reason given by the Board for finding in favour of the officers regarding Sheppard's 'alleged' request was because the Major could not remember whom he asked and each officer 'strongly denied that any such request was ever made to either one of them'.[29] On behalf of the two officers, the Board reasoned there were strong grounds for favourable treatment as a result of the difficult situation they often found themselves during the Inquiry when cross-examined by counsel for Sheppard. Moore and Woods were reprimanded and cautioned, and transferred in the interest of the force. The disciplinary sanctions were announced in Police Orders on 19 November 1925[30] and the House of Commons the following week.[31]

Major Sheppard did not formally complain about the treatment he was subjected to, the matter was taken up after he was obliged to inform the War Office of his arrest. In his letter to his commanding officer explaining what had happened, he requested that the Army Council endeavour to obtain an apology from the Met Commissioner and for his defence costs to be paid out of public funds. The Home Office desisted from this course of action on grounds that it was an exceptional mistaken identity case where the charge had been brought by a member of the public. Rawlinson had not found that Sheppard faced criminal proceedings as the result of misconduct on the part of the police, and it would set a dangerous precedent if public funds should be used to defray his legal costs.[32]

Lessons were learned as a result of Sheppard's misfortune. Although initiated by the Met Commissioner, change was driven by the Home Secretary whose appointee, Rawlinson, identified flawed custody procedures that did not protect the rights of the suspect. After receiving the Commissioner's comments on Rawlinson's findings the Home Secretary determined the areas where police regulations required revision,[33] and arranged for chief constables around the country to be informed. Sheppard played the part of the good citizen who had to pay his own defence costs and, although he saw the officers responsible for his misfortune provide the Inquiry with their accounts of what happened he did not have the satisfaction of seeing them answer before a court for their misconduct. The disciplinary outcomes were announced in the House of Commons and reported in the press, but the details remained secret for 75 years, and from a complainant standpoint it is clear that five experienced police officers accused of serious misconduct were treated leniently under internal Met procedures.

Major Graham Bell Murray and Francis Champain

Two years after the Shepherd case another senior army officer, Major Graham Bell Murray, was arrested and held in custody in Vine Street police station (*The Times*, 25 August 1927). Separated by five years, there were also similarities with the Fitzroy case: both men having been convicted solely on the evidence of constables before the same Police Court Magistrate, Frederick Mead, overturned on appeal by the same Chairman of benches of justices sitting at the London Sessions. The day after Bell Murray's successful appeal against his drunk and disorderly conviction, schoolmaster Francis Champain's conviction for importuning at Bow Street Police Court on the uncorroborated evidence of PC Reginald Handford was also quashed on appeal at the London Sessions (*The Times*, 22 September 1927). Under pressure from the Association for Moral and Social Hygiene (Self 2005; Slater 2012), Home Secretary Joynson-Hicks eventually appointed members of a departmental committee to examine the policing of prostitution, solicitation and other offences against decency and good order (Street Offences Committee 1928).[34] He also appointed a sub-committee, comprising three members of the Street Offences Committee to examine the conduct of the officers connected with the Bell Murray and Champain cases (*The Times*, 6 October 1927). Hearings were held in private and the Home Secretary decided not to publish the Sub-Committee's *Report*: it was not opened to the public until 1997.[35]

In advance of the Sub-Committee hearings the Met gathered intelligence on the character of the two complainants; namely, the financial circumstances of Murray[36] and Champain's Birmingham Police record.[37] Following reports in the press on the appointment of the Sub-Committee to examine Champain's arrest (*The Times*, 15 October 1927) there was no further mention of his case and it can be quickly dispensed with here. Champain decided not to participate in proceedings and, although the Home Secretary forwarded the Birmingham Police file to the Sub-Committee and an officer was on standby to give evidence, his police record did not figure in proceedings. The Sub-Committee did not find fault with the conduct of PC Handford or police procedures in the case. The constable admitted to making an error when giving evidence in proceedings which was grounds for the Sessions finding the conviction unsafe.[38]

The enquiry into the Bell Murray case was not as simple and straightforward. Bell Murray complained by letter to the Home Secretary, highlighting that he had been denied the opportunity when held in custody at Vine Street police station to communicate with his friends and call a private doctor. Suspicious about the purpose of the enquiry and the risk that it may be used to undermine his innocence, Bell Murray and his brother-in-law, James Russell, wrote separately to Sub-Committee Chairman Macmillan challenging the decision to hear evidence in private. Reassured at a meeting with the Chairman that the enquiry would not take the form of a retrial the pair changed their minds and agreed to fully cooperate, and Bell Murray thanked Macmillan for allowing Russell to attend all evidence hearings.[39] The Report of the Sub-Committee contains no record of their receiving or giving consideration to the intelligence gathered by the Met relating to Bell Murray's character. It is open to speculation whether the Sub-Committee's preference for holding the enquiry in private was on grounds that members were aware that the Met had every intention of shaping the enquiry into a retrial by focusing on Bell Murray's character.

The Sub-Committee concluded their Report on 2 March 1928 and a Home Office lawyer wrote to Bell Murray on 26 May informing him of their findings, which Bell Murray shared with *The Times* (31 May 1928). The Sub-Committee found that PC John Thurston failed to exhibit 'due care and judgment' when arresting Bell Murray for being drunk and disorderly and molesting women, and the evidence given by the constable at the appeal hearing was 'recklessly inaccurate'. Police at Vine Street police station were found to have failed to inform Bell Murray of his rights to communicate with friends or call a private doctor.[40] Bell Murray was paid £500 out of the police fund to cover expenses and the anxiety caused, which he complained was inadequate (*The Times*, 4 June 1928) and the Home Secretary declined his requests for a transcript of the evidence and copy of the Report. Unable to answer a question in the House of Commons on disciplinary proceedings against PC Thurston, the Home Secretary explained that police regulations did not provide for extra-judicial proceedings of the kind performed by the Sub-Committee.[41] Following a conference between the Met Commissioner and Home Office the Commissioner drafted the charge of negligently making misleading and exaggerated statements when giving evidence at Sessions, and the constable was punished by reduction in his rate of pay.

Unlike Sheppard, Bell Murray did not have the opportunity of hearing officers, in his case PC Thurston and Inspector John Clark in charge of Vine Street police station, provide their accounts of what happened to the Sub-Committee, nor was he informed of PC Thurston's punishment. After seeing Inspector Clark on duty in Piccadilly, Bell Murray wrote to the Home Office to complain that the inspector had not been punished for failing to protect the rights of a suspect held in police custody.[42] The Home Office did not respond to his complaint when informing him by letter that the decision not to publish the Report was final. Marylebone Street Police Court Magistrate Frederick Mead determinedly kept the case alive for a further 15 months in an unsuccessful attempt to rescind the disciplinary sanction imposed on PC Thurston.[43]

Sir Leo George Chiozza Money and Irene Savidge

A pattern of complaints was emerging, which gave rise to concerns that police resorted to 'third degree' methods to obtain evidence, and behind the scenes attempts to undermine the characters of Bell Murray and Champain were soon overshadowed by serious allegations that captured the full attention of the press. The reason given by the Home Secretary for his inability to inform the House of Commons of the disciplinary outcome against PC Thurston was because proceedings had been delayed as a result of similarities with another Hyde Park scandal. Former Member of Parliament Sir Leo Money and Miss Irene Savidge (mistakenly reported as Savage in early press reports) were acquitted of charges of public indecency when sitting on a bench in the Park at Marlborough Street Police Court on 2 May (*The Times*, 3 May 1928). The charges were dismissed after Money gave evidence that the two plain clothes officers, PCs Maclean and Badger based at Hyde Park police station, failed to act on his request to take down the details of an independent witness who returned his umbrella to him upon his arrest. Asked about the case, Joynson-Hicks informed the House of Commons that the proper way to proceed would be for him to consider with the appropriate authorities, the DPP and Met Commissioner, whether perjury or breach of duty were involved on the part of the arresting officers.[44] The situation rapidly deteriorated following revelation that a chief inspector, having been directed by DPP Sir Archibald Bodkin, arranged for 22-year-old Savidge to attend unaccompanied for interview at Scotland Yard as part of a preliminary investigation to determine whether there was evidence of perjury by the two constables. Two days later, on 17 May it was evident that an embarrassed Home Secretary was not abreast of what had taken place when questioned about the circumstances surrounding what was by then referred to as an 'interrogation'. There was indignation at the way in which Savidge was taken by police from her workplace to Scotland Yard, the duration of the interrogation and the way in which it was conducted, and the impact of events on the health of the young woman.[45] The serious allegation made was that Savidge, alone, tired and vulnerable, was put under pressure to provide a statement to two experienced male detectives that was favourable to the two constables and damaging to herself and Money. Moreover, reference was made in the House of Commons debate to similar allegations of police around the country failing to adhere to the Judges' Rules and pressurise suspects into providing involuntary statements.

In response to the rising tide of outrage at the manner in which police had treated a young woman, Joynson-Hicks reasoned that the DPP was an independent law officer who did not answer to the Home Secretary, and for him to interfere in proceedings would gravely risk impeding the course of justice. Introducing an adjournment debate Thomas Johnston MP captured the mood of the House when summing up the issues before them.

> We have here a case which has been heard before a learned magistrate and dismissed, with £10 costs awarded against the police. An inquiry into the conduct of the police is set on foot by the right hon. Gentleman [Home Secretary Joynson-Hicks]. The inquiry into the conduct of the police turns out to be an attempt by the police, using third degree methods of inquiry, to endeavour to trip up in some way or other Miss Savidge and her co-defendant in the recent police court proceedings.[46]

Seriously concerned by the questions asked of him earlier in the day the Home Secretary told the House that he had taken the unusual step of sending at once for the DPP and the officers involved—Chief Inspector Alfred Collins, Inspector Lilian Wyles and Sergeant William Clark—and had personally taken statements from them. Although they rejected the allegations made, he concluded in the interest of Metropolitan Police morale and discipline that there had to be an inquiry. There was agreement across the House that two inquiries were required: firstly, to urgently examine police treatment of Irene Savidge and, subsequently, to consider more generally complaints against the police and their criminal investigation methods (*The Times*, 18 May 1928). The following week three Commissioners of Inquiry—Sir John Eldon Bankes, retired Lord Justice of Appeal (Chairman), Sir John Withers, MP and Hastings Lees-Smith, MP—were appointed with strictly limited terms of reference to examine 'the action of the police in connection with their interrogation of Miss Savidge on the 15th day of May, 1928'.[47] Conservative Party Home Secretary Joynson-Hicks was at pains to point out that the Commission of Inquiry represented the entire House: Withers was a Conservative MP and Lees-Smith was a Liberal turned Labour Party MP. Given that the Inquiry concerned the treatment of a woman, and the role of women was accepted to be of increasing importance to the development of the police, criticism was made of the failure to appoint a female Commissioner.

After hearing the conflicting evidence over five days between 6 and 12 June, fully reported in the press, the Commissioners divided on party lines and concluded with two reports (Savidge Inquiry 1928). In their Majority Report Bankes and Withers concluded that the DPP was under a duty to obtain a statement from Savidge, and found that he along with senior Met officers involved in the planning of the perjury inquiry conducted by CI Collins followed established procedure. They countered allegations by Savidge in regard to what took place at Scotland Yard on 15 May: that Collins (a) terrorised her; (b) dismissed Inspector Wyles in order that a woman would not interfere with the interrogation; (c) improperly suggested she had not had connection with a man; (d) improperly and indelicately carried out a demonstration of how it was suggested she was sitting with Money in Hyde Park; (e) inserted words and distorted meanings in her statement; and (f) tired after a lengthy interrogation, Savidge did not care what was in her statement. The Majority Report found that Savidge was not intimidated and freely answered questions put to her by CI Collins and PS Clark; she was content to be interrogated without Inspector Wyles in attendance; there was no impropriety on the part of the two male detectives; although tired at the end of a long day she was 'quite competent to understand what was said and done' (Savidge Inquiry 1928: 15). After finding the accused public servants blameless, the Majority Report concluded that there was room for improvement in three areas: (a) a witness should be clearly informed if as a consequence of making a statement they may prejudice themselves; (b) police should attend the home of a person from whom they wish to take a statement and not their place of work and (c) unless she expressly objects, when police take a statement from a woman that intimately affects her morals a woman should always be present.

The approach of Lees-Smith in his Minority Report was to consider whether the Met operation on 15 May was open to criticism (Savidge Inquiry 1928: 17–30). He concluded, firstly, that CI Collins was deserving of censure for the way in which he secured Savidge's attendance at Scotland Yard: having sent a car to her workplace without notice; requiring that she immediately decide whether or not to accompany the officers; failing to give her the opportunity to ask her parents for advice; and misleading her about the nature of the inquiry. Secondly, Inspector Wyles's attendance at Savidge's workplace was material to her agreeing to attend Scotland Yard and, although it was not possible to determine the reason why CI Collins allowed the Inspector to leave the room, he was to blame for what transpired. Thirdly, after referring extensively to the manner in which Savidge, Collins and Clark gave their evidence, and cross-referencing with evidence given by other witnesses, Lees-Smith found Savidge a more credible witness than the two police officers. He found that CI Collins was blameworthy for asking Savidge questions that he should not have asked and misrepresenting what she intended to say.

In regard to the possibility that CI Collins had attempted to pervert the course of justice, Lees-Smith observed:

> It has been suggested that Chief Inspector Collins had seen the two constables in the Hyde Park case, and was working to secure their acquittal. Such an assumption is not necessary as an explanation of what occurred. This can be fully accounted for by the presence of an unconscious bias in

favour of the police arising out of the *esprit de corps* which marks the Force, and which was shown in another direction by the mechanical corroboration of each other's evidence by the chief police witnesses. It would be a result of the system by which police offences are investigated by the police themselves. (Savidge Inquiry 1928: 28)

The Minority Report concluded with the recommendation that 15 evidence-based questions, one of which addressed the institutional bias that protected police officers from prosecution, required further examination. Lees-Smith proposed that consideration be given to independent investigation of the police, by providing the DPP with the necessary powers and staff rather than creating a bespoke independent police complaints investigation body.

Mistreatment by police of Irene Savidge, including what amounted to serious allegations of misconduct against named officers, was lost sight of in what became a highly charged political arena. The politicisation of policing was apparent in press coverage and parliamentary debates. In early July, there were unattributed news reports that Met Commissioner Horwood was resigning as a result of fall-out from the Savidge case (*Evening News*, 2 July 1928); and that the Home Secretary had decided that PCs Maclean and Badger would not face perjury or disciplinary proceedings (*Daily Mail*, 5 July 1928). In the House of Commons on 11 July, the same day that he received the Savidge Inquiry *Report*, the Home Secretary did not mention his decision regarding the two constables when asked[48] and he was repeatedly challenged about the reasons for Horwood's pending retirement.[49] Majority and Minority Report findings were condemned in the press by unnamed police officers (e.g., *Daily Telegraph*, 14 July 1928), and the *Daily Express* (14 and 17 July 1928) warned against appointment of yet another Commission and shackling the police with more regulations. During the 20 July House of Commons debate on the Savidge Inquiry *Report*[50] the DPP was criticised for misdirecting himself on the law, which, although picked up in three legal practitioner journals, lawyers Bankes and Withers ignored in their Majority Report. Accusations were made that Bodkin intended to go further than exonerate the constables and obtain evidence to prosecute Money for perjury. The Home Secretary was held responsible by some for asking the DPP to become involved in the first instance, when there was no need as justice had been done by the Magistrate in the police court.

Lessons were learned from Savidge's complaint. Joynson-Hicks was insistent that the Majority Report must hold sway and he informed the House that after consultation with the Met Commissioner regulations would be revised to require that vulnerable witnesses would be informed of the risk of making prejudicial statements, and that a woman should be present when asked intimate questions by a male officer.[51] Consistent with the majority finding that no blame attached to CI Collins or PS Clark there are no records of disciplinary proceedings against either officer.[52]

Police Investigation of Police

This chapter started with a Royal Commission endorsing police investigation of police and ends two decades later with a Royal Commission considering whether police should investigate police. In the intervening years the Home Secretary refused to appoint a public inquiry into complaints against Met officers by over 100 women, and appointed three public inquiries and two quasi-judicial inquiries into alleged officer misconduct. Not one of the complainants that participated in the inquiries had the satisfaction of hearing an officer answer charges relating to misconduct in a court of law or quasi-judicial internal police inquiry as proposed by the 1906–08 Commission. Three officers accused of misconduct in the inquiries were disciplined, although full details remained undisclosed for 75 years. In criminal proceedings brought by the DPP over the same period, five Met officers were convicted of criminal offences and imprisoned arising from complaints by three people. Proceedings against PCs Clayton and Stephens for bringing false charges against 21-year-old Helene Adele were commenced shortly after conclusion of the Savidge Inquiry and, like the Savidge case, attracted the undivided attention of the press (Wood 2014).

Six of the eight incidents[53] that gave rise to the complaints examined in some detail in this chapter took place on Met Commissioner Horwood's watch; five with Joynson-Hicks serving as Home Secretary, and four in the 11 months prior to confirmation of Horwood's retirement and appointment of Viscount Lord Byng of Vimy as his replacement.[54] Before Horwood left Scotland Yard there was further scandal as a result of the dismissal of Sergeant George Goddard in October 1928 and his conviction the following year on charges of corruption (Shore 2013). Contrary to claims that Goddard was a rogue officer, high officer turnover in subsequent months and years in 'C' Division, comprising West End police stations on Vine Street, Great Marlborough Street and Tottenham Court Road, demonstrates that corruption in the Division was systemic and the Met chose to deal with it in house (Commissioner of Police of the Metropolis 1932; Emsley 2005, 2009).

Putting to one side any personal differences between Home Secretary Joynson-Hicks and Met Commissioner Horwood it is apparent that the Met were in crisis management mode as they tried to keep pace with a changing criminal justice landscape, which was reflected in widely held beliefs that the police were corrupt and access to justice was denied to victims of officer misconduct. The state of flux was captured in the House of Commons debate on the Savidge Inquiry *Report*, which was held in the form of an opposition amendment to reduce the government grant to the Metropolitan Police by the sum of £100. There were speeches in support of the majority and minority findings, expressions of despair at the division and stalemate caused and conciliatory statements that attempted to show that the two sides were not far apart. Addressing Lees-Smith's criticisms of the police investigating police, Joynson-Hicks countered that during his term as Home Secretary 'scores' of officers had been investigated and brought to justice by their colleagues, and managers were determined to root out any officer that offends against the law or discipline.[55] His claim was not supported by evidence: when giving evidence to the 1928/29 Commission the Met Commissioner and DPP testified that few officers were prosecuted or disciplined (see below). On grounds that justice had been served in the police court, several speakers pointed to the appointment of the Commission of Inquiry as the cause of the crisis in public confidence in the criminal justice system. In defence of his decision to refer the Money and Savidge case to the DPP, Jonson-Hicks referred, inaccurately, to a 'definite rule' laid down by the Home Secretary in 1868 which was supported by the 1906–08 Commission. He asserted that the rule, which according to his interpretation required that if there was a possibility that officer conduct involved a serious offence against the law the matter must be determined by the courts and not the Commissioner, was introduced for the protection of the public and not the police (see above Chaps. 2 and 3).[56] Referring to the Savidge Inquiry, Street Offences Committee and the pending Royal Commission, Leslie Horshe-Bella MP was sceptical of the use of public inquiries *per se* and advised that executive action was the best means of dealing with the crisis. Arguing that cunning cranks, lunatics and wrongdoers would come forward to give evidence, Captain Terence O'Connor MP cautioned against appointment of a Royal Commission to examine complaints against the police.[57] James Ramsay MacDonald MP, soon to take office as Prime Minister of a minority Labour Government, although critical of the DPP was among those that adopted a conciliatory approach. He urged the Home Secretary to take steps to improve police organisation and professionalism, for which legislation was not required.[58] The opposition amendment to reduce the Met grant was easily defeated by 211 votes to 63.

In the interest of averting the haemorrhaging of public confidence in the criminal justice system there was a retreat from the politicisation of policing that occurred as a result of the Savidge scandal. Contrary to the original intention, there was no mention of complaints in the terms of reference of the 1928/29 Commission (1929), which were to consider the powers and duties of the police across England and Wales to investigate crime, and the functions of the DPP with regard to rights and civil liberties and observance of the Judges' Rules. The Commission approached their task by sending preliminary questionnaires to criminal justice stakeholders which took into consideration the 15 questions drafted by Lees-Smith in his minority report. Question 8[59] addressed procedures for handling complaints arising from criminal investigations and whether the DPP should have a staff of investigators. There was some nervousness in the Met when preparing their written evidence to the 1928/29 Commission in the expectation that the force would be 'shot at' for having unilaterally decided not to continue with a legally qualified Assistant Commissioner at the helm of complaints investigations as recommended by the 1906–08 Commission (see Chap. 3).[60] There proved to be no need to worry and Horwood was given an easy ride when giving evidence to the 1928/29 Commission early in October 1928, shortly before his retirement as Met Commissioner.[61] The Met submitted less than 300 words in answer to Question 8 in their written evidence, and the Commissioners did not dwell on the subject of complaints during the oral evidence hearing with the Met Commissioner. No references were made to the 1906–08 Commission's recommendations or changes to complaints procedures introduced in the previous 20 years. Horwood spoke of the right of a complainant to commence criminal proceedings privately and, without mention of a role for the DPP assured the Commissioners that if investigation of a complaint by a divisional senior detective appeared to establish a case against the officer proceedings would 'almost invariably' be brought. Asked to provide the 1928/29 Commission with an analysis of complaints for one or two years, after checking that they meant both substantiated and unsubstantiated complaints Horwood said 'we might be able to do something in that way. I do not know how comprehensive it would be.'[62] The Commissioners accepted without further question that there were very few complaints that came within their terms of reference, and there is no record of the Met having forwarded further details to the Commission. The Met Commissioner dismissed the suggestion that the DPP investigate police on grounds that an officer should be treated the same as any other citizen suspected of an offence. DPP Bodkin gave more detail than Horwood in his written submission and two oral evidence hearings before the Commission. Believing that transfer of responsibility to the DPP for investigating police would reflect badly on the police, he was implacably opposed and declared it to be impossible and unnecessary.[63] Confirming that he was responsible for the preparation of all prosecutions of Met officers, including recent proceedings against PS Goddard, Bodkin suggested that it was undesirable for the DPP to be the sole prosecutor of police officers around the country. If introduced, however, there were so few cases that it would not add much to his duties and additional staff would not be required.[64]

The 1928/29 Commission (1929) quickly concluded business and reported in March 1929. Events had moved on and press coverage was cursory: the editorial in *The Manchester Guardian* (23 March 1929) reminded readers that the nationwide inquiry had been triggered by the Savidge case which had prompted scrutiny of the Met. Concluding with a list of observations and few recommendations, some of which were ignored, the Commission were unanimous in their commendation of the police and courts for delivering fair and effective criminal justice. They found very little evidence of misconduct on the part of police in the investigation of crime, including resort to the third degree, and attributed blame for what corruption there was to enforcement of unpopular laws or insufficient police powers. Agreeing with Bodkin that DPP investigations of police were unnecessary and undesirable, forces were encouraged to bring criminal proceedings rather than leave complainants to prosecute privately. On a more cautionary note, the Commissioners commented on the existence of a culture among officers serving with the CID who considered themselves to be 'above and apart' from the rules and regulations that restrained uniformed officers. In light of the problems Met Commissioners subsequently faced when tackling corruption (Ascoli 1979), which erupted into scandal some 50 years later (Mark 1978; Cox et al. 1977) the 1928/29 Commission were to presciently observe, 'This error, if not checked, is bound to lead to abuses which may grow until they bring discredit upon the whole Police Force' (1928/29 Commission 1929: 102).

If the Home Secretary had not been the Police Authority for the Metropolitan Police District it is inconceivable that the complaints against police discussed in this chapter, excepting the Mr. and Mrs. Chapman, Fitzroy and Adele cases, would have been subjected to the degree of public scrutiny that they were. It is also difficult to imagine the Home Secretary being asked to appoint an inquiry to examine allegations of officer misconduct made by a complainant from a poor and disadvantaged working-class background. The allegations of officer violence when policing protests by suffragettes and striking dockworkers in 1910 and 1912, respectively, are distinguishable from complaints in the following decade of abuse associated with police powers to enforce the law. The complainants that alleged officers abused their law enforcement powers and failed to respect their rights were of good character and high social status. Victimisation by police is a great leveller, and it is evident that the lives of each of the complainants were disrupted and they suffered as a result of their ordeals. Mention was made in court and inquiry hearings that people from less privileged backgrounds would not have been in a similar financial position to defend themselves against charges and vindicate their reputations, or possess the social capital to draw attention to officer misconduct. Also, and especially in regard to the experiences of Sheppard, as evidenced by Bell Murray's subsequent treatment at the same police station, it was presumed that police would interfere with the rights of less fortunate and more vulnerable people. The ignorance and disregard to regulations and the demeanour of officers when giving their evidence were taken as evidence of a police culture of disrespect for the rights of suspects. Rather than exist as isolated cases, it is apparent that the cases that were scrutinised by public inquiries reflected a less just criminal justice system than the authorities were willing to admit to.

The purpose of the inquiries appointed by Home Secretary Joynson-Hicks to examine complaints raised in the House of Commons was to identify flaws in policy and practice and make recommendations on how to improve the criminal justice process. The primary objective of each was to restore public confidence in the effectiveness of police to enforce the law, and the public interest in holding officers accountable for misconduct was of secondary importance. It is evident that the inquiries played a part in clarifying police powers and suspects' rights, and public acceptance of police as gatekeepers to the criminal justice system may be traced to the 1920s, signalled perhaps by the 1928/29 Commission generally approving their criminal investigation and prosecution responsibilities. At a time when the Met were struggling to maintain public support, it is held that the Savidge Inquiry represented a critical moment in the development of police. It is difficult to envisage a thorough and impartial inquiry into a complaint concerning the conduct of police when investigating police not raising serious questions about officer accountability. However, rather than raise the profile of officer accountability and address unconscious bias in internal police complaints procedures, the political fall-out that followed publication of the Inquiry Report was to lead in a different direction entirely.

Notes

1. National Archives, HO 73/121, Royal Commission on Police Powers of Procedure (1928–29) Minutes of Oral Evidence, Sir Archibold Bodkin DPP, p. 84.
2. In the other three cases, two detective sergeants were acquitted of conspiracy to obtain money in 1917; two constables were acquitted of perjury in 1923; and a constable was convicted of larceny and forgery in 1927. The DPP was also responsible for the successful prosecution of Sergeant George Goddard in 1929.
3. *Old Bailey Proceedings Online* (www.oldbaileyonline.org, version 6.0, 11 March 2015), February 1913, trial of BROOKS, Albert (27, police constable) WETHERILL, Maurice (24, police constable) SMITHE, William (27, police constable) (t19130204-64).
4. At the same time as the 1906–08 Commission was deliberating, and after inquiries into miscarriages of justice experienced on two occasions by Adolf Beck (Committee of Inquiry into the case of Mr. Adolf Beck 1904), and George Edalji (Home Office 1907) mounting pressure for a court of criminal appeal was realised under the Criminal Appeal Act 1907 (Whiteway 2008).
5. Having been examined by three public inquiries in the 1920s the Judges' Rules were scrutinised again half-a-century later as the result of a miscarriage of justice involving Met officers (Fisher 1977) and the ensuing Royal Commission on Criminal Procedure (1981), before they were replaced by a code of practice for the detention, treatment and questioning of suspects under Section 66 of the Police and Criminal Evidence Act 1984.
6. Within days of deploying 1400 Met officers to South Wales to assist with the policing of a mine workers' strike in the Rhondda Valley (Critchley 1967; O'Brien 1994).
7. *Hansard*, Parl Debs HC: 24 November 1910, col 389; Written answers HC: 10 March 1911, col 1834.
8. National Archives, MEPO 3/203, Memorandum on the conduct of the Metropolitan Police on 18, 22 and 23 November 1910 to accompany the collected evidence.
9. *Hansard*, Parl Debs HC: 1 March 1911, col 367.

10. National Archives, MEPO 3/203, Analysis of the complaints by suffragettes put forward by Mr. Brailsford; Memorandum by Commissioner of Police on allegations contained in Mr. Brailsford's Memorial.
11. Some of the complainants having been arrested on separate days, or having faced more than one charge.
12. National Archives, MEPO 3/192, 25 June 1910 G.O. Complaints against police.
13. National Archives, MEPO 3/203, Analysis of the complaints by suffragettes put forward by Mr. Brailsford.
14. Christabel Pankhurst was reported to have said about the *Memorandum*: 'We are soldiers and we don't think complaint is our first duty, but to go on fighting is the right attitude': National Archives, MEPO 3/203. Notes taken from a suffragette meeting: 23 February 1911.
15. *Hansard*, Written answers HC: 10 March 1911, col 1834.
16. Met officers deployed against striking mine workers in South Wales were also alleged to have used their rolled-up capes as weapons (O'Brien 1994).
17. *Hansard*, Parl Debs HC: 12 June 1912, col 869.
18. *Hansard*, Parl Debs HC: 10 October 1912, col 526.
19. National Archives, MEPO 3/217, Disturbances at Rotherhithe; complaints against police—Home Office enquiry and report.
20. National Archives, MEPO 3/217, Disturbances at Rotherhithe; complaints against police—Home Office enquiry and report, p. 7.
21. *Hansard*, Written answers HC: 12 December 1922, col 2638.
22. National Archives, MEPO 10/9, The 'Fitzroy' Case. The earlier charge could not be raised in the 1922 case because the defence had carefully avoided making character an issue.
23. National Archives, MEPO 3/297, letter re appeal of Sir Almeric Fitzroy.
24. *Hansard*, Parl Debs HC: 16 July 1925, cols 1509–1511.
25. National Archives, HO 144/6596, Metropolitan Police Orders, October 12, 1925.
26. National Archives, HO 144/6596, Report on Major Sheppard's case.
27. National Archives, HO 144/6596, covering letter of 27th August 1925.
28. National Archives, HO 144/6596, Defaulters disciplinary boards.
29. National Archives, HO 144/6596, Defaulters disciplinary boards.
30. National Archives, HO 144/6596, Police Order 19 November 1925.
31. *Hansard*, Parl Debs HC: 26 November 1925, Col 1583.
32. National Archives, HO 144/6596, Sir William Davison HC written question 8 December 1925.

33. Primary legislation was also introduced to allow for bail prior to charge under S. 45 of the Criminal Justice Act 1925.

34. The Home Secretary having already obtained the agreement of Hugh Macmillan, KC, MP to chair the Committee and the terms of reference (*Hansard*, Parl Debs HC, 29 June 1927, col 400).

35. National Archives, MEPO 3/1856, *Report of Sub-Committee consisting of The Chairman (The Right Hon. H. P. Macmillan, K.C.), Sir Joseph Priestley, K.C. and Mr W.A. Jowitt, K.C. on the Cases of MAJOR GRAHAM BELL MURRAY and MR. FRANCIS HENRY BATEMAN CHAPMAN, with Appendices* (hereafter, *Report of Sub-Committee*).

36. National Archives, MEPO 3/1856, 18 August 1927 Mrs Ashworth letter; 3 October and 18 November 1927 Commissioner Horwood letters.

37. National Archives, MEPO 3/405, 26 September 1927 Birmingham Chief Constable letter.

38. National Archives, MEPO 3/1856, *Report of Sub-Committee.*

39. Correspondence between the two witnesses and Sub-Committee Chairman reproduced in Appendix B of the *Report* (National Archives, MEPO 3/1856, *Report of Sub-Committee*): Russell also shared his letter to the Chairman with the press (*Daily Mail*, 17 November 1927).

40. The Sub-Committee was particularly disturbed to find that the steps taken to address Rawlinson's findings regarding failure to safeguard the rights of suspects at Vine Street police station had not proved effective: (National Archives, MEPO 3/1856, *Report of Sub-Committee*, p. 6).

41. *Hansard*, Parl Debs HC: 7 June 1928, col 318.

42. National Archives, MEPO 3/1856, Bell Murray letter 4 September 1928.

43. National Archives, MEPO 3/1856, Mr F. Mead: The Bell Murray case.

44. *Hansard*, Parl Debs HC: 7 May 1928, col 17.

45. *Hansard*, Parl Debs HC: 17 May 1928, cols 1216–1220.

46. *Hansard*, Parl Debs HC: 17 May 1928, Col 1310.

47. *Hansard*, Parl Debs HC: 23 May 1928, 1921–1931.

48. *Hansard*, Parl Debs HC: 11 July 1928, col 2241–2243. The Home Secretary informed the House of the decision not to bring proceedings five days later (*Hansard*, Parl Debs HC: 16 July 1928, col 35).

49. *Hansard*, Parl Debs HC: 11 July 1928, cols 2273–2327.

50. *Hansard*, Parl Debs HC: 20 July 1928, cols 805–891. The Report was discussed in the House of Lords six days later (*Hansard*, Parl Debs HL: 26 July 1928, cols 1352–1404).

51. National Archives, MEPO 3/554, Police Orders: 1 August 1928.

52. The attachment of blame to CI Collins in the minority report was briefly discussed in both Houses of Parliament with the opinion expressed that an experienced officer with more than 30 years' service he was a victim of the system (*Hansard*, Parl Debs HC: 20 July 1928, col 850).
53. Suffragette protests; Rotherhithe disturbance; Fitzroy arrest; Sheppard arrest; Bell Murray arrest; Champain arrest; Money and Savidge arrests; Savidge complaint.
54. *Hansard*, Parl Debs HC: 2 July 1928, cols 982–986.
55. *Hansard*, Parl Debs HC: 20 July 1928, col 833.
56. *Hansard*, Parl Debs HC: 20 July 1928, col 827.
57. *Hansard*, Parl Debs HC: 20 July 1928, col 856–857.
58. *Hansard*, Parl Debs HC: 20 July 1928, col 881–882
59. Complaints against the police

    '(a) What is the existing practice in your force with regard to the investigation of complaints received from the public against the conduct of the police in the investigation of crimes and offences? Can you suggest any improvements in the existing practice in this matter?'
    '(b) Would you be in favour of any change whereby the Director of Public Prosecutions would be furnished with a staff that would enable him, when deciding whether or not a prosecution should be instituted for an alleged offence in which police officers are concerned, to conduct his enquiries and to take statements without dependence upon the police for assistance.' (1928/29 Commission 1929: 134)

60. National Archives, MEPO 2/1902, Minute sheet L, 1 October 1928.
61. National Archives, HO/73/121, Royal Commission on Police Powers and Procedure, Minutes of oral evidence, pp. 37–38.
62. National Archives, HO/73/121, Royal Commission on Police Powers and Procedure, Minutes of oral evidence, p. 38.
63. National Archives, HO/73/121, Royal Commission on Police Powers and Procedure, Minutes of oral evidence, pp. 83 and 95.
64. National Archives, HO/73/123, Royal Commission on Police Powers and Procedure, Minutes of oral evidence Vol 3, p. 42.

References

1906–08 Commission, see Royal Commission upon the Duties of the Metropolitan Police.

1928/29 Commission, see Royal Commission on Police Powers and Procedure.

Ascoli, D. (1979). *The Queen's Peace: The Origins and Development of the Metropolitan Police, 1829–1979.* London: Hamish Hamilton.

Bearman, C. J. (2010). The Legend of Black Friday. *Historical Research, 83*(222), 693–718.

Brien, A. M. O. (1994). Churchill and the Tonypandy Riots. *Welsh History Review= Cylchgrawn Hanes Cymru, 17*(1), 67.

Commissioner of Police of the Metropolis. (1932). *Report of the Commissioner of Police of the Metropolis for the Year 1931*, Cmd. 4137. ProQuest Parliamentary Papers Online.

Committee of Inquiry into the Case of Mr Adolf Beck. (1904). *Report from the Committee: Together with Minutes of Evidence, Appendix, and Various Facsimiles of Documents*, Cd. 2315. ProQuest Parliamentary Papers Online.

Cox, B., Shirley, J., & Short, M. (1977). *The Fall of Scotland Yard.* Harmondsworth: Penguin.

Critchley, T. A. (1967). *A History of Police in England and Wales.* London: Constable.

Emsley, C. (2005). Sergeant Goddard: The Story of a Rotten Apple or a Diseased Orchard? In A. G. Srebnik & R. Levy (Eds.), *Crime and Culture: An Historical Perspective* (Advances in Criminology) (pp. 85–104). Aldershot: Ashgate.

Emsley, C. (2009). *The Great British Bobby: A History of British Policing from the 18th Century to the Present.* London: Quercus.

Fisher, S. H. (1977). *Report of an Inquiry by the Hon. Sir Henry Fisher of the Circumstances Leading to the Trial of Three Persons on Chargers Arising Out of the Death of Maxwell Confait and the Fire at Doggett Road, London SE6, HC 90.* London: Her Majesty's Stationery Office.

Hansard. ProQuest Parliamentary Papers Online.

Home Office. (1907). *Papers Relating to the Case of George Edalji*, Cd. 3503. ProQuest Parliamentary Papers Online.

Inquiry in Regard to the Interrogation by the Police of Miss Savidge. (1928). *Report of the Tribunal Appointed Under the Tribunals of Inquiry (Evidence) Act, 1921*, Cmd. 3147. ProQuest Parliamentary Papers Online.

Jones, C. (1912). *Report by Mr Chester Jones on Certain Disturbances at Rotherhithe on June 11ᵗʰ, 1912, and Complaints Against the Conduct of the Police in Connection Therewith*, Cd. 6367. ProQuest Parliamentary Papers Online.

Mark, R. (1978). *In the Office of Constable*. London: Collins.

Morrell, C. (1981). *"Black Friday" and Violence Against Women in the Suffragette Movement*. London: Women's Research and Resources Centre.

Rawlinson, J. F. P. (1925). *Arrest of Major R. O. Sheppard, D.S.O., R.A.O.C.: Report by the Right Hon. J. F. P. Rawlinson, K.C., M.P. of Enquiry Held under Tribunals of Enquiry (Evidence) Act, 1921*, Cmd. 2497. ProQuest Parliamentary Papers Online.

Royal Commission on Criminal Procedure. (1981). *Report*, Cmnd 8092. ProQuest Parliamentary Papers Online.

Royal Commission on Police Powers and Procedure. (1929). *Report of the Royal Commission on Police Powers and Procedure*, Cmd. 3297. ProQuest Parliamentary Papers Online.

Royal Commission upon the Duties of the Metropolitan Police. (1908a). *Report of the Royal Commission upon the Duties of the Metropolitan Police Along with Appendices, Vol. I*, Cd. 4156. ProQuest Parliamentary Papers Online.

Royal Commission upon the Duties of the Metropolitan Police. (1908b). *Minutes of Evidence Taken before the Royal Commission upon the Duties of the Metropolitan Police together with Appendices and Index. Vol. II.*, Cd. 4260. ProQuest Parliamentary Papers Online.

Royal Commission upon the Duties of the Metropolitan Police. (1908c). *Minutes of Evidence Taken before the Royal Commission upon the Duties of the Metropolitan Police Together with Appendices and Index. Vol. III.*, Cd. 4261. ProQuest Parliamentary Papers Online.

Savidge Inquiry. (1928). See Inquiry in regard to the interrogation by the police of Miss Savidge.

Self, H. J. (2005). *Prostitution, Women and Misuse of the Law: The Fallen Daughters of Eve*. London: Routledge.

Shore, H. (2013). 'Constable Dances with Instructress': The Police and the Queen of Nightclubs in Inter-war London. *Social History, 38*(2), 183–202.

Slater, S. (2012). Lady Astor and the Ladies of the Night: The Home Office, the Metropolitan Police and the Politics of the Street Offences Committee, 1927–28. *Law and History Review, 30*(2), 533–573.

Slater, S. A. (2010). Containment: Managing Street Prostitution in London, 1918–1959. *Journal of British studies, 49*(2), 332–357.

Street Offences Committee. (1928). *Report of the Street Offences Committee,* Cmd. 3231. London: HMSO.

Waddy, H. T. (1925). *The Police Court and its Work.* London: Butterworths.

Whiteway, K. (2008). The Origins of the English Court of Criminal Appeal. *Canadian Law Library Review, 33*(2), 309–312.

Wood, J. C. (2010). 'The Third Degree': Press Reporting, Crime Fiction and Police Powers in 1920s Britain. *Twentieth Century British History, 21*(4), 464–485.

Wood, J. C. (2012). Press, Politics and the 'Police and Public' Debates in late 1920s Britain. *Crime, Histoire & Sociétés/Crime, History & Societies, 16*(1), 75–98.

Wood, J. C. (2014). The Constables and the 'Garage Girl' The Police, the Press and the Case of Helene Adele. *Media History, 20*(4), 384–399.

5

Adjusted Responsibilities of the Home Secretary and Met Commissioner (*Fisher* v. *Oldham Corporation* and Constabulary Independence)

Appointed by the Home Secretary under the Tribunals of Inquiry (Evidence) Act 1921, the Inquiry in regard to the interrogation by the police of Miss Savidge (Savidge Inquiry) was the last of its kind to examine the conduct of officers serving with the Metropolitan Police (Met).[1] Several times in the 1930s when raising a complaint against the Met MPs asked the Home Secretary to appoint an independent inquiry, and they were unsuccessful on each occasion.[2] Discontinuation of the inquiry, whether appointed under the 1921 Act or set up as a quasi-judicial inquisition, as an independent review mechanism was signalled by Home Secretary Sir John Gilmour's determination not to intervene following an allegation of police abuse in the summer of 1933. MPs took exception to the Home Secretary's response to a complaint that when conducting a stop and question[3] (as stop and search was then known) plain clothes officers assaulted Flying Officer Douglas Fitzpatrick.[4] Relying on a report of the incident that he had received from the Met, Gilmour presented the police version of what had occurred as a factual account despite knowing that the complainant had not been spoken to. Resisting pressure to appoint an independent inquiry Gilmour insisted that discipline was not his responsibility and managed to persuade MPs, having obtained the

© The Author(s) 2020
G. Smith, *On the Wrong Side of The Law*, Palgrave's Critical Policing Studies,
https://doi.org/10.1007/978-3-030-48222-0_5

agreement of Met Commissioner Air Marshall Lord Trenchard to personally investigate, that the Flying Officer's complaint was being taken seriously.[5] The Home Office kept the press informed of the progress of the
internal investigation, and details of Trenchard's interview with
Fitzpatrick[6] and his final report were published in full (*The Times*, 1 and
18 August 1933). Finding that the complaint was the result of a misun-
derstanding, Trenchard criticised the refusal of Police Sergeant Donald
Fish to apologise to Fitzpatrick as soon as the matter had been cleared up.
Noting that Fitzpatrick's complaint had not been reported to senior officers the Commissioner announced that he would issue instructions
requiring officers to immediately report incidents where innocent persons attended a police station under circumstances that gave rise to a
grievance.[7] Trenchard did not state what action, if any, would be taken
against PS Fish.

Comparison may easily be made between Fitzpatrick's complaint and
those that were examined by inquiries appointed by Home Secretary
Joynson-Hicks in the 1920s. Home Office openness regarding the progress of the Commissioner Trenchard's investigation and reports of proceedings in the mainstream press contributed to the impression that the
internal inquiry was no different to a public inquiry. Moreover, Trenchard's
decision to revise regulations resembled action taken by Home Secretary
Joynson-Hicks after receiving reports of the Sheppard and Savidge inquiries (see Chap. 4, above). The approach pursued by Gilmour and
Trenchard suggest that the Home Secretary and Met Commissioner had
a different understanding of their responsibilities and the nature of their
working relationship, on which arrangements for the governance of the
Met were based, than their predecessors.

There is consensus among policing scholars (Brogden 1982; Critchley
1967; Jefferson and Grimshaw 1984; Lustgarten 1986; Marshall 1965;
Rawlings 2002; Reiner 1992) that relations between chief officers and
their local police authorities were rearranged throughout England and
Wales in the 1930s as police operational independence was established.
The origin of what came to be known as the doctrine of constabulary
independence is traced to a civil claim for damages for false imprisonment in the case of *Fisher* v. *Oldham Corporation* [1930] 2 K.B. 364. In
April 1929 Oldham police believed that a man they suspected of fraud

had fled to London and they contacted the Met. Timber merchant William Fisher was known to police, having been convicted several times six or seven years previously for fraud, and Met officers arrested him at his business premises in Plaistow, East London. Detained overnight in a local police station he was handed over to Oldham officers the following morning and taken by train to Manchester and, then, on to Oldham by car. He was released from custody several hours later that day when it was realised he was not the wanted man. Fisher sought damages for false imprisonment, but instead of suing the police officers responsible for his arrest he claimed that Oldham Corporation were liable on grounds that the officers were acting as their agents. Relying on Sections 190 and 191 of the Municipal Corporations Act 1882,[8] which required the local authority to establish a watch committee (police authority), appoint constables, issue regulations and serve as discipline authority, he sought to establish that a master-servant relationship existed between Oldham Corporation and Oldham police officers, which would render the police authority liable for damages. *Fisher* v. *Oldham Corporation* hinged on the nature of the relationship between police officer and police authority, and the judgment of McCardie J. was that the local authority was not liable for the false imprisonment of the claimant. In performing their law enforcement duties the police officers were fulfilling their duties as public servants and officers of the Crown and were not acting as servants or agents of the local authority. Although McCardie's interpretation of the law has been questioned and the judgment criticised for not giving due regard to the policing realities of the time, the decision was not appealed and the importance of *Fisher* to the realignment of relations between a chief officer of police and police authority, leading to police operational independence, has been accepted as conventional wisdom (Keith-Lucas 1960; Marshall 1960).

Fisher was the first occasion that a victim of a mistake by police had sought to retrieve damages from a police authority. Oldham Corporation admitted to the false imprisonment of the claimant and the parties agreed damages at a sum of £125; the only issue for the Court to decide was whether the local authority was liable. Pausing there for a moment, it is worth contemplating the options that were available to Mr Fisher to achieve redress. It was widely recognised that obtaining significant damages from a constable, a defendant with limited means, was a worthless exercise (Allen 1935). If Met officers had been responsible for Fisher's misfortune, lawyers acting for him may have advised proceeding against the officers knowing that the Met practice, as in the case of *Wilson* v. *Worsley* discussed above in Chap. 3, was to support constables defend claims for damages when performing their law enforcement duties.[9] Furthermore, the mistaken identity case was in the same category of complaint that the Home Secretary had recently been accustomed to addressing, and Fisher may have been tempted to seek satisfaction by raising the case with his MP. This opportunity was denied to him because the officers were members of the Oldham constabulary, and there is no record in *Hansard* of his case having been raised in Parliament. Although unprecedented, Fisher's attempt to establish that the police authority was liable was far from speculative. In consideration of the recent controversy surrounding the interrogation of Irene Savidge and pronouncements by senior office holders on police governance arrangements, there were sound reasons for proceeding with a claim against the local authority. A lively debate on police powers and responsibilities unfolded at the end of the 1920s that could not have escaped the attention of a litigation lawyer. Participants in the discussion, whether writing in practitioner or academic journals, for the press or speaking on the floor of the House of Commons, were agreed that control of the police rested with the police authority. Opinion subtly but noticeably shifted, however, and a new vocabulary was insinuated into police governance discourse which gathered pace after publication of the *Report* of the Savidge Inquiry (1928). As a matter of doctrinal law McCardie's judgment in *Fisher* v. *Oldham Corporation* may be the source of the constitutional convention of constabulary independence (Marshall 1978); it is contended in this chapter that major importance for the shift in the balance of power between chief officer of police and police authority, the Commissioner and Home Secretary in the Met, was the political fall-out from the Savidge scandal.

Police governance was an especially complex area of law in the middle part of the twentieth century. The existence of local police forces created under separate pieces of legislation in the nineteenth century, which laid down different governance arrangements for the Met, City of London,[10] borough (cities and towns) and county police forces, combined with developments at statute and common law, ensured that the responsibilities of constables, chief officers, watch committees, standing joint committees and the Home Secretary were open to interpretation. Uncertainty and a lack of clarity on the legal status of constables and the responsibilities of principal office holders, magistrates and elected representatives (who served on watch committees and standing joint committees) was compounded by ambiguous and inconsistent statements by government ministers on the floor of the House of Commons. Putting arrangements for the Met to one side for a moment, there were three key players: the Chief Constable, Police Authority and Home Secretary. The early police statutes more or less uniformly[11] laid down the responsibilities of chief constables to manage constables and deliver law enforcement services. Police authorities (watch committees in borough forces and standing joint committees in county forces) were responsible for ensuring the maintenance and efficiency of police forces. With central government funding increasing from a quarter to half the cost, force efficiency was overseen by the Home Secretary (assisted by annual reports on the condition of forces by inspectors of constabulary). The autonomy granted to local forces ensured that across England and Wales there were variations in the working relationships between chief constables and police authorities and, in consequence, the extent of democratic oversight exerted over the police. This was dependent on the scrutiny exercised by elected local councillors that served on watch committees and joint standing committees. Under these circumstances it was not possible to reach a clear and common understanding of policing arrangements at the national level and, although intended to standardise police practice and officer terms and conditions, the responsibility of the Home Secretary to draft national regulations under Section 4 of the Police Act 1919 obfuscated whether a chief constable, police authority or the Home Secretary was ultimately responsible for policing.

Governance arrangements for the Metropolitan Police were ostensibly less confusing. Section 1 of the Metropolitan Police Act 1829 established the Home Secretary as the Police Authority for the Metropolitan Police District with the Commissioner, a Crown appointment who was responsible for the direction and control of the force, 'acting under the immediate authority' of the Secretary of State. The Home Secretary was authorised 'from time to time' to give directions to the Met Commissioner whom, under Section 5 of the Act,[12] was responsible for framing orders and regulations, subject to the approval of the Home Secretary, and maintaining discipline. Thus, responsibility for policing was shared between the Home Secretary and Commissioner, and unpicking the statutory responsibilities of police authority and secretary of state was unnecessary to understanding the constitutional arrangement for control of the Met. Moreover, a form of democratic oversight in the shape of MPs raising petitions and complaints on behalf of their constituents on the floor of the House of Commons, which required a response by the Home Secretary, contrasted with the limited opportunities available to citizens to voice their concerns with borough and county constabularies.

Greater statutory clarity regarding governance arrangements for the Met there may have been, but it is equally evident that there were adjustments to the respective responsibilities of the Home Secretary and Commissioner over the years. Before formation it was understood that the Met would be controlled by the Home Secretary, and in his speech introducing the Metropolitan Police Bill for its first reading Sir Robert Peel sought to reassure opponents that increased protection against crime would compensate for any perceived disadvantages attributed to central government control of the new police.[13] It is evident from the outset that the first Met Commissioners, Rowan and Mayne, were junior partners and their responsibilities were exercised largely at the discretion of the Home Secretary. Lord Melbourne's 1833 instruction to the Commissioners to deploy constables to prevent the meeting of the National Political Union of the Working Classes at Cold Bath Fields was early indication of a hands on approach; and the Commissioners' appreciation of where authority for law enforcement ultimately lay was apparent in their request to the Home Secretary to permit them to establish a small cadre of detectives nearly a decade later. Ministerial directions were regularly issued in regard to the policing of public meetings and protests and, as a matter of course, commissioners sought the approval of the Home Secretary for decisions that were not routine operational matters or if unforeseen costs may arise. Although central government control of the police was objected to on political grounds, deployment of Met officers to South Wales and instructions in relation to the policing of suffragette protesters and subsequent criminal proceedings by Churchill in 1910 for example (see above,

Chap. 3), the subordinate position of the Commissioner as an executive officer was uncontroversial.[14]

Further evidence of the Home Secretary's superior authority was when Sir George Grey publicly issued directions to Met Commissioner Rowan after receiving the Report of the Royal Commission on the alleged disturbance of the public peace in Hyde Park on Sunday, July 1st, 1855 (1856) (see above, Chap. 2). In his letter, published in *The Times* (22 November 1855), the Home Secretary set out his reasons for instructing the Commissioner to convey his disapproval to a superintendent, bring criminal proceedings against three officers and issue disciplinary sanctions in other cases. There is no record of Rowan having taken exception to Grey's forthright directions, which disregarded his statutory position as Met discipline authority.[15] Furthermore, the 1868 instruction to refer complainants to a magistrate if there was conflicting evidence that an officer may possibly have committed a criminal offence went unnoticed until mentioned by Home Secretary Henry Bruce in the House of Commons the following year. On its face, the little-known instruction issued when police capacity to investigate crime and prepare criminal proceedings were in their infancy may have been uncontroversial at the time. The position of the Commissioner as discipline authority had been settled by the time Sir Edward Henry gave evidence to the Royal Commission upon the Duties of the Metropolitan Police (1906–08 Commission) (1908). Asked a few years later if a constable aggrieved by a decision of the Met Commissioner could ask the Home Secretary as statutory head of the Met to review the decision, Churchill confirmed that the Commissioner was 'the ultimate authority in all matters of discipline'.[16] Yet, the Home Secretary continued to exercise disciplinary responsibilities and, on the recommendation of the Committee on the Police Service (Desborough Committee) (1920), an officer suspended or required to resign by an internal police disciplinary board had the right of appeal to the Home Secretary.[17] The Met Commissioner's statutory authority for discipline did not deter Home Secretary Joynson-Hicks from intervening in disciplinary matters. Joynson-Hicks deferred to the authority of Commissioner Horwood regarding action to be taken against officers censured by the inquiry into the arrest of Major Sheppard (Rawlinson 1925) and, then, took it upon himself a few years later to decide that constables who had arrested Sir Leo Money and Irene Savidge would not face disciplinary proceedings.[18]

According to Plehwe (1974: 329) home secretaries 'exercised authority over most types of decision' up to the 1920s and routinely issued instructions, in most cases orally rather than in writing, which were uncontentious. There was much controversy, however, as the result of an instruction issued by Home Secretary Henry Matthews to Sir Charles Warren which culminated with the Met Commissioner's resignation in 1888. The altercation between the two men perfectly illustrates that the parameters of the statutory responsibilities of the Home Secretary and Commissioner were dependent on the two high office holders having a shared understanding of Met governance as a collaborative exercise. It follows that in the absence of a common understanding of their respective responsibilities and the nature of their working relationship their statutory duties were open to interpretation. Widely criticised that he had militarised the Met in the aftermath of Bloody Sunday, Warren (1888) personally defended his stewardship of the force in an article published in *Murray's Magazine*. Emphasising the broad range of law enforcement and regulatory 'statutory duties which devolve on the Commissioner', with only incidental references to the Home Secretary's overall responsibility for the force included in the article, following publication the Met Commissioner's attention was drawn to an instruction that the permission of the Home Secretary was required before heads of departments published personal opinions. Rather than undertake not to publish his views on the management and discipline of the Met in future without the prior authority of the Home Secretary, the Commissioner resigned. In his resignation letter Warren set out his understanding of his statutory responsibilities: 'I have to point out that my duties and those of the Metropolitan Police are governed by statute, and that the Secretary of State for the Home Department has not the power under the statute of issuing orders for the Police Force.'[19] A subsequent speech in the House of Commons by former home secretary Sir William Harcourt, in which he said the Home Secretary and Met Commissioner should work together as confidential colleagues, has often been cited (Marshall 1965; Plehwe 1974) as definitive of the Home Secretary's control of the Metropolitan Police.

There cannot be any doubt about the matter. It is not a dual control at all. The man who is responsible to the House for the police is, and ought to be, the Secretary of State, and the Commissioner of Police is no more independent of the authority of the Secretary of State than the Under Secretary of State for the Home Department. It is a matter entirely at the discretion of the Secretary how far the principle of responsible authority shall interfere with Executive action, and the less any interference happens the better. Of course, the Commissioner is the man who knows the Force under him, what is its work, and how it can be best accomplished; but for the policy of the police, so to speak, the Secretary of State must be, and is solely, responsible.[20]

In holding that democratic control of the Met in the form of the Home Secretary's answerability to parliament applied in regard to all aspects of the policing of the Metropolis, Harcourt referred to a separation between policy and executive action without explanation other than to caution that it would be unwise for the Home Secretary to interfere unduly with the Commissioner's executive duties.[21] Home Secretary Matthews fully endorsed Harcourt's speech, adding that the same principle of ministerial responsibility ought to apply the same in large towns as in the Metropolis.[22]

Arising from a publicly aired dispute the circumstances that gave rise to Harcourt's statement on the responsibilities of the Home Secretary and Commissioner for the governance of the Met were not dissimilar to the barely concealed tension that characterised Joynson-Hicks and Horwood's working relationship 40 years later. Despite the law enforcement powers, duties and expertise of the police having expanded considerably over the years, the constitutional position as set out by Harcourt was still held to apply in 1928. It is evident that there was room for improvement and the statutory responsibilities and nature of the Home Secretary and Met Commissioner's working relationship were once again open to interpretation and a subject for discussion, as were arrangements between police authorities and chief officers around the country. Significantly, perhaps, in light of the political rancour that had embroiled policing at the time, two senior civil servants were to play a prominent part in the debate: Sir Edward Troup whom, having joined the Home Office in 1880, had given evidence to the 1906–08 Commission and subsequently served as Permanent Under-Secretary of State in the Home Office between 1908 and 1922, and his successor Sir John Anderson.

Published on 1 January 1928 the first issue of the *Police Journal* carried articles by Troup (1928) and Sir Lionel Dunning (1928), one of the serving inspectors of constabulary for England and Wales.[23] Both articles adhered to the conventional view that police were under the control of the police authority. In his article, Dunning considered an operational law enforcement dilemma in asking who was responsible for criminal justice dispositions. After establishing that there was no public prosecutor for England and Wales[24] and the police decide whether to bring proceedings in the majority of cases, he went on to consider where authority effectively lay for prosecution decision making. Concluding that local authorities were entrusted with the administration of the criminal law, he referred to an instruction issued in 1903 to Liverpool police that consideration should always be given to the necessity for prosecution, and whether it was the best means of deterring an offender from reoffending. The Home Secretary issued a similar instruction to the Met in 1916, and five years later a Home Office circular to forces across England and Wales commended the practice for adoption.

Troup addressed tricky questions of police administration and the responsibilities of the chief officer, local police authority and Home Secretary across England and Wales in the first article of the new journal. Concluding that policing was dependent on co-operation between the three institutions, he pointed out that a chief officer did not have statutory authority to resist instructions by the local police authority, which was responsible for maintaining a reasonably strong and efficient force, however ignorant or meddling they may be. Troup cited Harcourt's 1888 speech[25] as authority for the Home Secretary's control of the Met, and in so doing he sought to clarify the responsibilities of police authorities for policy. The retired permanent under-secretary was clear that the primary legal duties of police to suppress crime and maintain order could not be interfered with by police authority or home secretary, which were 'matters of law and not of policy' (Troup 1928: 15). He understood that *policy* was limited to the means and methods of performing legal duties, including preparations for ensuring that the law was enforced effectively. Although Troup pointed out, like Harcourt, that a police authority had unfettered responsibility for the police he went further in making clear that the chief officer of police had sole responsibility for delivering law enforcement services. This appears to be the first occasion when the responsibility of the police authority for law enforcement policy was distinguished from the chief officer of police's operational responsibilities. It is also important to note that Troup considered the responsibility of police authorities for policy solely in terms of executive responsibility, whether by central or local government, and did not comment on the importance of democratic oversight to policy making decisions.[26]

A few months after publication of Troup's article, in April 1928, the arrest of Sir Leo Money and Irene Savidge was quickly followed by blanket press coverage of the ramifications of the interrogation of Savidge at Scotland Yard. In House of Commons debates it was common ground that as Police Authority the Home Secretary controlled the Met, and Joynson-Hicks asserted in terms that he was the head of the Met[27] and control of the force was his responsibility.[28] The press took exception to the Home Secretary and MPs, whether speaking in the House of Commons or sitting on public inquiries, meddling in police affairs, and newspaper headlines constantly reminded the public that the police were under political control.[29]

Shortly after publication of the Savidge Inquiry *Report* Permanent Under-Secretary of State Anderson (1929) entered the debate when giving a speech to the Institute of Public Administration simply entitled 'The Police'. Citing extensively from his predecessor's recent article in the *Police Journal*, he juxtaposed two principles of policing: firstly, with the exception of the Met, that the police were a branch of local government and, secondly:

> the policeman is nobody's servant. He is not appointed merely as an agent for carrying out the will of a higher authority. He executes a public office under the Law, and it is the Law, with all the safeguards of personal liberty which it enshrines, which is the policeman's master. If he neglects his duty, and equally if he exceeds it, whether in the exercise of personal discretion or under instructions, the Law, as interpreted by the Courts, will hold him to account. (Anderson 1929: 192–193)

Anderson's first principle was unremarkable. The second departed from convention and was at variance with contemporary interpretations of the police statutory framework as set out above. In support of his proposition Anderson referred to the common law origins of the office of constable and development of police powers over the course of the first 100 years of modern police forces. The system of policing, he explained, had not been made like a machine but had grown like an organism, which created difficulties when attempting to identify causes of problems and appropriate remedies. In regard to complaints against the Met and the importance of public inquiries, from which in his opinion the force emerged purged but stronger, Anderson anticipated some of the conclusions of the 1928/29 Commission in their *Report* the following March. He argued that many of the complaints then levelled at the police were as a consequence of unpopular laws relating to motor cars, gambling and moral offences that local constabularies were required to enforce.

Anderson went appreciably further than Troup in outlining his understanding of police powers and responsibilities. Whereas Troup focused on the responsibilities of the police authority for force policy, Anderson addressed the authority of the individual constable to enforce the law. In holding that the constable was not subject to a 'higher authority' he removed the operational law enforcement duties of the police from the domain of public administration, and any standards of democratic oversight that may apply, concluding that the constable was accountable to the law as determined by the courts. According to this view, which was not expressly stated by Anderson in his speech, with the constable's authority derived from law ultimate responsibility for the police could not rest with either the police authority or Home Secretary. Serving in the office of constable and responsible for the direction and control of officers under their command the chief officer of police was in sole charge of operational law enforcement.

Using similar language to Anderson, in their *Report* the 1928/29 Commission (1929: 15) set out that chief officers of police were responsible to their police authorities and described the status of the constable: police powers 'are not delegated by superior authority', the constable is not an 'agent' and is 'personally liable for any misuse of his powers or any act in excess of his authority'.[30]

The 1928/29 Commission Report was published a few weeks before William Fisher's arrest, which was the same month that *Public Administration* published Anderson's (1929) speech. The weight of opinion, even after allowing for the caveats introduced by Troup and Anderson, was that the police authority was responsible for law enforcement and reasonable grounds for believing that the local authority was liable for damages in accordance with standard master and servant principles. In light of the immense public interest shown in police accountability dilemmas, in regard to the answerability of the Home Secretary for the Met generally and individual police officers for their conduct, it is unsurprising that the courts were called upon to test the law. As important as McCardie's decision in *Fisher* v. *Oldham Corporation* was to the future development of the police of England and Wales, rather than consider the case responsible for a step change in police governance, it is held that the judgment reflected the transformation of policing that commenced several years earlier and was made more pressing as a consequence of the political fall-out from the Savidge case.

Rethinking *Fisher* this way, drawing on a complainant-centred narrative, is to place the judgment in the broader context of a socio-legal discourse that opened around the end of the 1920s. A notable feature of that discourse, couched in terms of authority and responsibility before the concept of 'accountability' emerged as a popular measure of answerability and liability in the late twentieth century (Mulgan 2003), was the omission of references to democratic control of the police. The responsibilities of elected representatives were integral to the nineteenth-century statutes which allowed for an element of political oversight of police, although how effectively exercised was a matter of contention. Yet, the core participants in the discourse, including McCardie, did not refer to the democratic credentials of the Home Secretary and members of police authorities when considering their executive responsibilities in a discourse that was to radically reshape arrangements for police governance. The answerability of politicians for the police was not openly criticised, it would not have been politic to have done so, but it appears as a sub-text to the debate and for which explanation may be found in the press backlash against politicians meddling in police affairs and the nature of the House of Commons debate on the Savidge Inquiry *Report*. There was scepticism of the usefulness of public inquiries for developing policy and executive action was praised as an effective problem-solving endeavour. Most tellingly, perhaps, was the intervention by Ramsay Macdonald, now the Prime Minister, he urged the government to pay attention to police administration, which could be reformed without legislation. It is not suggested that there was a conspiracy to undermine parliamentary democracy, the initial direction taken by the debate was not as suggested by Ramsay Macdonald,[31] it was probably more the case that the politicisation of policing that occurred as a consequence of Savidge focused the minds of senior civil servants that were ideally placed to ensure that it would not happen again.

In judging that the police authority was not liable for the false imprisonment of the claimant, McCardie emphasised the risk to independent and impartial law enforcement if he were to find for the claimant: it would entitle the local authority 'to demand that they ought to secure a full measure of control over the arrest and prosecution of all offenders' (*Fisher* v. *Oldham Corporation* [1930] 2 K.B. 364, at 377). Although the risk the local authority posed to the legal duties of the police was not contemplated to be of a political nature in the judgment, a consequence of *Fisher* was that in performing their law enforcement duties police were protected from political interference. The *Police Journal* (Anon 1930) immediately picked up on the importance of the case to the status and independent authority of the police, and in his seminal study of police governance Lustgarten (1986: 47–48) held that *Fisher* was an 'enormous boost' to the notion of police independence which became the 'enshrined orthodoxy' within two decades. In protecting law enforcement from political intervention, *Fisher* was also to restrict opportunities for elected representatives to address their constituents' complaints with the police authority. Arguably, history had repeated itself. Mounting public pressure arising from allegations of Met officer misconduct, including excessive use of violence in poor and disadvantaged communities, had led to the Home Secretary appointing the 1906–08 Commission, which represented a window of opportunity for reform. Commission recommendations for reform of the internal complaints system were not implemented and police capacity building was prioritised as part of the drive to improve law enforcement. The public interest in holding officers to account for their misconduct was neglected, and without access to a remedy the voices of powerless and disenfranchised victims were rarely heard. As police powers to enforce the law continued to expand, complaints against Met officers alleging abuse of power and denial of civil rights by respectable complainants were taken up by MPs and the Home Secretary was compelled to appoint several inquiries. Mounting public pressure led to another window of opportunity for reform after Lees-Smith asked if police investigations of police were fair and effective in his Minority Report into the interrogation of Irene Savidge. That line of enquiry was shut down by the 1928/29 Commission, and the traditional means available to a complainant of asking their MP to request the Home Secretary to address their grievance was closed. In the absence of reform of the Metropolitan Police Act 1829 the Home Secretary and Met Commissioner adjusted their understanding of their responsibilities and the nature of their working relationship. This realignment of responsibilities took place simultaneously with *Fisher*, rather than over a period of time as a consequence of the judgment, and the doctrine of constabulary independence has been closely associated with the operation of internal complaints systems since.

Notes

1. An inquiry was appointed under the 1921 Act to examine an alleged assault by Caithness police officers at Thurso in 1957 (Tribunal appointed to inquire into the allegation of assault on John Waters 1959).

2. After the Home Secretary declined to appoint an inquiry into a British Union of Fascists meeting held at Olympia (*Hansard*, Parl Debs HC, 14 June 1934, cols 1913–2014) the National Council for Civil Liberties (NCCL, formed in 1934) drew up plans for an independent inquiry into the conduct of the police (Hull History Centre U DCL 9/2, Commission of inquiry into the conduct of the police). Police were criticised for discrimination and failing to impartially enforce the law in not taking action in response to excessive violence against ant-fascist protesters at the Olympia meeting and subsequent events, and their targeting of anti-fascist events and protesters. The NCCL general inquiry did not go ahead (Clark 2012) and two years later, following the refusal of Home Secretary Sir John Simon to appoint an inquiry into the policing of an anti-fascist meeting

held at Thurloe Square, London SW 7 on 22 March 1936 (*Hansard*, Parl Debs HC, 25 March 1936, cols 1361–1378) the NCCL set up an Independent Commission of Inquiry (Hull History Centre U DCL 9/4, *Baton charge by mounted police in Kensington: Report of a Commission of Inquiry*). Responding once again to a decision not to appoint an inquiry into use of force by mounted police when dispersing a lobby of the House of Commons in January 1955 organised by opponents of the rearmament of Germany, the NCCL published a report of an investigation into the protest (Hull History Centre U DCL 100/39, *By what authority?*).

3. Under S. 66 of the Metropolitan Police Act 1839.
4. *Hansard*, Parl Debs HC, 26 July 1933, cols 2738–2739.
5. Reference was made to the Savidge Inquiry during the House of Commons debate, not as a precedent for appointing an inquiry but to remind MPs that as a result of the House getting carried away with protecting civil liberties police activity was stifled and officers were afraid of censure: *Hansard*, Parl Debs HC, 26 July 1933, col 2737.
6. National Archives, MEPO 3/2461, Note of interview on 31 July 1933.
7. Paragraph 138 of the revised complaints regulations: National Archives, MEPO 2/1808, Police Orders. Thursday, November 23, 1933.
8. Sections 190–195 of the Municipal Corporations Act 1882 replaced ss. 76–81 of the Municipal Corporations Act 1835 which provided for cities and towns to establish police forces commonly referred to as borough forces.
9. See also National Archives, MEPO 2/1342, *Sadler* v. *PC Gillard*; and MEPO 2/1457, *Ricketts* v. *PC Young*. Following the *Fisher* judgment the Police Federation made representations to the Police Council for England and Wales in regard to the personal liability of their members for tortious conduct, and a Committee of the Council considered the matter in 1931 (Committee on Police Conditions of Service 1949). The decision of the Council was that officers subjected to civil proceedings would be reimbursed out of police funds if found liable for torts committed when acting in good faith, reasonably and with proper regard to instructions. This closely resembled the policy that had been in place in the Met for some 50 years, and similar reasons were put forward by the Police Council in support of the policy as presented in evidence by Met Commissioner Henry to the 1906–08 Commission (see above, Chap. 3).
10. Under the City of London Police Act 1839 the Common Council appointed the Commissioner, subject to the approval of the Crown, and the Court of the Common Council served as police authority, a responsibility which was delegated to a police committee.

11. One anomaly was that the watch committee was the discipline authority for borough police forces under s. 191 (4) of the Municipal Corporations Act 1882, whereas the chief officer was responsible for discipline in other forces, which was important grounds for Mr. Fisher seeking damages from Oldham Corporation. Government failed to act on a recommendation by the Committee on the Police Service (Desborough Committee) (1920) to amend the legislation, and it was not uncommon for watch committees to delegate responsibility for discipline to the chief constable.

12. 'The said Justices [Commissioners] may from time to time, subject to the approbation of one of His Majesty's Principal Secretaries of State, frame such orders and regulations as they shall deem expedient, relative to the general government of the men to be appointed members of the Police force under this Act; ... and the said Justices may at any time suspend or dismiss from his employment any man belonging to the said Police force whom they shall think remiss or negligent in the discharge of his duty, or otherwise unfit for the same; and when any man shall be dismissed or cease to belong to the said Police force, all powers vested in him as constable by virtue of this Act shall immediately cease and determine.'

13. *Hansard*, Parl Debs HC, 15 April 1829, col. 879.

14. On many occasions in the House of Commons MPs unfavourably compared central government control of the Met with the local watch committee system operating in all other cities and towns. Charles Bradlaugh MP's 1888 request for information on prosecutions of constables (see above Chap. 2) was part of an unsuccessful attempt to bring the Met under the control of London County Council: *Hansard*, Parl Debs HC, 31 May 1888, cols 750–751; 12 July 1888, cols 1105–1185.

15. Commissioners Rowan and Mayne did object to Home Secretary Lord Duncannon's instruction to dismiss two officers in 1834, and failed in their efforts to reinstate the men: Ascoli (1979) and Emsley (2009) attribute the intervention on that occasion to Duncannon and Bow Street Magistrate Sir Frederick Roe's vendetta against the Met.

16. *Hansard*, Parl Debs HC, 10 April 1911, col 3939.

17. Under Section 1 of the Police (Appeals) Act 1927, extended to other punishments under the Police (Appeals) Act 1943. In evidence to the 1928/29 Commission, Met Commissioner Horwood pointed out that as a consequence of the Act he was not the final authority on discipline: National Archives, HO/73/121, Royal Commission on Police Powers and Procedure, Minutes of oral evidence, p. 52.

18. *Hansard*, Parl Debs HC, 11 July 1928, col 2242; and 16 July 1928, col 35.

19. *Hansard*, Parl Debs HC, 13 November 1888, col 1036.

20. *Hansard*, Parl Debs HC, 14 November 1888, cols 1162–1163.

21. *Hansard*, Parl Debs HC, 14 November 1888, col 1161.

22. *Hansard*, Parl Debs HC, 14 November 1888, col 1174. Two years later Harcourt held Matthews responsible for the resignation of Met Commissioner James Monro arguing that the Home Secretary's interference in police administration by appointing an Assistant Commissioner over the head of the Commissioner was unjustified: *Hansard*, Parl Debs HC, 20 June 1890, cols 1510–1516.

23. *The Times* (5 January 1928) previewed the first issue and regularly commented on articles appearing in the journal.

24. In a subsequent issue of the *Police Journal*, DPP Sir Archibald Bodkin (1928) positively affirmed the DPP's limited responsibilities (*The Times*, 30 June 1928).

25. Although he combined elements of speeches by former Home Secretary Harcourt and incumbent Home Secretary Matthews in error.

26. Troup did refer to the answerability of the Home Secretary and local councillors to the House of Commons and provincial councils, but only when describing the nineteenth century police statutes.

27. *Hansard*, Parl Debs HC, 17 May 1928, col 1312.

28. *Hansard*, Parl Debs HC, 17 May 1928, col 1315; 20 July 1928, col 839–840.

29. Headlines in *The Times* (21 July 1928) on the Commons debate on the Savidge Report, for example, was 'Home Secretary's instructions' and the editorial of the same day was sub-headed 'New orders to police'.

30. The 1928/29 Commission (1929: Appendix 3, 137–142) referenced their account of police powers and responsibilities to a memorandum submitted by the Home Office, which did not define the status of the constable in terms used by Anderson (1929) or the 1928/29 Commission. It would appear that the authority, duties and responsibilities of police were considered a pressing policy issue in the Home Office.

31. Ramsay Macdonald's ideas were taken up with the 1928/29 Commission (1929: 19) stepping aside from the terms of reference to comment on police administration and training. Met Commissioner Trenchard enthusiastically ran with the idea of a police college (Commissioner of Police of the Metropolis 1933) with the full support of government (Secretary of State for the Home Department 1933).

References

1906–08 Commission. (1908). See Royal Commission upon the Duties of the Metropolitan Police.

1928/29 Commission. (1929). See Royal Commission on Police Powers and Procedure.

Allen, C. K. (1935). Case Law: An Unwarranted Intervention. *Law Quarterly Review, 51*(2), 333.

Anderson, J. (1929). The Police. *Public Administration, 7*(2), 192–202.

Anon. (1930). The Quarterly Record. *Police Journal, 3*(3), 469–481.

Ascoli, D. (1979). *The Queen's Peace: The Origins and Development of the Metropolitan Police, 1829–1979*. London: Hamish Hamilton.

Brogden, M. (1982). *The Police: Autonomy and Consent*. London: Academic Press.

Clark, J. (2012). *The National Council for Civil Liberties and the Policing of Interwar Politics*. Manchester: Manchester University Press.

Commissioner of Police of the Metropolis. (1933). *Report of the Commissioner of Police of the Metropolis for the year 1932*. Cmd. 4294. ProQuest Parliamentary Papers Online.

Committee on Police Conditions of Service. (1949). *Report of the Committee on Police Conditions of Service, Part II*. Cmnd. 7831. ProQuest Parliamentary Papers Online.

Critchley, T. A. (1967). *A History of Police in England and Wales*. London: Constable.

Dunning, L. (1928). Discretion in Prosecution. *The Police Journal, 1*(1), 39–47.

Emsley, C. (2009). *The Great British Bobby: A History of British Policing from the 18th Century to the Present*. London: Quercus.

Hansard. ProQuest Parliamentary Papers Online.

Inquiry in regard to the interrogation by the police of Miss Savidge (1928). *Report of the tribunal appointed under the Tribunals of Inquiry (Evidence) Act, 1921*, Cmd. 3147. ProQuest Parliamentary Papers Online.

Jefferson, T., & Grimshaw, R. (1984). *Controlling the Constable: Police Accountability in England and Wales*. London: F. Muller.

Keith-Lucas, B. (1960). The Independence of Chief Constables. *Public Administration, 38*(1), 1–15.

Lustgarten, L. (1986). *The Governance of Police*. London: Sweet & Maxwell.

Marshall, G. (1960). Police Responsibility. *Public Administration, 38*(3), 213–226.

Marshall, G. (1965). *Police and Government: The Status and Accountability of the English Constable*. London: Methuen.

Marshall, G. (1978). Police Accountability Revisited. In D. Butler & A. H. Halsey (Eds.), *Policy and Politics* (pp. 51–65). London: Methuen.

Mulgan, R. (2003). *Holding Power to Account: Accountability in Modern Democracies*. Basingstoke: Palgrave.

Plehwe, R. (1974). Police and Government: The Commissioner of Police for the Metropolis. *Public Law*, 316–335.

Rawlings, P. (2002). *Policing: A Short History*. Cullompton: Willan.

Rawlinson, J. F. P. (1925). *Arrest of Major R. O. Sheppard, D.S.O., R.A.O.C.: Report by the Right Hon. J. F. P. Rawlinson, K.C., M.P. of Enquiry Held Under Tribunals of Enquiry (Evidence) Act, 1921*. Cmd. 2497. ProQuest Parliamentary Papers Online.

Reiner, R. (1992). *The Politics of the Police* (2nd ed.). London: Harvester Wheatsheaf.

Royal Commission on Police Powers and Procedure. (1929). *Report of the Royal Commission on Police Powers and Procedure*, Cmd. 3297. ProQuest Parliamentary Papers Online.

Royal Commission upon the Duties of the Metropolitan Police. (1908). *Report of the Royal Commission upon the Duties of the Metropolitan Police Along with Appendices, Vol. I*. Cd. 4156. ProQuest Parliamentary Papers Online.

Savidge Inquiry, see Inquiry in regard to the interrogation by the police of Miss Savidge

Secretary of State for the Home Department. (1933). *Memorandum on the Subject of Certain Changes in the Organisation and Administration of the Metropolitan Police*. Cmd. 4320. ProQuest Parliamentary Papers Online.

Tribunal Appointed to Inquire Into the Allegation of Assault on John Waters. (1959). *Report of the Tribunal Appointed to Inquire Into the Allegation of Assault on John Waters*. Cmnd. 718. ProQuest Parliamentary Papers Online.

Troup, E. (1928). Police Administration, Local and National. *The Police Journal*, *1*(1), 5–18.

Warren, C. (1888). The Police of the Metropolis. *Murray's Magazine*, November, 4(23): 577–594.

6

Internal Affairs

Recalibration of the responsibilities of the Home Secretary and Metropolitan Police (Met) Commissioner with the innovation of police operational independence resulted in the removal of an external oversight mechanism. This would allow the Met to manage their internal affairs free from a form of public scrutiny that had identified errors and malpractice in the recent past. Replacing Sir William Horwood as Met Commissioner at the end of 1928, Viscount Byng of Vimy devoted a section of his first annual report to complaints (Commissioner of Police of the Metropolis 1929). Without comment he provided details of the Savidge case and Inquiry, Royal Commission on Police Powers and Procedure (1928/29 Commission) and Street Offences Committee that had beleaguered his predecessor. On complaints generally he stated that there had been an increase in volume as a consequence of the adverse publicity, which he also held responsible for damaging police efficiency. With press coverage of officer misconduct considered to have caused immense reputational damage, one way of managing the risk to public confidence was to make every effort to ensure that complaints were handled in house.

© The Author(s) 2020
G. Smith, *On the Wrong Side of The Law*, Palgrave's Critical Policing Studies,
https://doi.org/10.1007/978-3-030-48222-0_6

In order to limit public scrutiny the minimum required was to manage complaints more effectively. Whereas Commissioner Horwood had not been able to provide the 1928/29 Commission with a breakdown of complaints, some three years later Commissioner Lord Trenchard was asking to be kept informed of quarterly trends. Located in the Commissioner's Office, A-1 Branch had commenced recording complaints in 1930 and quarterly summaries of the statistics were disseminated to senior officers across the force. Arguably, the steps taken to record complaints and prepare for a centralised complaints system, introduced under-revised regulations in November 1933, should have taken place some 20 years earlier following the proposals of the Royal Commission upon the Duties of the Metropolitan Police (1906–08 Commission). On receiving a basic annual summary for 1931 soon after commencing in office, Trenchard asked to be forwarded quarterly returns including more detailed breakdowns of substantiation rates in future.[1] Despite the Commissioner's interest in allegations made against officers and how they were resolved he did not consider it necessary to share the data with the public. Complaints were not mentioned in any of his annual reports; there was no room for the openness displayed by the Home Office when keeping the press informed of his 1933 inquiry into Flying Officer Fitzpatrick's complaint.[2] Commissioner Trenchard evidently did not act on a recommendation by A-1 Branch that his report for 1933 should refer to the Fitzpatrick complaint, subsequent revisions to *General Orders* and appointment of a Chief Constable with complaints duties.[3] Since Byng had included a paragraph on complaints in his report for 1929 there were to be no references to complaints in commissioners' annual reports until Commissioner Sir Joseph Simpson's report for 1958. It was another six years, after Section 50 of the Police Act 1964 required police authorities to keep themselves informed of the manner in which complaints were handled, before an annual report included statistical data on complaints (Commissioner of Police of the Metropolis 1965).

Complaints statistics are notoriously difficult to analyse. Quantities are open to interpretation as evidence of public satisfaction or dissatisfaction with the police. Low volumes are often taken to indicate a high level of public confidence, even though the reason people do not complain may be due to their lack of confidence in the effectiveness of the complaints system including the belief that complaining will not make a difference (Smith 2009). Small numbers, together with frequent revision of data recording methodologies create problems for detailed inferential analysis of complaints outcomes, patterns and trends. There is much to be learned, however, from examination of recording methods, which reflect police priorities, and descriptive analysis of the statistical data. The first Met complaints statistics were the prototype of present-day records for England and Wales, currently compiled and published by the Independent Office for Police Conduct (2019), and they are of significance to understanding how a centralised internal complaints system was operationalised. Initially based on data provided by supervising officers in the districts that were directly responsible for recording and investigating complaints, it is important to bear in mind that the statistical records were not conceived and designed as a research project but reflected existing practice. Designed in-house, the priorities of police along with their working assumptions and biases founded on 100 years of operational experience are evident when examining the system from a complainant-centred standpoint.

Separated into three parts this chapter concludes the complainant-centred narrative developed in this book. Statistics and notes by senior officers contained in the force-wide summaries[4] are a useful framework for discussion of Met priorities and underlying trends, and the first part comprises an examination of the complaints system created by A-1 Branch in the 1930s. Police powers continued to develop at common and statute law during the 1930s (Ewing and Gearty 2000) and the National Council for Civil Liberties (NCCL), founded in 1934, campaigned in opposition to state interference with civil liberties and individual rights (Clark 2012). The NCCL quickly established a reputation as a civil society police 'watchdog'. In addition to monitoring the policing of protest the Council provided legal advice and support to victims of police misconduct and their publications and records are referred to in the pages below. The volume of recorded complaints dropped significantly during the war years and post-war, commonly regarded as the 'golden age' of policing, there were significant annual increases in numbers starting in the mid-1950s. A-1 Branch pointed to a growing awareness among the public of their civil liberties and rights to explain the rising figures, and the second part of the chapter is structured around the Branch's 1950s complaints summaries. Appointment of the Royal Commission on the Police (1960–62 Commission 1962) was announced by Home Secretary R. A. Butler during a House of Commons debate on the settlement of a claim for damages against a Met constable by Commissioner Simpson,[5] and the terms of reference of the Commission were to consider governance arrangements for police forces throughout Great Britain, including procedures for handling public complaints.[6] The chapter concludes with an examination of the Met evidence submitted to the Commission on complaints and the arrival of a discourse on independent oversight that challenged police control of their internal affairs.

A-1 Branch Complaints System

There were understandable methodological and design problems that A-1 Branch had to contend with when they commenced recording complaints statistics. Complaints records were kept in the four operational districts and it was November 1933 before regulations were revised to provide for a centralised Met complaints system.[7] Paragraph 139 (a) of the new regulations required a register of complaints, including outcomes, to be kept in every police station, and sub-paragraph (b) required districts to forward papers regarding all concluded complaints to A-1 Branch for the purpose of maintaining a central record.

When the allegation that Flying Officer Fitzpatrick was assaulted by a CID officer who stopped and questioned him was raised in the House of Commons[8] (*Daily Telegraph*, 2 July 1933; see above Chap. 5) discussion on revisions to the complaints regulations were already at an advanced stage.[9] Fitzpatrick's case captured some of the problems that A-1 was grappling with in consultation with command and senior district officers. Devolved responsibility for complaints to the districts and divisions was upheld on grounds of principle and effectiveness, and frontline supervisors were considered best placed to immediately deal with complaints and prevent them from escalating. A supervisor who believed they had managed to resolve differences between a member of the public and an officer would, naturally, be tempted to avoid unnecessary paperwork and not record the complaint. Obviously dissatisfied with the way he had been treated, Fitzpatrick did not formally complain at Rochester Row police station and no record was made of the fact that he bore a grievance against the police. The dilemma was how to allow for disputes to be informally resolved while ensuring that records were maintained. Paragraph 138 of the 1933 regulations sought to accommodate both types of good practice, which left much to the discretion of divisional and sub-divisional inspectors in charge of police stations. Supervisory officers were encouraged to take action to prevent or forestall a complaint from being made and, using the example of an innocent person who leaves the police station appearing to 'harbour a sense of grievance', matters should be immediately reported 'even though no formal complaint of police action has been made'.[10]

In light of critical comments by the 1928/29 Commission (1929) that CID officers considered themselves above and apart from the rules and regulations that governed uniformed officers, Paragraph 140 brought all officers under the purview of the complaints system, for which the Deputy Commissioner was responsible. Sub-paragraph (b) laid down that A-1 Branch was responsible for all communication with complainants, whom would not normally be notified of any disciplinary action taken against an officer as a consequence of their complaint.[11] The officer in charge of a district continued to have responsibility for the investigation of complaints. If there was a possibility that an officer may have committed a criminal offence, Paragraph 150 required the complaint to be referred to the Assistant Commissioner responsible for the CID and any enquiries to be made under the direction of the Divisional Detective Inspector. Paragraph 152 set out the instruction that if there was a possibility that criminal or civil legal proceedings may be brought in connection with a complaint, there should be no confrontation or cross-examination of the complainant until after the conclusion of proceedings unless the Commissioner directed otherwise.

The first A-1 Branch complaints summaries included three sets of figures, and annual statistics up to the first full year before the outbreak of World War II are presented in Table 6.1, below. Numbers of complaints recorded for the first two years were broken down into seven categories under a 'Particulars of complaints' sub-heading: wrongful arrest;

Table 6.1 Metropolitan Police complaints statistics: 1930–38

	1930	1931	1932	1933	1934	1935	1936	1937	1938
Number of complaints recorded	957	983	987	1184	1693	1863	1888	1811	1611
Particulars of complaints (allegations)									
Wrongful arrest or abuse of power	63	79	89	86	80	120	146	113	139
Incivility	290	316	273	247	339	393	269	229	236
Neglect of duty, irregularities, etc.	468	555	435	603	988	1137	1248	1271	1091
Bribery	41	50	66	130	174	170	193	187	183
False evidence	20	14	11	26	45	54	51	36	40
Domestic	85	60	103	91	105	66	98	82	77
Stop and question	n/a	n/a	n/a	19	81	92	88	80	79
Unclassified	59	37	54	33	40	24	23	18	21
Total no. allegations	1026	1111	1034	1223	1852	2056	2116	2016	1866
Per 1000 officers	*50.84*	*54.38*	*51.19*	*62.11*	*95.44*	*107.66*	*112.52*	*106.75*	*100.8*
Substantiated	n/a	n/a	178	192	303	309	272	267	258
Per 1000 officers	*n/a*	*n/a*	*8.81*	*9.75*	*15.62*	*16.18*	*14.46*	*14.14*	*13.94*
Particulars of complainants									
Persons reported for an offence	171	240	187	189	264	458	362	258	195
Prisoners and CRO men	25	29	37	31	87	74	104	76	66
Street traders, pedlars, musicians, etc.	15	11	n/a	n/a	n/a	n/a	n/a	n/a	n/a
Motorists	237	352	289	279	393	599	546	488	215
Unclassified	539	453	519	626	891	827	861	947	909
Anonymous	106	116	101	203	256	275	248	248	226
Male	696	721	n/a	n/a	n/a	n/a	n/a	n/a	n/a
Female	154	154	n/a	n/a	n/a	n/a	n/a	n/a	n/a
Results									
Not pursued by complainant	286	256	n/a	n/a	n/a	n/a	n/a	n/a	n/a
Not substantiated	471	542	774	971	1348	1541	1589	1521	1356
Substantiated	140	140	174	188	285	289	256	254	255
(% of no. of complaints)	(15.6)	(14.93)	(18.35)	(16.22)	(17.45)	(15.79)	(13.63)	(14.31)	(15.83)
Legal remedy: not for Commissioner	60	45	39	25	60	33	43	36	n/a
Force strength as at 31 December	*20180*	*20432*	*20200*	*19696*	*19404*	*19097*	*18805*	*18886*	*18511*

Source: National Archives, MEPO 2/7237 and 2/7238, summaries of complaints against the police 1931–39 and 1939–40

incivility; neglect of duty and so on. With some complaints containing more than one allegation, the annual totals of allegations were higher than the numbers of complaints recorded. Numbers of complainants were initially separated into eight categories according to their 'particulars' (referring to their circumstances or character): whether reported for an offence; a prisoner or person with a criminal record; a street trader, pedlar or musician for example. Motorists who were reported for an offence were double counted up to 1937. Results, or outcomes, presented per complainant and not per complaint were initially recorded under four headings: whether or not substantiated, not pursued by the complainant, and whether a legal remedy was pursued and, therefore, not a matter for the Met to determine. Statistics for the total number of allegations and substantiations per 1000 officers were not disseminated by A-1 Branch, and figures that are now widely used to analyse statistical trends have been included in Table 6.1 using 31 December force strength figures published in Commissioners' annual reports.

Data recording methods were changed after two years, and the separate results category of unpursued complaints was discontinued. Bribery allegations were separated into three sub-categories depending on whether or not made anonymously, and a sub-category was added for anonymous complaints connected to betting (the sub-categories are not shown in Table 6.1). Three of the initial complainant categories—'Street traders, pedlars, musicians, etc.', 'Male', 'Female'—were dispensed with, and motorists reported for an offence were separated out from the 'Persons reported for an offence' category and the 'Motorists' category was divided into private and licensed driver sub-categories (again, not shown in Table 6.1). As the result of Commissioner Trenchard's request for more detail, substantiation rates for each category of allegation commenced in 1932 (again, not shown, see further below). In the last quarter of 1933 'Stop and question' was included as a separate category at the direction of the Commissioner following the publicity surrounding the Fitzpatrick complaint.[12]

Double counting of motorists ceased at the end of the decade and legal remedy figures, the vast majority of which A-1 Branch noted were for 'Domestic' complaints, were also discontinued.[13] The complainant was A-1 Branch's preferred unit of measurement and served as the headline figure in statistical tables and, with the problem of double counting resolved, 1938 is the only year in Table 6.1 for which the aggregate figure for complaints recorded corresponds with the number of recorded complainants.

Starting from a low of 50.84 allegations per 1000 officers in 1930 the rate more than doubled to over 100 within five years, and substantiations also increased by over 80% from 8.81 in 1932 (the first year available) to 16.18 in 1935, increases which suggest a complaints system improving in effectiveness and attracting public confidence. Although A-1 Branch attributed the increase of more than 40% in allegations between 1933 and 1934 to the publicity surrounding the Fitzgerald complaint, it is likely that introduction of new regulations and the requirement that districts forward complaints papers to A-1 for recording purposes, including complaints against CID officers, will have contributed significantly to the increase.[14] A-1 monitoring of quarterly statistical returns from the operational divisions picked up where numbers of recorded complaints were disproportionately low compared with other divisions in the same district. This was attributed to complaints being dealt with informally within sub-divisional police stations and failure to record details as required under the regulations.[15] Despite more effective management of complaints closer inspection of the A-1 Branch summaries reveals (a) priority was not given to the grievances of complainants; (b) there were wide disparities in substantiation rates between complaints categories; (c) persons with serious allegations against officers were reluctant to complain; and (d) data recording methods were inconsistent and less than comprehensive.

Bias against complainants in the new complaints system is immediately apparent when consideration is given to complaints which included multiple allegations against more than one officer. Take, for example, a hypothetical case where one complainant alleges they were assaulted by at least one officer during an encounter with a group of four and, with none of the officers intervening to stop the assault, they are unable to identify any of the officers involved. Cases like this were recorded as one complaint by one complainant, and not four complaints which required the investigation of allegations against four officers. The way in which A-1 Branch prioritised the complainant, rather than their allegations against officers, was consistent with the practice of seeking to discredit the character of complainants as identified in previous chapters of this book. Particulars considered detrimental to the credit of the complainant were singled out for categorisation, and classification of complainants according to whether they were suspected or convicted of a criminal offence conformed to the stereotype of the anti-police, vindictive and malicious complainant (cf. Box and Russell 1975). It is unsurprising that members of the public that came into contact with the police should have had cause to complain about officer conduct, which applies equally to victims of crime as suspects and, although quickly dispensed with the 'Street traders, pedlars, musicians, etc.' category indicates an early bias in the recording of complaints.[16] Motorists were also liable to come into contact with police and appear in the records as a neutral category, yet, with more than 50% of complainants categorised as 'Unclassified' A-1 Branch were not disposed to include categories that reflected positive characteristics of complainants, householders or tenants, for example, and a minority that were considered discreditable continued to be separated out for attention. Bearing in mind that the Branch were not responsible for investigating or determining the outcome of complaints, and their categorisations and summaries represented decision making and practice in the operational districts, they could have sought to address bias by requesting that district officers ensure collection of additional data when recording details of complaints from the divisions. There would not appear to have been practical problems with introducing new complainant categories, as demonstrated by the inclusion of a 'Soldiers, sailors and airmen' category with the outbreak of World War II.[17]

Recording substantiation rates according to complainant characteristics, as requested by Trenchard in 1931, proved problematic and it was 1940 before they were included in statistical tables. Commissioner Air Vice-Marshall Sir Philip Game (1935–45) was uninterested in complainant figures and towards the end of his watch they were not recorded, which resulted in a four-year hiatus between 1943 and 1946. Commissioner Sir Henry Scott asked A-1 Branch to resume collating the figures in 1947[18] and, although persevered with until the late 1960s[19] accurate analysis of trends is limited by further methodological changes in 1952 and 1957. Nevertheless, between 1947 and 1957 two categories that remained unaltered were complaints from (a) persons reported for offences other than traffic offences and (b) prisoners and persons with a criminal record, unarguably the two most discreditable categories of complainant. Of a total number of 63 complainants who were reported for criminal offences between 1947 and 1957, 2 had their complaints substantiated, at a rate of 3.17%; of the 1021 prisoners and CRO persons who complained 3.23% (n = 33) had their complaints substantiated. This was about one quarter of the average substantiation rate of 12.39% (n = 1,289) for the total number of 10,401 complainants over the 11 years. Although complainant substantiation figures were not available until the 1940s, the statistics suggest that there was a bias against complainants considered by police to be of disreputable character in the new complaints system from the outset.

After removing the number of 'Legal remedy' results from the figures, fluctuating between a low of 13.63% and a high of 18.35% the overall substantiation rate between 1930 and 1938 was high by modern standards. Examination of substantiation rates for complaints categories, with recording having commenced in 1932 (not shown in Table 6.1), reveals wide disparities between different types of allegation. The overall aggregate substantiation rate for 1932–38 was 15.7%,[20] and at 41.63% the rate for 'Domestic' complaints (once again excluding legal cases from the calculation) was the highest by a considerable distance. 'Unclassified', 'Incivility' and 'Neglect of duty, irregularities, etc.' categories were also above the overall rate at 22%, 17.93% and 16.07%, respectively. At the bottom end, much below the average were the 'Bribery', 'Stop and question', 'False evidence' and 'Wrongful arrest' categories at 1.63%, 2.96%, 3.42% and 10.61%, respectively. The disparities reflect the implications that different types of allegation, if substantiated, had for the management of complaints. The consequences of a substantiated complaint of incivility, for example, would rarely lead to further action or pose a serious risk to the career development of a police officer. A more serious complaint, providing false evidence, for example, was likely to lead to criminal or disciplinary proceedings with serious consequences for the police officer if proved.

The relatively low volume of serious complaints recorded suggests reluctance on the part of persons with more serious allegations to complain. It is remarkable to find that assault complaints were not classified separately in the first statistical records, especially as reports in the press of police brutality towards unemployed marchers and anti-fascist protesters were commonplace during the 1930s (Clark 2012; Kingsford 1982).[21] Allegations of police violence were included in the 'Neglect of duty, irregularities, etc.' general category until 1944, when they commenced to be recorded separately under an 'Assault and brutality' category.[22] The explanation given by A-1 Branch for introduction of the new category was that 10 or more assault complaints had been consistently recorded in quarterly returns.[23] Given that annual totals of less than 40 'False evidence' complaints were consistently recorded in the 1930s, the threshold rationale for complaints categories does not stand up to scrutiny.

Closer examination of the 'Legal remedy' results category indicates another methodological inconsistency in the early statistical records, which suggest less than meticulous monitoring by A-1 Branch,[24] under-recording and, perhaps, some massaging of the figures. It is difficult to understand why the category was included in the early statistical summaries, especially as all legal remedies pursued were not recorded. Among the legal remedies available to complainants were private prosecutions, which were regularly brought against officers, particularly on charges of assault, up until 1964 at least,[25] and civil claims for damages were also brought, although less frequently. As noted in previous chapters private prosecutions against constables were rarely successful with the magistrate often refusing an application to issue a summons, and press reports of legal proceedings against officers in this period are difficult to find. Two cases that were reported include an unsuccessful private prosecution for assault brought by Henry Cole against PC William Bond (*The Times*, 14 December 1935), and Wilhelmina Urquhart accepted £50 paid by the Met Commissioner in settlement of a claim for false imprisonment (*The Times*, 19 February 1937; see further, below). The 'Neglect of duty, irregularities, etc.' general category included legal remedy sub-categories— 'Police officer alleged to have committee a criminal offence' and 'Action in civil disputes'[26]—yet, neither the legal remedies pursued by Cole or Urquhart appear to have been included in the A-1 Branch statistical summaries for 1935 and 1937, respectively. In 1935 A-1 Branch did not note any legal remedies in the 'Neglect of duty, irregularities, etc.' category and in 1937 all legal remedies were in the 'Domestic' category,[27] which lends support to the claim that serious complaints, including assault, were not recorded. The discretion available to local supervisory officers, noted above in regard to grievances considered to have been resolved informally, may explain omissions of this type. The policy not to investigate complaints where there was a possibility that the complainant may bring criminal or civil proceedings, included in Paragraphs 150–152 of the 1933 Complaints Regulations, may have been interpreted loosely and complaints that were not investigated were not recorded.

Continuing with the subject of legal remedies, in 1935 the Metropolitan Police Solicitor's Department was established in the Commissioner's Office to handle the increasing volume of casework generated (Commissioner of Police of the Metropolis 1936). Met Solicitor Thomas Baker soon addressed the conflict of interest involved in preparing criminal prosecutions against police officers. Contrasting the situation he faced with the standard practice of a firm of solicitors refusing to prosecute one client on behalf of another, Baker was concerned that he could be placed in the difficult position of advising an officer prosecuting one day and addressing a magistrate in proceedings against the same officer the next. Baker's suggestion that the Director of Public Prosecutions (DPP) should be requested to prepare all proceedings against police officers was opposed by the Assistant Commissioner responsible for the investigation of crime on grounds that this would give the impression that the Met were not able to manage their internal affairs.[28] Baker persisted with his proposal, and Commissioner Game eventually issued a direction that the DPP should only be asked to prosecute cases which were serious, of particular public importance, border-line or where there were particular reasons why the police could not prosecute.

One year later, prompted in part by the embarrassment caused by the Commissioner's *volte face* in apologising to Mrs. Uquhart when settling her claim for damages, the Met Solicitor turned his attention to the quality of reports written by constables in response to public complaints. In so doing Baker revisited the same concerns that the 1906–08 Commission had sought to address in their recommendations, and which the Met failed to implement (see above Chap. 3). Supported by the NCCL, Urquhart was arrested when selling copies of the *Daily Worker* and charged with obstructing the highway. The Hendon Police Court Magistrate dismissed the charge after hearing conflicting evidence from two constables, and her solicitor subsequently wrote a letter before action to the Met Commissioner asking that he investigate the detention of his client and the intrusive body search she was subjected to while in custody. Chief Constable Wilkinson responded on behalf of the Commissioner by stating that after making enquiries the Commissioner was satisfied that the police were justified in charging his client and officers had acted correctly throughout her detention. Four months later the Commissioner settled Mrs. Urquhart's claim for damages and sincerely apologised for the unfortunate experience she had suffered.[29] In a February 1937 memo to the Chief Constable responsible for A-1 Branch, ten days before *The Times* ran the Urquhart story, Baker set out his concerns that rather than provide accurate accounts of events officers' reports were written from a defensive frame of mind for the purpose of protecting against the risk of disciplinary proceedings.[30] Reports of this type were unhelpful in cases where the solicitor was instructed to defend claims for damages, and he proposed that the written report should be dispensed with in preference of a member of A-1 Branch taking a statement from the officer. Baker also questioned the accuracy of the standard letter sent to complainants which stated 'The Commissioner has caused enquiry to be made' on grounds that officer reports were often edited by supervisory officers, included a character reference and rarely was the officer cross-examined on the content. The Solicitor's intervention provoked considerable discussion among command officers, a round-table conference on the subject was considered, which reflected the working assumptions on which the complaints system was premised. The A-1 Branch Chief Constable countered that a substantial proportion of the 1888 complaints recorded the previous year, if true, would lead to disciplinary proceedings and 'complainants are no less prone to colour their complaints than are police officers to defend themselves without holding strictly to the truth.'[31] He went on, Baker's proposals would undermine the authority of senior officers in the districts who were responsible for discipline and create divisions between A-1 Branch, which was composed entirely of civil staff, and constables. He proposed that the problem could be solved by impressing upon district officers with responsibilities for discipline and complaints to monitor officer reports, and to especially look out for reports which rebutted complaints without regard for the true facts. It is apparent that there was considerable concern among Met managers with how an instruction on the veracity of officer reports on complaints may be received by frontline officers, including the effect it may have on officer morale, and rather than issue an order Commissioner Game decided to issue a confidential memo that was initially disseminated to superintendents only.[32] Adopting the approach proposed by the A-1 Branch Chief Constable the Commissioner reassured colleagues that he was satisfied the majority of reports were 'complete and accurate'. He referred to the reputational damage caused to the force where further enquiries revealed that officers had withheld information, and he asked senior officers to eradicate the feeling among the men that they were at risk of disciplinary action when required to write a report on a complaint. Primary responsibility for addressing the problem was devolved to subdivisional inspectors who were to explain to officers when informing them that they were required to submit a report that they were to write 'a full and true account of the incident in question'. Inspectors and other officers subsequently responsible for handling complaints were expected to check the content of officer reports instead of simply submitting them to a higher authority for consideration.

A-1 Branch was referred to as a 'hybrid' organisation in the discussion on the veracity of officer accounts of incidents that gave rise to complaints. It is apparent that operational law enforcement priorities, including force morale, trumped due process officer accountability concerns and, kept very much in-house, these competing public interests informed the design of the first complaints system. Police conduct was under the spotlight as a result of the reputational damage arising from complaints made by Savidge, Fitzpatrick and Urquhart, and there were signs of improvement in complaints procedures before the outbreak of World War II. Met defensiveness and aversion to the risk of reputational damage ensured that the new complaints system was inward looking and lacked openness and transparency. It was highly significant that after appointment of the first Met solicitor, he was soon to raise concerns with independent prosecutions and the quality of officer reports that had exercised the 1906–08 Commission. A more effective and fairer complaints system would have been created if the Met had invited complainants and those that represented them to participate in the construction of their hybrid organisation. For example, if the NCCL had been consulted they would most probably have asked the Met to justify the grounds on which Urquhart's complaints, presuming that a record was made, against the two officers that arrested her, the matron that subjected her to a body search at Golders Green police station and the officer in charge of the station, appeared in the aggregate statistics as one complaint. Unfortunately, the opposite was the case and the Met routinely dismissed approaches from the NCCL to co-operate, castigating the Council as a Communist Party front which was kept under observation by Special Branch (Clark 2009, 2012; Thurlow 1995).

End of Deference

A-1 Branch continued disseminating complaints summaries throughout World War II, and with some minor modifications the 1938 format was retained until 1957. In 1939 the 'Wrongful arrest or abuse of power' category was changed to 'Mistaken arrest', reflecting the belief that wrongful arrest unfairly implied wicked or malicious conduct on the part of the police[33] and, as already noted, an armed forces complainant category was introduced at the outbreak of the war and separate recording of assault complaints commenced in 1944. There was a significant drop in the number of complaints recorded in the final third of 1939 compared with the same four months of 1938[34] and figures were low throughout the war years (for the trend in complaints and substantiations per 1000 officers between 1930 and 1964 see Graph 6.1, below). Force strength was also reduced, partly offset by the recruitment of special constables on a full-time basis and auxiliaries, and the number of complaints per 1000 officers dropped to 33.31 in 1944.[35] The volume of complaints increased slightly in the last quarter of 1945 compared with the previous year and, with force strength starting to build up again in 1948, it was the late 1950s before complaints numbers approached the levels recorded in pre-war years. Although the trend in substantiations per 1000 officers was not dissimilar, dropping to 4.59 in 1944, the pre-war figures of over 14 per 1000 officers have not been achieved since.

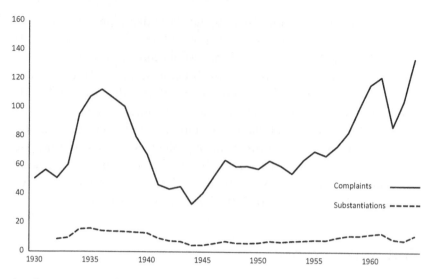

Graph 6.1 Metropolitan Police complaints and substantiations per 1000 officers: 1930–64. (Source: National Archives, MEPO 2/7237-38; 2/6031; 2/6034-36; 2/6038; 2/10769-785; 2/10272 A-1 Branch complaints summaries; the summary for 1964 is not yet open to the public and figures for that year have been taken from the 1965 summary, MEPO 2/10787)

Responding to the increasing number of complaints recorded, A-1 Branch reappraised their recording methods and presented a new statistical format for quarterly summaries to a Met Commanders' Conference in January 1958.[36] Noting that between 60% and 70% of complaints recorded each year were in the 'Neglect of duty, irregularities, etc.' category, which comprised 39 sub-categories, there was concern that the substantiation rate for the general category was also increasing. In the interest of more precisely identifying work areas which gave rise to complaints that were liable to be substantiated new statistical tables were introduced.[37] The variance in substantiation rates for the new complaints categories was as marked as it was in the 1930s. Rates were significantly lower than the 1930s, at 8.45% the average overall rate for the years 1956–64 was down over 45% on pre-war figures. For complaints of bribery, false evidence and stop and question, rates were significantly below the average and down on the 1930s rate at 0.25%, 1.11% and 2.63%, respectively. Assault complaints were not recorded separately in the 1930s and the substantiation rate in the 1950s/60s was about half the average at 4.15%, and the new stand-alone category of 'Victimization and persecution' (allegations of harassment) were also low at 2.28%. The exception to this trend were complaints in the 'Mistaken arrest and wrong accusation' category, for which the substantiation rate was up from 10.61% to 13.36%.

With numbers of complaints increasing post war, the Met Commissioner would routinely impress upon commanders when addressing them at district conferences on the need for officers to be civil when dealing with members of the public. Starting in 1952 A-1 Branch included in their summaries short commentaries of complaints which resulted in *ex gratia* payments or settlements of civil claims, numbers of which also steadily increased over the years. It was not uncommon for the Commissioner to pay out sums totalling several hundred pounds sterling when settling claims for damages for assault, false imprisonment and malicious prosecution, some of which are noteworthy for the insights they provide. In 1953 the Commissioner settled for £300 with £26 and 5 shillings costs a claim for personal injuries and damage to a motor car brought by two claimants against four plain clothes constables. One of the claimants received a truncheon blow to the head and the other had injuries to his head and face as the result of another officer smashing the car windscreen with his truncheon.[38] The A Department Commander commented on the case:

> I feel this case was very unfortunate as the four aides to CID were genuinely of the impression that they had two good crooks in the car. The car occupants turned out to be perfectly genuine and although the case cost the Service quite a bit of money, I feel the PCs were really alert and were most unlucky.[39]

Anthony Iseppl was acquitted of assaulting PC Bruce in the execution of his duty at Marylebone Magistrates' Court; the Magistrate awarding five guineas costs against the Met after Iseppi claimed in his defence that the officer struck him three times in the face (*West London Observer*, 25 June 1954). Iseppi had physical and mental health disabilities and, on

Council's advice of the risk of an award of substantial damages if defended at trial, the Commissioner settled his civil action for £300 without accepting liability.[40] In 1959 an *ex gratia* payment of 10 shillings was made to John Murphy after he had to rearrange a missed appointment with his solicitor having been delayed when he voluntarily accompanied an officer to Brentford police station to assist with the investigation of an offence.[41] Murphy was supported by the NCCL and their General Secretary engaged in lengthy correspondence with the Met and Home Office before it was agreed that his small loss would be covered by the police fund.[42] The £300 settlement of senior civil servant Gerald Garrett's claim for assault and false imprisonment against PC Ernest Eastmond (*The Times*, 27 October 1959), which triggered the 1960–62 Commission (see further below), was recorded in the 1960 complaints summary with a note on costs presumed to be £245.[43] That year A-1 Branch gave details of 18 complainants compensated by way of *ex gratia* payments or settlement of claims, and 25 the following year, including £650 plus costs of just over £100 to a restaurateur after the Met Solicitor discovered that an arresting constable had falsified an entry in his notebook.[44] Also in 1961, a claim for damages for false imprisonment brought by writer John Chandos against a constable and inspector was settled for the sum of £50 with £180 and 10 shillings costs. A-1 Branch described Chandos as 'obstructive' for declining to answer questions when stopped under Section 66 of the Metropolitan Police Act 1839 on Park Lane, W 1 in December 1958 and at Gerald Road police station.[45] Chandos (1962) later wrote an account of his experiences, which includes his correspondence with the Met, and the disregard for his rights shown by the constable who stopped him, the duty inspector at the police station and the divisional superintendent whom he met regarding his complaint. Chandos met Commissioner Simpson to discuss his complaint and, impressed with his understanding of the values and standards he was seeking to uphold, agreed to discontinue his claim on receipt of an apology from the officers. Unable to agree the wording of the apology, a writ was eventually issued before settlement was agreed. The final case worthy of mention, recorded in 1963, was Maurice Power's acceptance of £857 (comprising £750 general and £107 special damages) and £197 costs in settlement of his claim against two officers for assault, false imprisonment and malicious prosecution. Power required six sutures to a wound to his forehead after struck by an officer with a truncheon, and he was acquitted of charges of violence to police and possession of an offensive weapon, with costs of 20 guineas awarded against the Met, at criminal trial.[46] A-1 Branch did not include further details of the case and the absence of press coverage of what is presumed to have then been a record settlement would have come as a great relief to the Met in light of the controversy that accompanied the £300 settlement to Garrett.

There was no mention of criminal or disciplinary action taken against any of the officers involved in the six cases noted above. Indeed, in regard to the *Garrett* v. *Eastmond* settlement the absence of proceedings against PC Eastmond provoked the ire of politicians with MPs demanding to know why public money had been paid out if the constable had done nothing wrong.[47] In their complaints summaries between 1952 and 1963[48] A-1 Branch provided notes on a total of 123 payments to complainants and in only one of the cases was a disciplinary finding against a constable noted. An officer pleaded guilty to a disciplinary charge following an *ex gratia* payment of £100 with 15 guineas costs to a tenant who complained that police assisted in evicting her from furnished rooms.[49] The reluctance to proceed against officers is evident in the commentaries and in another case it was recorded that 'no useful purpose would be served by instituting disciplinary proceedings' against PC Bennett after he was found to have given untruthful evidence in a hearing against two 16-year-old youths at Lambeth Juvenile Court. The officer was given advice by his Chief Superintendent and transferred to another division after the youths' claims for damages were settled in the sum of £50 each and they received letters of apology from the Commissioner.[50] In one other case two sergeants were spoken to by their Chief Superintendent about properly recording property after an *ex gratia* payment of £7 and 10 shillings was paid to the owner of a wallet that went missing after handed in at Barking police station by a member of the public.[51]

Statistical tables of complaints may have been revised in the interest of improving understanding of complaints, but A-1 Branch was taken over by events as the number of complaints per 1000 officers continued to increase: by over 75% between 1957 and 1960 (see Graph 6.1, above).

First mention of an explanation for the rise in complaints that quickly gained currency appears to have been in March 1959, when Commander Townsend of A Department attributed the increase to growing numbers of officers on the street and, 'with improved education and enlightenment, some members of the public are becoming increasingly conscious of their civil liberties and rights.'[52] Commissioner Simpson used similar language in his annual report for 1958, his first (Commissioner of Police of the Metropolis 1959), and Townsend returned to the subject the following year to explain the 60% increase in complaints of assault: 'I have no doubt the bulk of these complaints are trivial and are due to the present day tendency for people to make complaints against police which at one time they would not have made.'[53] Later the same year, with news breaking of a series of scandals around the country, he attributed the increasing volume of complaints to adverse publicity surrounding the alleged 'cover up' of an assault by Caithness police in Thurso, Scotland which was the subject of a public inquiry (Tribunal appointed to inquire into the allegation of assault on John Waters 1959); the *Garrett* v. *Eastmond* civil action; and injuries suffered by Guenter Fritz Podola after his arrest for the murder of a police officer (*The Times*, 20 July 1959[54]).[55] The prevailing view expressed in A-1 Branch minutes on the steady rise in complaints was that members of the public did not understand that coercive powers were available to police to enforce the law and they were complaining about use of force which had been exercised legitimately.

An inexplicable 28.37% drop in recorded complaints was warmly welcomed in 1962, but A-1 Branch hopes that numbers had peaked were soon dashed with a further rise in 1963. Commander Townsend suggested that this increase was due to 'many complaints received by Members of Parliament which have received a great deal of publicity and which were largely designed to embarrass the Government prior to the election'.[56] References were also made to the increasing number of complaints of assault and improperly dealing with property made by 'coloured' people. Introduction of a 'Coloured person' category in statistical tables in 1960 reflected the changing nature of police relations with black communities following the Notting Hill riots of 1958 and the unsolved murder of Kelso Cochrane the following year (Pilkington 1988; Phillips and Phillips 1998).

An interesting debate was opened in 1959 by District 2 Acting Sub-Commander Frederick Fieldsend who was responsible for reviewing the investigation of a complaint against CID officers by three men convicted of being in the possession of offensive weapons, convictions that were eventually quashed in 1964 (see below, Chap. 7). Concerned with the way complaints were investigated Fieldsend submitted a short paper to the Research and Planning Branch proposing that inquiries should be conducted into all complaints received.[57] His primary concern was with the standard practice of taking a statement from the complainant, which the officer would then be informed of and given the opportunity to respond to. Fieldsend held that it was fully appreciated by district senior officers with responsibilities for complaints and A-1 Branch that in the absence of an admission by the officer there was rarely evidence on which to substantiate a complaint. This was a primary cause of public dissatisfaction as it was understood that complainants were disbelieved and the word of the constable was taken as the truth. Fieldsend argued that, rather than at the discretion of the District Commander as provided for in regulations, a more satisfactory way of arriving at the truth would be for all complainants to be invited to attend an inquiry so that the constable would be confronted by their accuser in the presence of their superior officer. This would benefit public confidence in the complaints system, deter constables from behaving in a manner which gave rise to complaints and discourage malicious complainants. Responding to Feildsend's proposal, the Commander of Research and Planning pointed out that the 1906–08 Commission had recommended the same (see above Chap. 3), and Commander Townsend challenged the idea that there was a lack of confidence in the complaints system and dismissed the Chief Superintendent's suggestion as impractical, on grounds that the great bulk of complaints were trivial and did not warrant the resources required.[58] Undeterred, Fieldsend, who was initially unaware of the 1906–08 Commission's recommendations, responded by drawing attention to their criticism of Met procedures for failing to command public confidence and he asked that the 1960–62 Commission, then about to consider police complaints, be made aware of his proposal.[59] Deputy Commissioner Alexander Robinson had the final word, reassuring colleagues that the 1960–62 Commission would be appraised of Met procedures and discussions he concluded: 'The main point is to support our men within reason and to ensure at all costs that the Commissioner must have full responsibility for the Force and not any outside or independent authority.'[60]

Royal Commission on the Police

Appointed to examine policing throughout Great Britain, the 1960–62 Commission planned to publish comparative research on police complaints, including statistical analyses. The Commission Secretariat forwarded a questionnaire to all police forces asking for details of complaints recorded between 1 August 1959 and 31 July 1960.[61] The questionnaire asked for information on when and how the complaint was received; its substance; how dealt with; action subsequently taken; comments on the officer complained against; and steps taken to inform the complainant of the result of the investigation. The Met returned 1568 completed questionnaires,[62] and their interpretation of the data was set out in a covering letter and statistical tables.[63] A forthright exchange of views ensued[64] when the Secretariat shared with the Met their own interpretation of the Met data and analyses of the national data.[65] The principal differences between the two parties were that the Secretariat (i) did not double count complaints, recording only once under the category determined most serious; (ii) held there were twice as many complaints recorded against Met officers as elsewhere in the country; (iii) determined that 23% of Met complaints were substantiated; and (iv) there was evidence of reluctance on the part of the Met to initiate disciplinary proceedings. Met Commissioner Simpson countered that the Met recorded all complaints, including trivial ones, whereas other forces only recorded fairly serious complaints in their returns; the substantiation rate was 10%; and, in light of the Met practice of recording all complaints regardless of seriousness, the impression that disciplinary proceedings were rarely initiated was mistaken.[66] The upshot of the disagreement was that statistical data collected by the 1960–62 Commission were not published in the *Final Report*.

A different quality of data was provided in the Met returns to the 1960–62 Commission to the data set out in A-1 Branch summaries.

Close examination of the narratives in the two returns comprising 200 assault and mistaken arrest/wrongful accusation questionnaires,[67] some of which contained multiple complaints and 19 were recorded by the Met as substantiated, clearly show that disciplinary proceedings against officers were infrequent, private prosecutions were unsuccessful and there was some success for complainants in civil proceedings. Of the 145 officers accused of assault, two faced disciplinary proceedings with one officer fined and no details provided in the other case. A further 37 officers were admonished, transferred, advised or reminded of their duties, although in only nine of these cases does it appear that management action was as a consequence of substantiation of the complaint. No criminal prosecutions were recorded as having been brought following a decision by the DPP. One officer summonsed for assault by a complainant was discharged after the Magistrate found he had committed a technical assault, and attempts to prosecute a further 12 officers were unsuccessful; another case was waiting to be heard. Four claims for damages were recorded: one claim for assault was settled and another was unsuccessful, and two claims for assault and false imprisonment, one against three officers, had not been heard. Of the 137 complainants that alleged they had been assaulted, 40 were charged with a criminal offence: 33 for offences directly connected with their complaint, assaulting or obstructing a police officer in the execution of his duty, or use of threatening words or behaviour, for example. Of the 75 questionnaires in the mistaken arrest/wrong accusation category, 66 did not include a complaint of assault. In these questionnaires, disciplinary proceedings against one officer had not yet concluded, and were under consideration against another. A further 21 officers were transferred, warned or advised of their duties. Two false imprisonment civil claims had been settled, one for £200 with costs, another was approaching settlement and another was proceeding. There was no record of the Met providing information on the result of the investigation to the complainant in a third of the 200 questionnaires ($n = 63$); six complainants were apologised to for the conduct of officers; and no complainant was informed of disciplinary or management action taken against an office as the result of their complaint. There was indication of the ethnicity of complainants in nine of the questionnaires, which recorded complainants as 'black', 'coloured' or 'negro'.

In evidence to the 1960–62 Commission (1961b) several organisations, including the NCCL, Justice[68] and Law Society were critical of the secrecy surrounding the police complaints system, especially the Met practice of not disclosing to a complainant the action taken following substantiation. On this point Commissioner Simpson was unrepentant, 'it is not the practice to indicate what punishment has been imposed, nor is it desirable.' (1960–62 Commission 1961b: 1161). The Met Commissioner opened his written evidence on complaints to the 1960–62 Commission (1961b: 1158) by acknowledging that the public were less deferential than the police had been accustomed to, and he went on to conclude that a chief officer of police should have complete control over the determination of complaints in accordance with the operational independence afforded by constitutional convention. Concerns expressed within the Met that the 1960–62 Commission may recommend withdrawing from police responsibility for complaints and discipline (see above Chap. 6) proved unfounded. In contrast to the sometimes gruelling cross-examination Commissioner Henry was subjected to on several occasions by the 1906–08 Commission, Commissioner Simpson, like Commissioner Horwood when giving evidence to the 1928/29 Commission, appeared once before the 1960–62 Commission (1961b: 1173–1183) and was quickly taken through his written evidence.[69] Simpson was not examined about the Met complaints data which were the subject of disagreement with the Secretariat of the 1960–62 Commission and he readily agreed when asked by the Chairman if they could publish A-1 Branch figures for 1958 and 1959 (1960–62 Commission 1961b: 1170–1171). It is believed that this was the first occasion that complaints statistics by any police force in Britain were placed on public record.

The NCCL submitted lengthy written evidence to the 1960–62 Commission (1961b: 728–763) which included details of their complaints, freedom of expression and assembly casework, public protests monitored by their observers and a section on police relations with black people. Evidence was presented of discrimination and racism with particular reference to Notting Hill following the unsolved murder of Kelso Cochrane, and details were given of several NCCL recorded complaints of police failure to respond when members of the African Caribbean community reported white on black incidents of violence. Problems potential complainants faced accessing the complaints system were identified: arrests of persons for obstructing the police when trying to write down the number of a constable or attending a police station to record a complaint, for example, were noted in the NCCL evidence. The Council referred to what was known about the disciplinary history of PC Ernest Eastmond to highlight the questionable integrity of the Met complaints system. In December 1958 Gerald Garrett stopped his car to offer assistance to the actor Brian Rix who had been stopped by the constable for speeding. Rix was reported to have said that after he saw Garrett go to take the officer's number the next thing he knew the two men were on the ground (*Daily Herald*, 18 December 1959). PC Eastmond arrested Garrett and the charge of assaulting a police officer while in the execution of his duty was refused by the officer in charge of Putney police station, and Eastmond was suspended from duty pending investigation of a complaint alleging assault and false imprisonment. The following August PC Eastmond was admonished after a disciplinary hearing for having given evidence against colleagues at court (*Daily Herald*, 14 August 1959), which was shortly before the furore over the Met decision not to bring disciplinary charges against the constable despite the Commissioner settling Garrett's claim for damages.

A major concern of the NCCL was that the Met complaints and discipline procedures operated in secret and they recommended that all grievance against police should be referred to an independent tribunal which would determine whether to hear a complaint in public. In regard to discipline the NCCL, along with Justice and other lobbyists, held that this was not solely a police matter but of public concern and if a complainant was dissatisfied with police proceedings or the outcome they should be able to refer the case back to the independent tribunal. The Law Society and Society of Labour Lawyers also supported the introduction of independent tribunals, the former proposing an appellate-type body with powers to investigate complaints and police investigation of them following referral by complainants who were dissatisfied with the way police had initially handled their complaint (1960–62 Commission 1961b: 1079–1080). Citing from their recently published report recommending the introduction of an ombudsman-type figure to the United

Kingdom (Whyatt 1961), Justice proposed that a Parliamentary Commissioner would be an appropriate independent authority to consider complaints against the police (1960–62 Commission 1961b: 5–7).

Arraigned against the legal associations and lobbyists the Home Office, police forces and police professional bodies were implacably opposed to outside intervention in complaints and discipline procedures. Their opposition was based on arguments that creation of an independent body would be contrary to the doctrine of constabulary independence and undermine chief officer control of their forces; interfere with the duties of the chief officer as discipline authority; and seriously damage officer morale. In support of the status quo, police stakeholders insisted that chief officers took complaints seriously; all complaints were thoroughly investigated; and the correct balance existed between the rights of citizens and police officers (1960–62 Commission 1962: 137).

The proposal put forward by Justice to create a police ombudsman attracted the support of a minority of the 1960–62 Commission and at a March 1962 meeting Alastair Hetherington (Editor of *The Guardian*), supported by Leslie Hale MP (Oldham West) failed to persuade the majority of Commissioners that they should not shy away from recommending what was considered at the time a novel and foreign institution. Six Commissioners spoke against the proposal. Sir George Turner (retired Permanent Under-Secretary of State for War) cautioned that new machinery may create more problems than intended to solve, and Sir James Robertson (retired Rector of Aberdeen Grammar School[70]) warned that formation of an independent body 'might well have the effect of discouraging the police in their primary task of fighting crime'.[71] Hetherington and Hale, joined by Baron Geddes (retired General Secretary of the Union of Postal Workers), put their names to a short appendix proposing the appointment of a Commissioner of Rights (1960–62 Commission 1962: 193–194). Careful not to be misunderstood to be recommending independent investigation of complaints against the police they proposed that under certain conditions the Commissioner of Rights would have the discretion to examine a complaint which a chief officer of police had refused to investigate; or after investigation refused to hold disciplinary proceedings; or was alleged to have arrived at an improper outcome. Alternatively, the Home Secretary or a police authority could refer a complaint to the Commissioner of Rights for consideration. The three held that the ombudsman-type scheme would address the primary reason for public dissatisfaction with existing procedures by ensuring that police would no longer serve as the final judge in their own cause.

The primary purpose of the 1960–62 Commission was to consider police governance and the majority of their *Final Report* was devoted to the responsibilities of chief officers of police, police authorities and the Home Secretary. Their recommendations to formalise police operational independence by means of a tripartite arrangement was accepted by government and duly provided for under the Police Act 1964 (Lustgarten 1986; Marshall 1965). The 1960–62 Commission (1962: 101) declared 'it was difficult to explain completely' the evidence submitted by representatives of respectable bodies with much experience of police conduct that relations with the public had deteriorated in recent years. After refuting any suggestion that relations between the police and the public were difficult, they turned their attention to the handling of complaints. Modelling their proposals on the A-1 Branch complaints system, despite the reservations of the Secretariat, the Commission were evidently impressed by the Met evidence and persuaded of the effectiveness of their procedures.

The 1960–62 Commission's rationale for a police misconduct package comprising legal remedies for complainants in criminal and civil proceedings, and by way of administrative procedure under the complaints system was remarkably similar to the one given by the 1906–08 Commission (1908: 143; see above Chap. 3).

> We have no reason to think that the police are unfit to deal with complaints: on the contrary, we are satisfied that complaints are dealt with thoroughly and impartially. Moreover, we have proposed substantial improvements in the present system which meet any reasonable criticism. If the complaint is of conduct amounting to a crime the question of prosecution will have been decided by the Director of Public Prosecutions in England and Wales or by the Crown Office in Scotland. If it amounts to a civil wrong the complainant will be entitled to sue the police authority, whether or not he can identify the police officer concerned. Hence the only clear field in which disposal of a complaint will still be dependent on the unaided decision of a chief constable will comprise complaints either not

so serious as to give rise to legal action, or in which the complainant for reasons that may appear reasonable to him does not wish for a prosecution or is unwilling to sue. But even in this field our proposals for the reform of disciplinary procedure, for the systematic recording of complaints, for a measure of surveillance by the police authority and the inspectorate over the treatment of complaints, and for ensuring courtesy in the replies that are sent to complainants should go a very long way towards removing the last risks of an unfair or careless inquiry, and towards commending the procedure to any reasonable member of the public. To go further than this would in our view be unnecessary and unwise, and might in the end produce much greater dissatisfaction among the public than it would remove. Above all we think that the interests of the public can best be served by resisting any innovation which may weaken the strength and resolve of the police in their fight against crime. (1960–62 Commission 1962: 138)

After interrogation of Met and Home Office documents it is difficult to explain on the evidence how the 1960–62 Commission arrived at their conclusions. The final sentence of the above quote indicates that a political decision was reached, and it is clear that the perception of the Commission was that the public interest in law enforcement outweighed any benefits that may be gained by developing an independent and effective mechanism to hold law enforcement officers accountable for their conduct. The spat between the Secretariat and Met in regard to the difficulties encountered analysing the statistical data before members of the Commission considered the evidence were glossed over. It is interesting to note that Secretary T. A. Critchley, when sharing the Secretariat's analyses of the national statistical data with police forces, expressed his disappointment with the finding that only half of complainants were satisfied with internal complaints procedures He concluded, 'Perhaps this result is all that could be expected as long as the investigation remains wholly in the hands of the police.'[72] In contrast, in their *Final Report* the 1960–62 Commission (1962: 124–125) welcomed the very low incidence of complaints and 'police success in convincing complainants that their grievances have been fairly dealt with', which was taken as evidence that police forces were 'in general, scrupulously fair and thorough in the way in which they investigate complaints'.

Government broadly accepted the recommendations of the Commission. Determining that the chief officer of police more closely resembled the employer of a constable than the police authority, under Section 48 of the Police Act 1964 a vicarious liability was attached to the chief officer as well as the constable alleged to have committed the tort. Section 49 of the Act required the chief officer to record and investigate complaints received, and refer to another police force for investigation if considered appropriate; and sub-section (3) required investigation reports to be forwarded to the DPP unless the chief officer was satisfied that a criminal offence had been committed. Section 50 required the police authority and inspectors of constabulary to keep themselves informed of the manner in which complaints were handled.

Notes

1. National Archives, MEPO 2/7237, Complaints against police, Minute sheet no. 2.
2. There was less coverage of police misconduct in the press after the Fitzpatrick case. One complaint picked up by court reporters was made by Alice Neri, and was to conclude with a Met Disciplinary Board acquitting three officers, PC Copeland and DCs Gowan and Sutherland, of bringing discredit upon the force (*The Times*, 30 September 1936). Acquitted by a London Sessions jury of stealing off-duty PC Copeland's wallet, Neri's defence was that the constable had arrested her after she refused his advances in Hyde Park. Detained in Hyde Park police station for two and a half hours, DC Gowan and another officer suggested to her that as PC Copeland had been drinking there would be no further action if she were to say nothing more about the matter. She declined their offer and was, then, charged with the offence (*Daily Telegraph*, 27 August 1936).
3. National Archives, MEPO 2/6278, A-1 Branch: The Commissioner's Annual Report for 1933.
4. Held in the National Archives, MEPO 2/7237-38; 2/6031; 2/6034-36; 2/6038; 2/10769-785; 2/10272; the summary for 1964 is not yet open to the public and figures for that year have been taken from the 1965 summary National Archives, MEPO 2/10787.

5. *Hansard*, Parl Debs HC, 12 November 1959, Cols 1254–1255.
6. Also tasked with considering police remuneration, the 1960–62 Commission (1961a) published an interim report on pay before deliberating on their other terms of reference.
7. National Archives, MEPO 2/1808, Police Orders: Complaints against police by members of the public (*General Orders*, pages 72–75, paras 137–158).
8. *Hansard*, Parl Debs HC, 1 July 1933, cols 2719–2739.
9. National Archives, MEPO 2/1808, Summary of minutes, 16 November 1932.
10. National Archives, MEPO 2/1808, Police Orders: Complaints against police by members of the public.
11. Discipline was co-ordinated by A-3 Branch, and A-1 documents examined rarely referred to disciplinary proceedings or outcomes.
12. National Archives, MEPO 2/7237, Minute sheet No. 7.
13. Of the total legal remedies pursued between 1932 and 1937 ($n = 236$) the vast majority were for domestic complaints ($n = 220$). Details of proceedings were not included in the summaries and this category is presumed to primarily include claims against officers for failing to honour their marital or parental obligations.
14. An interesting trend over the nine years was the increase in multiple allegations recorded, particularly after introduction of the new regime. There were 39 more allegations than recorded complaints in 1933, which increased to 159 in 1934 and continued to rise to 255 in 1938.
15. See, for example, National Archives, MEPO 2/7238, Minute sheet no. 5.
16. The failure of a complainant to pursue their complaint, a result category that was also discontinued at an early stage, was also considered to reflect poorly on the character of a complainant. In his 1929 annual report, Commissioner Byng made a barbed comment on the large number of complainants that were unwilling to go to the extra trouble of attending a police station (Commissioner of Police of the Metropolis 1930).
17. Few complaints were made by members of the armed forces, and the complainant category was retained until 1957.
18. National Archives, MEPO 2/10770, Minute sheet no. 4.
19. Although not included in the Commissioner's annual reports after publication of complaints statistics commenced in 1964, the Met continued to keep internal records of the characteristics of complainants up to the late 1960s: National Archives, MEPO 2/10791, Types of complaints and complainants.

20. Aggregate figures are provided in order to reduce distortion arising from low annual numbers, particularly false evidence complaints.
21. A-1 Branch noted that 24 complaints were made following dispersal by mounted police of an anti-fascist protest at Thurloe Square, SW 7, on 22 March 1936 (National Archives, MEPO 2/7237, Minute sheet no. 31), which was the subject of an NCCL organised independent Commission of Inquiry into allegations of brutality (see Chap. 5, above Endnote 2). On 4 October the Battle of Cable Street took place in the heart of London's East End Jewish community. The Met rerouted a British Union of Fascists (BUF) march away from where anti-fascists and local people had made barricades to prevent their entry, and fighting broke out between anti-fascists and police. Forty police and 30 members of the public were injured and 79 arrests made, and police powers to curb political protests under the Public Order Act 1936 soon followed (Thurlow 1998; Weinberger 1995). The following year, on 14 July, NCCL observers reported on police use of batons to disperse local people who had attended a BUF outdoor meeting in Stepney Green (Hull History Centre, U DCL 38/4, Police baton charge Stepney Green). Local and national newspapers picked up on a comment by Thames Police Court Magistrate Everard Dickson: 'When the police are dealing with cases of mob-disorder they cannot do so in kid gloves. It may be that following these events someone is arrested in circumstances which lead to complaints of people being ill-treated, but of course the police have their work to do, and sometimes they have to do it in a way that is not gentle. Therefore I am not much impressed by these sort of complaints.' (*The Manchester Guardian*, 30 July 1937)
22. 'Neglect of duty, irregularities, etc.' complaints ranged from idling on duty to victimisation of members of the public and threats of assault: after assault and battery complaints were separated out the category remained unchanged until revised in 1957: National Archives, MEPO 2/10780, Classification of types of complaint.
23. For the three years 1942–44, 44, 52 and 43 assault and brutality complaints were recorded, respectively, of which 13.67%, 15.38% and 9.3% were substantiated: National Archives, MEPO 2/6036, Comparative summary of complaints and complainants, 1944.
24. The complaints register held at South Mimms police station (S Division) evidently slipped through the net: seven complaints were registered between 1930 and 1934 and none thereafter until non-recording was

discovered in 1970: National Archives, MEPO 8/36, South Mimms police station complaints book.

25. In 1964 Commissioner Simpson recorded that 44 officers received financial assistance from the Police Fund: 19 to defend civil claims and 25 to defend criminal charges, mainly privately brought charges of assault (Commissioner of Police of the Metropolis 1965: 16).

26. National Archives, MEPO 2/10780, Classification of types of complaint.

27. *Elias* v. *Pasmore* [1934] 2 K.B 164, in which £20 damages for trespass and £10 costs were awarded against the police, may have been included in the A-1 return for 1934 as one legal remedy was pursued for one complaint in the 'Neglect of duty, irregularities, etc.' category.

28. National Archives, MEPO 2/5887, Cases involving prosecution of police officers.

29. Hull History Centre, U DCL 9/2, DCL, Mrs. Urquhart case.

30. National Archives, MEPO 3/2460, Complaints and threatened actions against police officers.

31. National Archives, MEPO 3/2460, Minute sheet no. 1.

32. National Archives, MEPO 3/2460, Confidential memorandum: Complaints against police—reports.

33. National Archives, MEPO 2/7237, Minute sheet No. 45.

34. Three hundred and eighty-two complaints were recorded between 1 September and 31 December 1939 compared with 617 in 1938: National Archives, MEPO 2/7237, Minute sheet no. 47.

35. National Archives, MEPO 2/6035, Comparative summary of complaints and complainants recorded during the year ended 31 December 1943 and the year ended 31 December 1942 and Commissioner of Police of the Metropolis (1944).

36. National Archives, MEPO 2/10780, Complaints against police.

37. The 'Neglect of duty, irregularities, etc.' and 'Unclassified' complaint categories were discontinued and replaced by six new categories: 'Failure to attend incidents, etc.'; 'Incorrect traffic regulation, etc'; 'Lack of assistance to public'; 'Other neglect of duty'; 'Victimization, etc.'; 'Improperly at premises'; 'Improperly dealing with property'; and 'Other irregularities'. A-1 Branch continued to provide a separate table of figures for complainants in their quarterly summaries, on which internal aggregate figures and substantiation rates were based, removing the armed forces category in 1957 and introducing ethnic minority recording of complainants on 1 July 1960 with the inclusion of a 'Coloured persons' category.

38. National Archives, MEPO 2/10776, 4E.
39. National Archives, MEPO 2/10776, Minute sheet no. 3.
40. National Archives, MEPO 2/10778, Cases included in the return of complaints for the quarter ended 31 December 1955, in which compensation was paid.
41. National Archives, MEPO 2/10782, Cases included in the return of complaints for the quarter ended 31 March 1959, in which compensation was paid.
42. Hull History Centre, U DCL, Case of John Murphy.
43. National Archives, MEPO 2/10783, Cases included in the return of complaints for the quarter ended 31 March 1960, in which compensation was paid.
44. National Archives, MEPO 2/10784, Summaries of compensation cases noted during the first quarter of 1961.
45. National Archives, MEPO 2/10784, Summaries of compensation cases noted during the third quarter of 1961.
46. National Archives, MEPO 2/10272, Summaries of compensation cases noted during the first quarter of 1963.
47. See above, Endnote 5.
48. The 1964 A-1 Branch complaints summary is not open to the public until 2049.
49. National Archives, MEPO 2/10783, Cases included in the return of complaints for the quarter ended 30 June 1960, in which compensation was paid.
50. National Archives, MEPO 2/10778, Cases included in the return of complaints for the quarter ended 30 June 1955, in which compensation was paid.
51. National Archives, MEPO 2/10776, 1E.
52. National Archives, MEPO 2/10781, Minute sheet no. 4.
53. National Archives, MEPO 2/10782, Minute sheet no. 3.
54. *Hansard*, Parl Debs HC, 20 July 1959, cols 873–882. Podola was convicted of the murder of Detective Sergeant Raymond Purdy at the Central Criminal Court and sentenced to be hanged (*The Guardian*, 25 September 1959).
55. National Archives, MEPO 2/10782, Minute sheet no. 7.
56. National Archives, MEPO 2/10272, Minute sheet no. 4.
57. National Archives, MEPO 2/9846, Complaints against police by members of the public.

58. National Archives, MEPO 2/9846, Minutes sheet no. 2.
59. As Divisional Chief Superintendent Fieldsend was responsible for complaints and discipline, and in 1959 he was disturbed with the impartiality and thoroughness of a CID investigation into complaints by three men convicted of offences alleging that officers had fabricated evidence against them. The solicitor of the three persisted with the case and reporting to the Home Secretary on the complaints investigation five years later William Mars-Jones QC (1964: 127) commended Fieldsend as an 'extremely efficient, fearless and conscientious police officer' and the only officer to have 'done any real detective work' (see further Chap. 7, below).
60. National Archives, MEPO 2/9846, Minute 12, 9 May 1960, unnumbered sheet.
61. National Archives, HO/272/139, Commission Assistant Secretary D. G. Mackay letter of 16 August 1960.
62. National Archives, HO/272/141–HO/272/147, Files 12/12/1–12/12/7 Complaints of Treatment: Metropolitan Police.
63. National Archives, HO/272/139, Metropolitan Police secretary Richardson letter of 10 October 1960; Summary of Complaints and Complainants Table I.
64. National Archives, HO/272/139,1960–62 Commission Assistant Secretary D. G. Mackay letter of 24 November 1961; Commissioner Simpson letter of 28 December 1961; Commission Secretary T. E. Critchley 'Criticisms by the Commissioner of Police of the Metropolis of 63/61 (summary of information about complaints)'.
65. National Archives, HO/272/139, 63/61 Complaints by the public against the police: summary of information provided by chief constables.
66. A detailed description of Met procedures was forwarded to the 1960–62 Commission: National Archives, HO/272/139, Metropolitan Police procedure for investigating complaints against police.
67. National Archives, HO/272/141, Files 12/12/1 Complaints of Treatment: Metropolitan Police, Assault 0001-0125; and HO/272/142, Files 12/12/2 Complaints of Treatment: Metropolitan Police, Mistaken Arrest/Wrong Accusation 0255-0329.
68. Founded in 1957, Justice became the UK section of the International Commission of Jurists the following year and quickly rose to prominence for their work promoting the rule of law and fair administration of justice.

69. Accompanied by Deputy Commissioner Robertson; Assistant Commissioners Webb and Jackson and Secretary Richardson: the Commissioner was the only Met representative to answer questions put by the 1960–62 Commission.
70. Robertson was a member of the Tribunal appointed to inquire into the allegation of assault on John Waters (1959).
71. National Archives, HO 272/139, Extracts of minutes of a meeting held on 6 and 7 March 1962.
72. National Archives, HO 272/139, Summary of information provided by chief constables.

References

1906–08 Commission, see Royal Commission upon the duties of the Metropolitan Police

1928/29 Commission, see Royal Commission on Police Powers and Procedure

1960–62 Commission, see Royal Commission on the Police

Box, S., & Russell, K. (1975). The Politics of Discreditability: Disarming Complaints Against the Police. *The Sociological Review, 23*(2), 315–346.

Chandos, J. (1962). Constabulary Duty. In C. H. Rolph (Ed.), *The Police and the Public*. London: Heinemann.

Clark, J. (2009). Sincere and Reasonable Men? The Origins of the National Council for Civil Liberties. *Twentieth Century British History, 20*(4), 513–537.

Clark, J. (2012). *The National Council for Civil Liberties and the Policing of Interwar Politics*. Manchester: Manchester University Press.

Commissioner of Police of the Metropolis. (1929). *Report of the Commissioner of Police of the Metropolis for the Year 1928*, Cmd. 3335. ProQuest Parliamentary Papers Online.

Commissioner of Police of the Metropolis. (1930). *Report of the Commissioner of Police of the Metropolis for the Year 1929*, Cmd. 3600. ProQuest Parliamentary Papers Online.

Commissioner of Police of the Metropolis. (1936). *Report of the Commissioner of Police of the Metropolis for the Year 1935*, Cmd. 5165. ProQuest Parliamentary Papers Online.

Commissioner of Police of the Metropolis. (1944). *Report of the Commissioner of Police of the Metropolis for the Year 1943*, Cmd. 6536. ProQuest Parliamentary Papers Online.

Commissioner of Police of the Metropolis. (1959). *Report of the Commissioner of Police of the Metropolis for the Year 1958*, Cmnd. 800. ProQuest Parliamentary Papers Online.

Commissioner of Police of the Metropolis. (1965). *Report of the Commissioner of Police of the Metropolis for the Year 1964*, Cmnd. 2710. ProQuest Parliamentary Papers Online.

Ewing, K. D., & Gearty, C. A. (2000). *The Struggle for Civil Liberties: Political Freedom and the Rule of law in Britain, 1914–1945*. Oxford: Oxford University Press.

Hansard. ProQuest Parliamentary Papers Online.

Independent Office for Police Conduct. (2019). *Police Complaints: Statistics for England and Wales 2018/19*. London: IOPC.

Kingsford, P. (1982). *The Hunger Marchers in Britain, 1920–1939*. London: Lawrence and Wishart.

Lustgarten, L. (1986). *The Governance of Police*. London: Sweet & Maxwell.

Marshall, G. (1965). *Police and Government: The Status and Accountability of the English Constable*. London: Methuen.

Mars-Jones, W. (1964). *Report of Inquiry into the Inquiries Made, for the Information of the Secretary of State for the Home Department, into the Case of Thomas Hallron and Patrick Joseph Cox and the case of Patrick Albert Tisdall, Thomas Alfred Kingston and Sidney Hill-Burton*, Cmnd. 2526. ProQuest Parliamentary Papers Online.

Phillips, M., & Phillips, T. (1998). *Windrush: The Irresistible Rise of Multi-racial Britain*. Scarborough, Canada: Harper Collins.

Pilkington, E. (1988). *Beyond the Mother Country: West Indians and the Notting Hill White Riots*. London: IB Tauris.

Royal Commission on Police Powers and Procedure. (1929). *Report of the Royal Commission on Police Powers and Procedure*, Cmd. 3297. ProQuest Parliamentary Papers Online.

Royal Commission on the Police. (1961a). *Interim Report*, Cmnd. 1222. ProQuest Parliamentary Papers Online.

Royal Commission on the Police. (1961b). *Royal Commission on the Police Minutes of Evidence*. London: HMSO.

Royal Commission on the Police. (1962). *Final Report of the Royal Commission on the Police*, Cmnd. 1728. ProQuest Parliamentary Papers Online.

Royal Commission upon the Duties of the Metropolitan Police. (1908). *Report of the Royal Commission Upon the Duties of the Metropolitan Police Along with Appendices, Vol. I*, Cd. 4156. ProQuest Parliamentary Papers Online.

Smith, G. (2009). Why Don't More People Complain Against the Police? *European Journal of Criminology*, 6(3), 249–266.

Thurlow, R. C. (1995). *The Secret State: British Internal Security in the Twentieth Century*. Blackwell.

Thurlow, R. C. (1998). The Straw that Broke the Camel's Back: Public Order, Civil Liberties and the Battle of Cable Street. *Jewish Culture and History*, 1(2), 74–94.

Tribunal Appointed to Inquire into the Allegation of Assault on John Waters. (1959). *Report of a Tribunal Appointed to Inquire into the Allegation of Assault on John Waters*, Cmnd 718. ProQuest Parliamentary Papers Online.

Weinberger, B. (1995). *The Best Police in the World: An Oral History of English Policing from the 1930s to the 1960s*. Aldershot: Routledge.

Whyatt, S. J. (1961). *The Citizen and the Administration. The Redress of Grievances*. London: Stevens & Sons.

7

To Be Continued

The evidence presented in this study of complaints against officers serving with the Metropolitan Police (Met) demonstrates that procedures have developed incrementally, and the history of reform has been characterised by continuity rather than moments of upheaval and discontinuity. Three remedies to misconduct were available to complainants before their codification under Sections 48 and 49 of the Police Act 1964. A complainant could apply to a court to bring criminal proceedings or claim damages from a constable, or make a formal complaint which would be handled by internal administrative procedures. The effectiveness of each as a means of holding an officer to account has been shown in the pages above to have been problematic and codification was intended to resolve difficulties complainants faced accessing an appropriate remedy. After 1964 private prosecutions ceased and Section 49 (3) of the Police Act provided for the Director of Public Prosecutions (DPP) to determine whether criminal proceedings should be brought against a constable following investigation of a complaint by the police. Under Section 48 a vicarious liability rule was introduced which allowed a complainant to claim damages from the Met Commissioner as well as the constable alleged to have committed a tort. Under Section 49 (1) the Met

© The Author(s) 2020
G. Smith, *On the Wrong Side of The Law*, Palgrave's Critical Policing Studies,
https://doi.org/10.1007/978-3-030-48222-0_7

Commissioner was required to record and investigate complaints, with the discretion to refer to another police force for investigation or if directed to do so by the Home Secretary. In addition, Section 50 of the Act provided for limited oversight by requiring the Home Secretary as the Police Authority for the Metropolitan Police District to keep him or herself informed of the way in which the Met handled complaints.

In modelling their recommendations for legislative reform on the A-1 Branch complaints system that the Met had operated in secret for more than 30 years, the Royal Commission on the Police (1960–62 Commission) rejected introduction of an independent oversight body and cautioned against radical change for fear of weakening the capacity of police to fight crime. In the early 1960s Met opposition to external intervention in the complaints system was founded on the statutory responsibility of the Commissioner for discipline, the common law office of constable as defined in *Fisher* v. *Oldham Corporation* ([1930] 2 K.B. 364) and the constitutional convention of constabulary independence. In addition to the legal grounds for retention of internal complaints procedures the system developed by A-1 Branch was presented by the Met as fair and effective to complainants and officers, and in accepting this evidence the 1960–62 Commission determined that external intervention was unnecessary. In dismissing the evidence of a growing body of opinion that was coalescing around concerns raised by the National Council for Civil Liberties (NCCL), Justice and legal practitioner associations with a system that allowed police to judge in their own cause, a majority of the members of the Commission ensured that the biases associated with unmonitored investigation of police by police survived legislative reform. Reforms proposed by civil society and professional bodies were not unprecedented and the need for more independent, impartial and thorough procedures had been acknowledged decades earlier, most notably by the Royal Commission upon the Duties of the Metropolitan Police (1906–08 Commission) and the Minority Report of the 1928 Inquiry in regard to the interrogation by the police of Miss Savidge (Savidge Inquiry). On both occasions the Met successfully resisted proposals for reform which they considered to involve unwarranted external intervention in their internal affairs, and police opposition to the introduction of independent and effective mechanisms is a permanent feature of complaints discourse.

In the five years between appointment of the 1960–62 Commission and the 1964 Act public concern with internal complaints procedures continued to grow, particularly in regard to the conduct of Met officers. In their quarterly summaries A-1 Branch commented on the increasing number of complaints made by black people alleging assault and interfering with property, and by 1964 complaints of assault were the second largest category after incivility. With the Branch taking solace in low substantiation rates of less than 2% for assault and 8.5% for all complaints Commissioner Simpson was to advise: 'A low percentage of substantiation is not always encouraging: it may lead – rightly or wrongly to the accusation that our investigation is weak and that we cover up! Of course many unsubstantiated are "not proven" by Scottish standards.'[1] Published for the first time in the Commissioner's 1964 Annual Report (Commissioner of Police for the Metropolis 1965) complaints figures revealed that action was seldom taken against officers as the result of a complaint. The total number of persons that complained in 1964 was 1870, 138 complaints reports were forwarded to the DPP and criminal proceedings were brought in 5 non-traffic cases (17 in total) and an unstated number of officers were found guilty in 3. Disciplinary proceedings were brought in five cases after the DPP determined criminal proceedings should not be brought, without comment on the outcomes, and reference was made to officers having been given advice following an unspecified number of substantiated complaints.

1964 was a challenging year for the Met and several high-profile cases ensured that officer conduct remained under the spotlight. Within two years of publication of the *Final Report* of the 1960–62 Commission (1962) and with the Police Bill progressing through Parliament it was increasingly difficult for police to maintain that they could be trusted with outright control of the complaints system. Mrs. Woolf complained in November 1963 that despite reporting her former husband Herman Woolf missing she had not been informed of his death in police custody, for which the Met Commissioner apologised (O'Higgins 1964). Taken unconscious to hospital after a road traffic accident Woolf was released into police custody after discovery of what was suspected to be Indian hemp in his possession. Suspicious that Woolf suffered further injury after his release from hospital, relying on grounds of insufficient evidence Mrs. Woolf unsuccessfully applied to quash the verdict of the coroner's inquest that his death had been caused by a contusion of the brain following collision with a motor car (*Woolf* v. *Baron* [1963] 1 WLUK 843). With media interest in the case unabated Norman Skelhorn QC (1964), asked by Home Secretary Henry Brooke to conduct a private inquiry into the case,[2] reported his findings in March 1964 that Woolf had not been ill-treated by police.

In June, PCs David Oakey, Keith Goldsmith and Frank Battes were convicted of conspiracy to pervert the course of justice at the Central Criminal Court and received prison sentences of four and three years (*Daily Mail*, 24 June 1964).[3] Under the supervision of co-defendant Detective Sergeant Harold Challenor, found insane and unfit to plead at an earlier Old Bailey hearing, the officers had fabricated evidence against four protesters arrested the previous July. Charged with possession of an offensive weapon, one of the protesters and NCCL member, Donald Rooum, was acquitted after forensic evidence proved that he had not been carrying a broken brick that he alleged had been 'planted'. Co-defendant John Apostolou's conviction was subsequently quashed on appeal after the prosecution offered no evidence, and proceedings at Chelsea Juvenile Court against two other protesters were discontinued (Morton 1993). The NCCL carried out their own enquiries into cases involving Challenor and having discovered evidence of a pattern of complaints lobbied for convictions to be quashed (Grigg 1965; Moores 2017). Announcing that five persons convicted on the evidence of the Detective Sergeant were to receive a pardon and another five to have their cases referred to the Court of Appeal, the Home Secretary appointed Arthur James QC to hold an inquiry under Section 32 of the Police Act 1964 to consider Challenor's mental health while performing his policing duties.[4] After examining multiple allegations by 25 complainants including fabrication of evidence, assault and intimidation, James (1965) rejected the allegation that there was a culture of corruption at West End Central police station and concluded that Challenor continued in post four months after the onset of paranoid schizophrenia. Included in his *Report* were details of the Met Commissioner settling claims for damages for assault, false imprisonment and malicious prosecution by eight complainants, which amounted to several thousands of pounds sterling, with a further five claims outstanding.

At the end of 1964 the *Report* of an inquiry held in private by William Mars-Jones QC (1964) was published into complaints made in 1959 before appointment of the 1960–62 Commission (Morton 1993).[5] Patrick Tisdall, Thomas Kingston and Sidney Hill-Burton alleged that razors and lead tubing had been planted on them by CID officers at Hornsey police station in August 1959, which resulted in convictions and prison sentences for possession of offensive weapons.[6] Unable to prove beyond reasonable doubt that officers were guilty of the allegations, Mars-Jones concluded that five officers had lied and the defendants would have been acquitted if the evidence before him had been available at trial.[7] Reluctant to blame individual officers Mars-Jones was scathing of the partiality demonstrated by CID officers towards their colleagues and the absence of a thorough investigation into the three men's complaints. Chief Superintendent Frederick Fieldsend, whose proposals for complaints reform were discussed above in Chap. 6 and who retired from the Met shortly before publication of Mars-Jones's *Report*, was singled out for praise. As the No. 2 District Acting Deputy Commander Fieldsend had identified several inadequacies with the investigation of the complaints and his recommendation that an officer from another district should take over responsibility was not acted upon by his superiors. Disciplinary proceedings against the officers did not follow publication of the *Report*, three of whom were no longer serving and they had all been granted immunity from proceedings in advance of the Inquiry. Home Secretary Sir Frank Soskice recommended free pardons for the three complainants.[8]

Coming in the same year as codification of the complaints system, rather than post mortems on past misconduct and mismanagement the three inquiries were to signal worse times ahead. In public the Home Secretary and Met Commissioner offered reassurance that the discord between uniformed and CID officers highlighted by Mars-Jones was limited to one Met division, statutory referrals to the DPP would protect against the same happening again and lessons had been learned from the inquiries. In private Mars-Jones's reflections on the evidence he heard from Met officers in regard to their truculence, dishonesty, forgetfulness, disaffection and mistrust of senior officers fed into concerns in the Home Office that the Met were out of control.[9] T. A. Critchley, who returned to the Home Office after serving as Secretary to the 1960–62 Commission, considered it imperative to address Met aversion to 'outsiders' and press ahead with the appointment of provincial chief constables to command positions in the Met.[10] More widely, the inquiry reports contributed to the quickly growing critical discourse on police investigation of police ignited in part by the deliberations of the 1960–62 Commission. In addition to CID corruption and deaths in custody or following contact with police, complaints of racism in regard to targeting members of ethnic minority communities as suspects or failing to protect from crime were to increasingly result in calls for complaints reform. Moreover, a new type of civil society activism was developing. Defence campaigns were to emerge, especially in black and Asian communities, which introduced new dimensions to the complainant-centred narrative developed in this book.

This study of complaints against officers serving with the Metropolitan Police has been undertaken in an attempt to advance understanding of an elusive problem of modern policing. Since codified in 1964 primary legislation has been introduced on four further occasions for the purpose of improving the effectiveness of the police complaints system; and the Independent Office for Police Conduct (IOPC) currently serves as the fourth statutory body established to oversee complaints across England and Wales. Shortly after operationalisation of the Independent Police Complaints Commission (IPCC), precursor of the IOPC, Smith (2006) identified two constant and connected features of a reform cycle. Firstly, police successfully resisted widespread support for the introduction of independent and effective complaints mechanisms and, secondly, the interests of complainants have been marginalised in both the reform process and operation of complaints systems. In an attempt to counteract under-representation of their interests, and in the belief that obstacles to progress may only be overcome by better appreciation of the experiences of victims of police misconduct, a complainant-centred standpoint has been developed in this study. The first of a two-volume study, this book presents research on the antecedents and trends leading up to codification and the second will examine statutory reform to the present day.

This book tells a tale of two public interests, law enforcement and the accountability of law enforcement officers. Perceived by those responsible for policing to be competing, prioritisation of law enforcement in the interest of the majority has been taken as given and weighed against the accountability of officers for their conduct, which has been considered a minority interest. This zero-sum approach was captured by the 1960–62 Commission in pitting an independent oversight body against police 'strength and resolve' to enforce the law, concluding that police should have sole responsibility for handling complaints. The complainant-centred narrative shows that greater consideration has been given to officer accountability only when deemed necessary to ensure public confidence in the capacity of police to effectively enforce the law. This was apparent in the mid-nineteenth century when the Met were proactively working to establish public support. Successive home secretaries and the first Met Commissioners took every opportunity available to promote the new police as an effective and efficient force for the prevention and detection of crime. A hard line was taken against officer indiscipline and the Met Commissioners stated their preference for magistrates to hear complaints against constables, which were offences at common law and under Section 14 of the Metropolitan Police Act 1839. With Met statistical returns to parliament revealing that constables appeared far more frequently before criminal courts to answer charges in the mid-nineteenth century than at any time since, concerns were raised in the House of Commons of bias on the part of magistrates in their reluctance to find against constables. This was a common refrain, and it was widely perceived that the tendency of magistrates to uncritically accept the evidence of constables was much to blame for public dissatisfaction with the police and criminal justice system.

As police developed their powers to investigate crime and prepare prosecutions, eventually establishing their reputation as gatekeepers to the criminal justice system, numbers of officers brought before the police courts fell appreciably. Although not repealed until the Police Act 1964, Section 14 of the Metropolitan Police Act 1839 fell into disuse in the late nineteenth century. In 1868 the Home Secretary issued an instruction to the Met Commissioner that serious complaints involving a conflict of evidence should not be investigated by police, which left complainants in the position of having to apply to a magistrate for a summons or not proceed with their complaint. Whereas police increasingly provided a prosecution service to victims of crime which relieved them of the burden of bringing charges against offenders, the same did not apply where the suspect was a constable. Although claims for damages against constables were rare, it was also in the 1860s that subject to the approval of the Home Secretary provision was made for the Met police fund to cover the expense of defending constables in civil proceedings.

The status, wealth and character of complainants were factors that had a considerable bearing on their prospects of achieving redress. For the less advantaged civil society emerged as interlocutor and defender of rights, raised funds to defend complainants and supported private prosecutions against constables. The short-lived Law and Liberty League, which was formed to assist protestors on the eve of Bloody Sunday, November 1887, ensured that the death of Alfred Linnell was suitably marked by holding a funeral cortège along London's streets. The Personal Rights Association supported Elizabeth Cass who unsuccessfully prosecuted PC Bowen Endacott for perjury after she was cleared of charges of solicitation and common prostitution; and the Society for the Protection of Women and Children supported Rosa Parton in her unsuccessful attempts before magistrates at two police courts to bring a charge of assault against PC James Butler.

Emergence of police complaints and officer accountability centre stage in the first decade of the twentieth century had much to do with the efforts of the Police and Public Vigilance Society (PPVS). Formed in 1903 by dynamic General Secretary James Timewell and flamboyant Chairman Earl Russell, the PPVS supported complainants in the criminal and civil courts and the pair were to play prominent roles in the proceedings of the 1906–08 Commission. Unequivocal in their condemnation of officer abuse the PPVS was particularly active in opposing the use of violence against suspects detained by police, whether in the streets after having restrained their prisoner or in the police station. The 1906–08 Commission was appointed by the Home Secretary in response to outrage surrounding two cases a few weeks apart where magistrates discharged three respectable defendants, arrested on the word of constables and charged with drunk and disorderly behaviour and behaving in a riotous and indecent manner. Much of the time of the Commission, however, was devoted to examining allegations against constables made by complainants of a lower social status that were brought before them by the PPVS: Timewell acting as agent of the Commission and Russell as counsel for the PPVS.

It is held that the proceedings and findings of the 1906–08 Commission and the response of the Met represented missed opportunities relatively early in the history of the modern police to adequately address the public interest in holding officers accountable for misconduct. Evidently disturbed by the evidence of complainants and accused officers, in over 40% of the complaints they heard the Commission found that officers were guilty of misconduct and several changes were proposed to Met procedures. Questioning the effectiveness of criminal and civil proceedings as a means of redress for complainants, the Commissioners expressed their concerns with the adequacy of internal police enquiries into complaints. Endorsing a system of police investigating police, yet finding that existing procedures lacked independence, impartiality and thoroughness the 1906–08 Commission recommended introduction of a quasi-judicial complaints system under the leadership of a legally qualified Assistant Commissioner reporting directly to the Met Commissioner. For cases in which evidence was available that a criminal offence may have been committed, it was proposed that investigation of the complaint should be postponed pending a decision by the DPP on whether to prefer criminal proceedings, and the investigation resumed in the event that proceedings were not brought. Although accepted by the Home Secretary, the 1906–08 Commission proposals were not fully implemented and it was business as usual for the Met: the drive to improve the efficiency and effectiveness of law enforcement overshadowing concerns with officer accountability.

Left alone to handle public complaints free from external interference after the 1906–08 Commission, internal Met complaints procedures lacked openness and transparency. Despite regular reports in the press of violence at public protests and strikes in the years leading up to World War I and between the wars, little evidence is available of complaints of excessive police use of force which were so prevalent before the 1906–08

Commission. As police law enforcement powers continued to expand and their responsibilities for the pre-trial stages of the criminal justice process developed, a pattern of complaints alleging abuse of power and denial of rights emerged. Disseminated to police forces across England and Wales in 1918 the Judges' Rules laid down administrative guidelines for the questioning of suspects, and it was not long before confusion as to where the balance lay between the powers of police to enforce the law and their duty to protect the rights of suspects gave rise to a series of allegations of abuse. Complaints by respectable complainants who objected to the way in which they were treated by police were highlighted by the press and raised in Parliament.

As Police Authority for the Metropolitan Police District the Home Secretary was often asked by Members of Parliament when raising complaints on behalf of their constituents to appoint an inquiry to examine police conduct. Two inquiries appointed under the Tribunals of Inquiry (Evidence) Act 1921, into the arrest of Major Robert Sheppard (Rawlinson 1925) and interrogation of Irene Savidge (Savidge Inquiry 1928) were of particular significance. The primary purpose of the inquiries in each instance was to establish what happened and make recommendations on how police procedures to effectively and fairly enforce the law may be improved, for which the Home Secretary had an overarching statutory responsibility. In both cases complaints were made that clearly amounted to allegations of misconduct on the part of named police officers, for which the Met Commissioner had an express statutory responsibility. In addition to Rawlinson's findings that Sheppard had been unnecessarily detained in custody, not informed of his rights and the Judges' Rules breached, *prima facie* evidence of misconduct was obtained during inquiry proceedings. Having received Rawlinson's Inquiry *Report* Home Secretary Joynson-Hicks took charge of the situation and, ignoring the suggestion by Met Commissioner Horwood to respond to Rawlinson's criticisms, personally arranged for the revision of police regulations and left the Commissioner to deal with the misconduct allegations.

Escorted to Scotland Yard and interrogated alone by two experienced male detectives as part of an investigation to determine whether two constables should be charged with perjury, it was alleged that 22-year-old Miss Savidge had been subjected to third degree methods in an attempt to obtain evidence that would be of assistance to the officers. The circumstances surrounding the Savidge complaint represented another occasion when there was serious risk to public confidence in the police and greater consideration was given to officer accountability. The Commission of Inquiry appointed to examine the allegations divided on party political lines and Hastings Lees-Smith MP forthrightly pointed out in his Minority Report that unconscious bias was inherent in a system in which police investigated alleged offences committed by police. Once again the Home Secretary stepped forward to take charge, this time side-lining the Met Commissioner in announcing that the two constables would not face criminal or disciplinary proceedings in regard to the perjury investigation and arranging for the revision of regulations.

Whereas the 1906–08 Commission had little impact on police policy, coming soon after the Sheppard Inquiry the political fall-out from the Savidge Inquiry was a catalyst for change and followed by recalibration of the working relationship between the Home Secretary and Met Commissioner. The authority of the Home Secretary to appoint an independent inquiry, rather than perceived positively as a mechanism for addressing the grievances of citizens, improving police performance and maintaining public confidence, was negatively regarded for the reputational damage public scrutiny caused to the police institution. The Savidge Inquiry was the last independent inquiry of its type to examine complaints against Met officers: although comparison could arguably be made with the inquiry 70 years later by Sir William Macpherson (1999) into the circumstances surrounding the death of Stephen Lawrence.

After 100 years of police developing their powers and responsibilities, traditional interpretations of the statutory responsibilities of the Home Secretary and Met Commissioner for the governance of the Met were no longer considered fit for purpose. The working relationship between the two high office holders needed to be realigned in accordance with the transformation of Met administration which would allow the force to develop structures, procedures and technology to enforce the law with minimal external interference. There was no need for legislation; administrative reform could be introduced by executive action on the basis of a shared understanding between the Home Secretary and Met Commissioner of what was required. Appreciation of what took place behind the scenes at this time is helped by contributions to debate on policing by senior Home Office civil servants. Conceptualisation of the separation of responsibilities between the Home Secretary and Met Commissioner for law enforcement policy and operations was introduced to discourse on police governance by Sir Edward Troup (1928). Sir John Anderson (1929) reinforced the separation between policing and politics in tracing the development of the office of constable at common law to demonstrate that the police officer exercised an original authority and was accountable to the law.

Adjustment of the Home Secretary and Met Commissioner's responsibilities coincided with developments at common law to the status of the constable in the case of *Fisher* v. *Oldham Corporation* [1930] 2 K.B. 364. Judgment by McCardie J. that the local authority was not liable for damages for a tort committed by a constable when performing their law enforcement function is commonly accepted as the source of the doctrine of constabulary independence. Rather than the cause of a radical break with the past, in this complainant-centred narrative *Fisher* is held to have reflected the changing shape of police governance arrangements at the time. Clarification of the office of constable at common law, then, conveniently served to legitimise the Commissioner's control of the Met and refusal by the Home Secretary to intervene in operational policing matters, including complaints and discipline.

What is understood to be the first centralised police complaints system in England and Wales was also developed away from public view after the Savidge Inquiry. Records held in the National Archives show that the first tentative steps involved A-1 Branch of the Met Commissioner's Office disseminating quarterly complaints summaries, including a breakdown of statistics from the four operational districts, to command and senior officers across the force. Revised regulations introduced in November 1933, including the requirement that districts forward completed complaints documents to A-1 Branch for recording purposes, provided a framework for the new system. Although tweaked on occasion in the next three decades this was the system on which the 1960–62 Commission modelled their recommendations for nationwide complaints reform.

Effective management of complaints is far from synonymous with addressing the grievances of complainants, a reason why standpoint is fundamental to understanding the enduring nature of this policy dilemma. The inherent bias identified in police investigation of police by Lees-Smith is rooted in internally conceived, designed, developed and managed procedures and may only be overcome by police, or an oversight body, engaging meaningfully with complainants and their representatives in regard to process as well as on grievances. The Met complaints system has been discussed internally, when problems were raised by the first Met Solicitor, Thomas Baker, soon after appointment in 1935 and No. 2 District Acting Deputy Commander Fieldsend in 1959, for example. Their concerns with the reliability and accuracy of officer reports on which complaints investigations were based and opportunities for complainants to attend hearings, had been previously addressed in the unimplemented recommendations of the 1906–08 Commission. After giving consideration to their proposals, command officers rejected them on grounds that procedures were adequate for the vast majority of complaints.

Experience-based perceptions are important to understanding behaviour, and may also be understood in terms of the mind-set or working assumptions of professionals that underpin standard operating procedures. It is apparent from this historical study that where the evidence has been conflicting, as in the majority of complaints against police, officers have been given the benefit of the doubt. Prevailing perceptions within the Met, as regularly placed on record by senior officers, were that complaints against officers were trivial, and many were tactical, malicious or vexatious. With the commonly held view among officers that complaints were an unfortunate consequence of good policing, effective management of complaints involved reassuring the officer considered to have acted in good faith that their efforts to catch criminals would not be deterred by substantiation of a complaint. Given this priority, reassuring the complainant that their complaint had been taken seriously and thoroughly investigated, so important to maintaining good public relations, was not always possible. An inevitable consequence of the zero-sum complaints management model is that officer morale, essential to effective law enforcement and considered at risk from the substantiation of complaints, trumps public dissatisfaction with the lack of officer accountability. Herein lies the crux of the problem. It is fully understood that public dissatisfaction with officer unaccountability, or the perception that officers are unaccountable, damages public confidence with police generally. It is equally understood that the publicity surrounding misconduct and the openness of procedures to establish officer accountability, which ensure respect for the rights of complainant and officer, damages public confidence with police generally. This antonym inevitably results in a cyclical pattern of relations between police and public, where mounting concern with police conduct and officer accountability give rise to demands for reform of complaints procedures. Whereas in the last 55 years or so a series of complaints reform cycles have been signposted by legislation,[11] the same is not the case for the first 135 years of the Met. In the absence of legislative reform, however, government appointed inquiries signposted occasions when officer accountability emerged as a policing priority prior to the Police Act 1964.[12] Looking back over close to two centuries of Met history it is apparent that there have been a series of cycles of concern with officer accountability. The duration of the first cycles which concluded without statutory reform was between 20 and 32 years, and since first codified a further five cycles have lasted between 8 and 15 years and each has featured legislation setting out new oversight arrangements.

By way of conclusion, and in anticipation of the second volume of this study, all that remains is to comment on the international dimensions of police complaints discourse. At the same time that the 1960–62 Commission were considering the effectiveness of complaints procedures across UK police forces an international reform trend was emerging. In October 1958 the Philadelphia Police Advisory Board, originally called the Police Review Board, was the first independent body created to oversee police complaints (Coxe 1965). New York followed suit in establishing the Civilian Complaint Review Board in 1966 and a succession of independent oversight bodies have operated since across English speaking jurisdictions in the USA, Canada, Australia, New Zealand and South Africa in addition to England and Wales, Scotland and Northern Ireland (Goldsmith and Lewis 2000).[13] Discourse on police complaints has always been inter-disciplinary and in addition to the traditional focus on police administration (Prenzler 2009; Punch 2009; Walker 2005) international human rights law has become increasingly important (Murdoch 1999; Smith 2010; Svandize 2014). The obligation under international human rights law that states protect individual human rights has led to the development of a set of standards intended to ensure the effective investigation of alleged violations, which are a core component of a global programme to combat impunity (Smith 2015b). Alongside the developing jurisprudence of international human rights courts, independent oversight bodies with powers to investigate the police are highly regarded as best practice (Council of Europe Commissioner for Human Rights 2009; United Nations Special Rapporteur on Extra-Judicial, Summary or Arbitrary Executions 2010).

In the first volume of this study of complaints against Metropolitan Police officers the complainant-centred standpoint has demonstrated the obstacles faced by victims of police misconduct in attempting to hold the officers responsible to account. If it were not for the complainants and civil society organisations who spoke truth to power, then, police would have exercised their power with virtual impunity. The second volume of the study will focus on the role played by civil society in combating the impunity of Met officers in the citizen oversight era.

Notes

1. National Archives, MEPO 2/1072, Minute sheet no. 4.
2. *Hansard*, Parl Debs HC, 23 January 1964, Col 1246.
3. PCs Oakey and Goldsmith had their four-year sentence reduced to three on appeal (*The Times*, 24 July 1964).
4. *Hansard*, Parl Debs HC, 2 July 1964, Cols 1547–49.
5. Eric Fletcher MP had lobbied for an inquiry after he received information from Met whistleblowers claiming that complaints were inadequately investigated (Mars-Jones 1964).
6. Mars-Jones found that complaints made in May 1959 by Thomas Halloran and Patrick Cox alleging officers had suppressed a report in an attempt to exonerate officers were not substantiated.
7. Solicitor for the three men, David Napley (1982), who had written to Home Secretary Brooke in 1959 about their complaints regretted that Mars-Jones was unable to come to a more courageous and robust finding.

8. *Hansard*, Parl Debs HC, 3 December 1964, Col 752.
9. National Archives, HO 287/25, The Secretary of State's role in relation to the Metropolitan Police, T. A. Critchley.
10. There was resentment in the Met to Home Secretary Roy Jenkins's appointment of Leicester Chief Constable Robert Mark to the position of Assistant Commissioner in February 1967 (Ascoli 1979).
11. Police Act 1964; Police Act 1976; Police and Criminal Evidence Act 1984; Police Reform Act 2002; Policing and Crime Act 2017.
12. Royal Commission on the Alleged Disturbance of the Public Peace in Hyde Park on Sunday, July 1st, 1855; 1887 Met inquiry into a complaint by Elizabeth Cass; 1906–08 Commission; 1928 Savidge Inquiry and 1928/29 Commission (considered in this study to have been of less significance to the Savidge Inquiry); 1960–62 Commission.
13. Non-English-speaking jurisdictions that have also introduced independent oversight bodies include Belgium, Brazil, Denmark and the Philippines (Smith 2015a).

References

1960–62 Commission. (1962). See Royal Commission on the Police.
Anderson, J. (1929). The Police. *Public Administration, 7*(2), 192–202.
Ascoli, D. (1979). *The Queen's Peace: The Origins and Development of the Metropolitan Police, 1829–1979.* London: Hamish Hamilton.
Commissioner of Police of the Metropolis. (1965). *Report of the Commissioner of Police of the Metropolis for the Year 1964.* Cmnd. 2710. ProQuest Parliamentary Papers Online.
Council of Europe Commissioner for Human Rights. (2009). *Opinion of the Commissioner for Human Rights Concerning Independent and Effective Determination of Complaints against the Police.* CommDH(2009)4. Strasbourg: Council of Europe.
Coxe, S. (1965). The Philadelphia Police Advisory Board. *Law in Transition Quarterly, 2*(3), 179–185.
Goldsmith, A. J., & Lewis, C. (2000). Introduction. In A. J. Goldsmith & C. Lewis (Eds.), *Civilian Oversight of Policing: Governance, Democracy and Human Rights* (pp. 1–15). Portland, OR: Hart Publishing.
Grigg, M. (1965). *The Challenor Case.* Harmondsworth: Penguin.
Hansard. ProQuest Parliamentary Papers Online.

Inquiry in regard to the interrogation by the police of Miss Savidge. (1928). *Report of the tribunal appointed under the Tribunals of Inquiry (Evidence) Act, 1921.* Cmd. 3147. ProQuest Parliamentary Papers Online.

James, A. E. (1965). *Report of an Inquiry Into the Circumstances in Which it was Possible for Detective Sergeant Harold Challenor of the Metropolitan Police to Continue on Duty at a Time When He Appears to Have Been Affected by the Onset of Mental Illness.* Cmnd 2735. ProQuest Parliamentary Papers Online.

Macpherson, W. (1999). *The Stephen Lawrence Inquiry: Report of an inquiry by Sir William Macpherson of Cluny.* 1998–99 Cm 4262. ProQuest Parliamentary Papers Online.

Mars-Jones, W. (1964). *Report of Inquiry Into the Inquiries Made, for the Information of the Secretary of State for the Home Department, Into the Case of Thomas Hallron and Patrick Joseph Cox and the Case of Patrick Albert Tisdall, Thomas Alfred Kingston and Sidney Hill-Burton.* Cmnd. 2526. ProQuest Parliamentary Papers Online.

Moores, C. (2017). *Civil Liberties and Human Rights in Twentieth-Century Britain.* Cambridge: Cambridge University Press.

Morton, J. (1993). *Bent Coppers: A Survey of Police Corruption.* London: Little, Brown.

Murdoch, J. (1999). CPT Standards Within the Context of the Council of Europe. In R. Morgan & M. D. Evans (Eds.), *Protecting Prisoners. The Standards of the European Committee for the Prevention of Torture in Context* (pp. 103–136). Oxford: Oxford University Press.

Napley, D. (1982). *Not Without Prejudice.* London: Harrap.

O'Higgins, P. (1964). Complaints Against the Police—Procedure for Investigation. *Cambridge Law Journal, 23*(1), 53–56.

Prenzler, T. (2009). *Police Corruption: Preventing Misconduct and Maintaining Integrity.* London: Routledge Cavendish.

Punch, M. (2009). *Police Corruption: Deviance, Accountability and Reform in Policing.* Cullompton: Willan.

Rawlinson, J. F. P. (1925). *Arrest of Major R. O. Sheppard, D.S.O., R.A.O.C.: Report by the Right Hon. J. F. P. Rawlinson, K.C., M.P. of enquiry held under Tribunals of Enquiry (Evidence) Act, 1921.* Cmd. 2497. ProQuest Parliamentary Papers Online.

Royal Commission on the Police. (1962). *Final Report of the Royal Commission on the Police.* Cmnd. 1728. ProQuest Parliamentary Papers Online.

Savidge Inquiry. See Inquiry in regard to the interrogation by the police of Miss Savidge.

Skelhorn, N. (1964). *Report of Inquiry Into the Action of the Metropolitan Police in Relation to the Case of Mr Herman Woolf.* Cmnd. 2319. ProQuest Parliamentary Papers Online.

Smith, G. (2006). A Most Enduring Problem: Police Complaints Reform in England and Wales. *Journal of Social Policy, 35*(1), 121–141.

Smith, G. (2010). Every Complaint Matters: Human Rights Commissioner's Opinion Concerning Independent and Effective Determination of Complaints Against the Police. *International Journal of Law, Crime and Justice, 38*(2), 59–74.

Smith, G. (2015a, March 2). International Complaints Reform. Paper Presented to *CPT at 25: Taking Stock and Moving Forward.* 25th Anniversary Conference of the CPT. Strasbourg, France. Retrieved from https://rm.coe.int/CoERMPublicCommonSearchServices/DisplayDCTMContent?documentId=09000016806dbbbd.

Smith, G. (2015b). The Interface Between Human Rights and Police Complaints. In T. Prenzler & G. den Heyer (Eds.), *Civilian Oversight of Police: Advancing Accountability in Law Enforcement* (pp. 159–178). Boca Raton: CRC.

United Nations Special Rapporteur on Extra-Judicial, Summary or Arbitrary Executions. (2010). *Study on police oversight mechanisms.* Geneva: UN Office of the High Commissioner for Human Rights.

Svandize, E. (2014). *Effective Investigation of Ill-Treatment—Guidelines on European Standards* (2nd ed.). Strasbourg: Council of Europe.

Troup, E. (1928). Police Administration, Local and National. *The Police Journal, 1*(1), 5–18.

Walker, S. (2005). *The New World of Police Accountability.* Thousand Oaks, CA: Sage.

Index[1]

---

[1] Note: Page numbers followed by 'n' refer to notes.

© The Author(s) 2020
G. Smith, *On the Wrong Side of The Law*, Palgrave's Critical Policing Studies,
https://doi.org/10.1007/978-3-030-48222-0

CPI Antony Rowe
Eastbourne, UK
August 27, 2020